WITHDRAWN
HARVARD LIBRARY
WITHDRAWN

Chronicling The Soul's Windings

Thomas Hooker and His Morphology of Conversion

JOHN H. BALL, III

UNIVERSITY PRESS OF AMERICA

Lanham • New York • London

Copyright © 1992 by
University Press of America®, Inc.
4720 Boston Way
Lanham, Maryland 20706

3 Henrietta Street
London WC2E 8LU England

All rights reserved
Printed in the United States of America
British Cataloging in Publication Information Available

Library of Congress Cataloging-in-Publication Data

Ball, John H., 1954-
Chronicling the soul's windings : Thomas Hooker
and his morphology of conversion / John H. Ball.
p. cm.
Includes bibliographical references and index.
1. Hooker, Thomas, 1586-1647. 2. Conversion
—History of doctrines—17th century. I. Title.
BX7260.H596B35 1991
285.8'092—dc20 91-21330 CIP

ISBN 0–8191–8362–8 (hard : alk. paper)

The paper used in this publication meets the minimum requirements of American National Standard for Information Sciences—Permanence of Paper for Printed Library Materials, ANSI Z39.48–1984.

FOR

LAURA EMILY AND MARTHA LOGAN

ACKNOWLEDGMENTS

The author owes special words of thanks to Dr. Samuel T. Logan, Professor of Church History at Westminster Theological Seminary, whose guidance has been invaluable. Great debt is also owed to Dr. Robert T. Handy, Henry Sloane Coffin Professor Emeritus, Union Theological Seminary, New York, who prompted my first written formulations of Hookerian thought. Professor Handy also kindly served as a reader of the dissertation of which the present work is an outgrowth.

Grace Mullen, Archivist at the Montgomery Library of Westminster Theological Seminary, cheerfully located and procured volumes and microfilms from various libraries across the country. William O. Harris, Archivist at the Speer Library, Princeton Theological Seminary, never tired of retrieving Hookerian material from the excellent Puritan Collection of the Speer Library Archives. Some of this material has been located nowhere else in our country. Without his patient indulgence my research would not have been possible.

Finally, with a grateful heart I must acknowledge the constant and loving encouragement of my wife Phyllis.

John H. Ball, III
Lent, 1991

TABLE OF CONTENTS

INTRODUCTION..1

CHAPTER ONE: THE LIFE AND WORK OF THOMAS HOOKER.......5

   Early Life and Education (7)
   Pastoral Career in England (10)
   The Chelmsford Period (13)
   Episcopal Scrutiny (17)
   The Netherlands Experiment (22)
   On To New England (33)
   The Case of Mr. Roger Williams (40)
   Sermonic and Literary Activity During the
      Newtown Period (44)
   The Removal To Connecticut (45)
   The Antinomian Crisis (56)
   The Final Years (67)

CHAPTER TWO: HOOKER'S MORPHOLOGY OF CONVERSION:
             CONTEXTUAL CONSIDERATIONS............. 73

   Hooker's Preparationism In Context: The Covenantal
      Milieu (74)
   Hooker's Orthodoxy and the Developing Federal
      Theology (81)
   Establishing Hooker's Morphology From His Published
      Works (85)
   Hooker's Voluntarism in the Context of the Faculty
      Psychology (88)

CHAPTER THREE: HOOKER'S MORPHOLOGY OF CONVERSION:
                 EARLY FORMULATIONS................... 95

   The Earliest Stages of the Morphology As Explicated
         During The Chelmsford Period, 1626-1630 (95)
   The Major Morphological Works: The Unbeleevers
         Preparing (1638) (106)
   The Major Morphological Works: The Soules
         Preparation (1632) (117)
   The Major Morphological Works: The Soules
         Humiliation (1637) (130)
   The Major Morphological Works: Transitional
         Volumes (142)
   The Major Morphological Works: The Soules
         Effectual Calling (1637) (149)
   The Major Morphological Works: The Soules
         Exaltation (1638) (161)
   The Major Morphological Works: Sanctification
         (173)
   Volumes Supplementary to the Major Morphological
         Works (181)

CHAPTER FOUR: HOOKER'S PREPARATIONIST THEOLOGY AS
                FORMULATED IN HIS WRITINGS FROM THE
                ANTINOMIAN PERIOD AND BEYOND..........199

   The Saints Dignitie and Dutie (1651) (200)
   The Application of Redemption   (1656) (212)
   A Comment Upon Christ's Last Prayer (1656) (238)

CHAPTER FIVE: THE VEHICLE FOR HOOKER'S MORPHOLOGY: THE
                PURITAN PLAIN STYLE...................247

CONCLUSION...255

WORKS CITED..259

                              viii

INTRODUCTION

The Reverend Thomas Hooker (1586-1647), "founder" of the Connecticut colony, and to some less than careful interpreters the "first democrat," was a pastor-teacher of exceptional piety and skill. His preaching had great impact in Old England as well as in New. To many today, Hooker is best known for his last great work, A Survey of the Summe of Church Discipline (1648), his definitive defense of the congregational way.
Because certain features of the extant Winthrop-Hooker correspondence show Hooker to be at odds with Winthrop's highly aristocratic and oligarchical views, some have been led rashly to assign to Hooker a democratic spirit, a sort of John the Baptist to Thomas Jefferson. Among the several of these seemingly wishful interpreters, with a growing intensity have been: George Leon Walker (1891); James Truslow Adams (1921); and especially Vernon Parrington (1927). Perry Miller has written with vigorous emotion, showing that Hooker remained as thoroughly orthodox and non-democratic as Thomas Shepard and John Cotton himself. Finally, it seems that the sane insights of Clinton Rossiter over three decades ago, should have laid this debate to rest. Nevertheless, the hagiographical tones of "Hooker the democrat" are still occasionally sounded, and still becloud our view of the most important contribution of this Puritan pastor. A mere glance at the titles of the published Hooker canon demonstrates that such continued debate misses the essence of the man.
This study attempts to demonstrate that Thomas

Hooker was first and foremost a "physician" to the soul who specialized as a psychologist of conversion. Remaining faithful to his Calvinistic theology, Hooker became a model pastor, with an intense concern for the spiritual welfare of his parishioners. Therein lies Hooker's significance for today, rather than in any supposed democratic ideals.

Hooker's greatest contribution to church and society was his collection of conversion sermons. The morphology that can be therein discerned, was put to use as by a skillful physician both to prod the complacent and to bring peace to the troubled.

Because several incidents in Hooker's early pastoral career molded and gave rise to certain marks of his entire ministry, the initial section of this work is biographical in nature. The Antinomian crisis of 1637, threatening as it did the very foundations of the New England authority structure, serves as the "pivot point" for the third and fourth sections of this book. These sections are designed to serve as much as an arrangement of the Hookerian corpus as a critical evaluation of the same. Of major concern is an examination of Hooker's sentiments prior to the Antinomian crisis during which he was labeled as one of the "legal preachers" by the Hutchinsonians. Hooker's views dating from 1637 and beyond will then be discussed as evidence for any post-Antinomian tailoring will be sought. This unfolding temporal schema, pivoting on the Antinomian crisis, has not been previously employed in studies of Hooker by scholars such as Emerson, Shuffelton, or Bush.

Given the central importance of Hooker's preparationism, the sources of his thought will also need to be traced. An evaluation of how preparationism relates to the more pristine form of Calvinism is essential to understanding the significance of Hooker's thought and how it should be judged as to its orthodoxy. An examination of the relative importance of the covenant concept will be made in order to demonstrate that Hooker remained an eloquent spokesman for the emerging federal theology and New England orthodoxy.

William Perkins' Reformed conception of the _ordo salutis_ is clearly mirrored and given new application in

INTRODUCTION

Hooker's pastoral theology, and specifically his conversion sermons. For this reason the great bulk of this book constitutes a systematic analysis of each of the Hookerian morphological works. By representative citations, the final section will demonstrate Hooker's overall use of the Puritan "plain style" which served as the vehicle for his morphology. Attention will also be given to Hooker's place in the Reformed tradition especially as it developed in the two centuries between John Calvin and Jonathan Edwards.

Ever seeking to promote "heart religion" Thomas Hooker was concerned to chronicle the "windings" of the soul during its halting sojourn along the low road of contrition and humiliation. Fearing empty professions of faith Hooker sounded his activist calls, positing as a basis for assurance the presence of sanctifying graces. Such sentiments placed him on a collision course with the Hutchinsonian party.

A systematic analysis of Hooker's entire corpus as it relates to his morphology of conversion will here be made. This work is especially concerned to show that despite the commotion of 1637, little if any evidence exists that Hooker felt the need to "tailor" his teaching, or to "firm up" his Calvinism in the face of the Antinomian crisis. Indeed his brand of preparationism had won the day. Hooker would continue to consider the presence or absence of sanctifying graces in his diagnoses as he sought to treat the spiritual maladies of his parishioners. While becoming a champion of preparationist theology, Hooker's high-Calvinism remained constant throughout his career.

CHAPTER ONE: THE LIFE AND WORK OF THOMAS HOOKER

Despite the high esteem in which Thomas Hooker came to be held, reconstructing the career of this trans-Atlantic Puritan presents some difficulty. In 1683 Samuel Clarke provided an early biographical sketch.[1] More well known is Cotton Mather's "Piscator Evangelicus. Or, the Life of Mr. Thomas Hooker, the Renowned, Pastor of Hartford-Church, the Pillar of Connecticut-Colony, in New-England," which was first published in 1695.[2] Mather prefaces his essay with a lament that "through want of information I have underdone in this" (Mather 1853, I, 332). Despite this apology, all other biographers have been indebted largely to Mather, even while noting his hagiographical tone. John Winthrop provided a contemporary voice in his The History of New England from 1630-1649,[3] with its occasional references to Hooker.

---

[1] Samuel Clarke, The Lives of Sundry Eminent Persons in this Later Age (London, 1683). Clarke had been sent to Emmanuel to study under Thomas Hooker. Cf. Haller 1938, 102, for the importance of Clarke as a Puritan biographer.
[2] Published as an Appendix to Mather's Johannes in Eremo. Memoirs Relating to the Lives, of . . . John Cotton . . . John Norton . . . John Wilson . . . John Davenport . . . and Mr. Thomas Hooker who dyed, 7d. 5m. 1647. Pastor of the Church at Hartford; New England (Boston, 1695). This work was later incorporated into Mather's Magnalia Christi Americana (London, 1702) as "The Light of the Western Churches: Or, the Life of Mr. Thomas Hooker."

[3] Despite considerable differences with Hooker, Winthrop's respect and admiration for Hooker are

Following a brief biographical account by Alexander Young published in 1846, Edward Hooker published his modest Life of Thomas Hooker (1849), consisting largely of quotations from Hooker and from the earlier works by Winthrop and Mather. In 1891 this work was superseded by what until recently had served as the standard biography, George Leon Walker's Thomas Hooker: Preacher, Founder, Democrat. More will be said regarding this work which emphasizes what the author portrays as Hooker's "democratic values." This evaluation received approbation and was intensified in the works of James Truslow Adams (1921) and Vernon Parrington (1927), but found a vigorous opponent in Perry Miller (1931).

Going beyond this more narrow controversy, Hookerian biographical interest was stirred anew in 1967 with two biographical essays by George Huntston Williams, and in 1973 with Keith Sprunger's "The Dutch Career of Thomas Hooker." Frank Shuffelton, building on his own doctoral dissertation, has now provided only the second full length critical biography of Thomas Hooker (Shuffelton 1972 and 1977). Displacing Walker's century old work, Shuffelton's biography, which also treats Hooker's published works, has become the new standard.

Notwithstanding this historiographical evolution, one may still concur with Mather's lament regarding our "want of information" regarding the life of the Reverend Thomas Hooker. Indeed, though our century has produced a new understanding of Stuart nonconformity, and though Hooker's works are now more accessible than they were a century ago, biographical knowledge of Hooker has not gone far beyond the portrait presented by Mather. In view of this "data-dearth," and given the tone of Mather's own work, the modern researcher does well to heed the warning of Andrew Denholm: "If great care is not exercised in the critical

---

nevertheless revealed throughout. Winthrop's history is referred to in this work as Winthrop's Journal, (ed. by J.K. Hosmer, New York: 1908).

THE LIFE AND WORK OF THOMAS HOOKER   7

examination and selective use of the few scraps of evidence that do exist, his life history is apt to resemble more clearly a classical epic than a critical appraisal" (Denholm 1961, 24).[1]

EARLY LIFE AND EDUCATION

Thomas Hooker was born at Marfield, in Leicester-shire, probably on July 7, 1586. The Hooker family was evidently a respected one with moderate but adequate means (Walker 1891, 4). Accompanying Thomas' cheerful and courteous temperament was a "sensible grandeur of mind" which produced the common verdict that this young man was "born to be considerable" (Mather 1853, I, 333). It is generally assumed that the place of Hooker's preparatory training was the school at Market-Bosworth[2] which had been established by Sir Wolston Dixie in 1586.

Sir Wolston's Puritan interests were manifested by his establishment of the Wolston-Dixie fellowships at Emmanuel College. Mather calmly notes that Emmanuel was at the time "designed for the study of divinity" (Mather 1853, I, 333). Yet the atmosphere there was less than serene. Sir Walter Mildmay, a Puritan nobleman, had received a charter from Queen Elizabeth in 1584 for the establishment of a college of divinity. Despite disdain

---

[1] "The undisputed facts of his life are so few that many accounts of him seem almost like fairy tales. No one knows what he looked like, but two splendid statues of him gaze out sternly over the bustling of the insurance peddlers. No one knows where he rests in dust, but a gravestone proclaims his triumphs and talents" (Rossiter 1953, 159).

[2] Market-Bosworth's proximity to Marfield, and the fact that Hooker received a Dixie fellowhip, provide the basis for the assumption regarding the location of Hooker's preparatory studies (Walker 1891, 9; Denholm 1961, 25-26).

from the Cambridge authorities, Emmanuel College, under the leadership of Laurence Chaderton, experienced a mercurial rise in popularity, becoming the second largest and possibly most influential of the Cambridge colleges.

Notwithstanding its financial difficulties, during the first half of the seventeenth-century Emmanuel admitted more members than even St. John's. For a time, during the 1620's, it was the largest college in the university (J. Morgan 1986, 253). The College has been consistently treated by historians as a house of non-conformity and the charged atmosphere there has been captured by characterizations such as the one by Hugh Trevor-Roper who called Emmanuel a "notorious hotbed of Puritanism" (Trevor-Roper 1962, 16). Into this tumultuous academic setting Thomas Hooker entered in 1604. James had ascended to the throne in 1603 arousing Puritan hopes for a sympathetic ear. But just two months before Hooker came to Cambridge, the Hampton Court Conference resulted in the dashing of these Puritan hopes as James, cheered by Archbishop Whitgift, concluded, "If this be all your party have to say, I will make them conform, or I will harry them out of the land, or else worse" (Neal 1837, I, 232).

The significance of this house of institutionalized Puritanism will receive further treatment below. It suffices here to recall Mather's report of Hooker that it was here at Emmanuel that "the more effectual grace of God gave him the experience of true regeneration." Mather speaks of a soul long distressed by terrors, anguish, and horror at the just wrath of heaven. The inner conflict is summarized by Mather:

> That in the time of his agonies, he could reason himself to the rule, and conclude that there was no way but submission to God, and lying at the foot of his mercy in Christ Jesus, and waiting humbly there, till he should please to perswade the soul of his favor: nevertheless, when he came to apply this rule to himself in his own condition, his

reasoning would fail him, he was able to do nothing (Mather 1853, I, 333).

It was a Mr. Ashe, sizer to Hooker, that finally brought spiritual comfort.[1] If indeed Hooker did experience an agonizing prolonged conversion followed by the pastoral comfort of another, this may well have had a molding influence upon the tenor of his own pastoral ministry. Subsequently Hooker received "well grounded perswasions of his interest in the new covenant." Nightly, upon retiring, Hooker made it his practice to single out some promise of God and rehearse it until he found satisfaction of soul whereupon he could pray, "I will lay me down in peace, and sleep; for Thou, O Lord, makest me dwell in assurance." Amid the storm at Emmanuel, Hooker had found the possibility and comfort of assurance of the soul's safety in Jesus Christ. To help others to seek the same course would become a hallmark of his pastoral ministry. Mather summarized well Hooker's conjunction of promise with assurance by noting that Hooker would counsel "that the promise was the boat which was to carry a perishing sinner over unto the Lord Jesus Christ" (Mather 1853, I, 334).

From Emmanuel Thomas Hooker received his B.A. in 1608. As a Dixie fellow he embarked upon his graduate career taking an active role in the religious life of his college. The M.A. was granted in 1611 and his career in the pulpit had become a foregone conclusion. Nevertheless, Hooker remained at Emmanuel in some capacity,[2] for it was not until 1618 that he departed from its somewhat unsettled security to assume the more precarious career as an Puritan pastor.

---

[1] Hooker's conversion experience receives it most in-depth treatment in Shuffelton 1977, 18-25.

[2] Walker suggests that while a catechist and lecturer, Hooker began the systematic development of his experimental religion (Walker 1891, 30).

PASTORAL CAREER IN ENGLAND

Little is known of Hooker's life between the years of 1618 when he left Cambridge, and 1625 when he took up his pastoral duties in Chelmsford. Upon leaving Cambridge, it is assumed that he went immediately to the village of Esher in Surrey.[1] Hooker's first charge was that of rector of St. George's Church. Coming to Esher he took up residence in the household of a certain Francis Drake, to whose family he also served as chaplain. Though little is known of Hooker's work with the little St. George's congregation, one incident has become notable from the period.

Mrs. Drake was at the time quite emotionally and spiritually disturbed, being convinced that she had committed the unpardonable sin and would invariably burn in hell. During this protracted time of melancholy, Joan Drake had convinced herself of her reprobate status. John Dod, a three-times-silenced nonconforming minister, was the first to try to minister unto her needs. Eventually exasperated by Mrs. Drake's theological argumentation, to say nothing of her outbursts of violence, Dod left the charge with the recommendation that a Thomas Hooker, newly come from the University, and equipped with a "new answering method" might lend some successful counsel.[2] Though Dod

---

[1] Yet by some accounts Hooker did not come to Esher until 1620 (Williams et al. 1975, 4).

[2] Jaspar Heartwell (pseudonymous), *Trodden Down Strength* (1647), p. 117. This narrative of Mrs. Drake's spiritual struggles is attributed on its title page to a Hart On-hi. It was early suggested that this was a pseudonym of John Hart, a parish pastor in Hamilton, Scotland. Williams has argued convincingly for the identification of Jaspar Heartwell (Hartwell) with this Hart On-hi (Williams 1968, 278-290). Frank Suffelton concurs with what he calls Williams' "convincing argument" against the John Hart identification (Shuffelton 1977, 30n).

THE LIFE AND WORK OF THOMAS HOOKER   11

had found some measured success with this argumentative woman, Hooker's Ramistic logic, personal piety, and gentle temperament in the end proved unassailable.[1] Mrs. Drake,

being visited with such distresses of soul as Mr. Hooker himself had passed through, it proved an unspeakable advantage unto both of them that he had the opportunity of being serviceable; for indeed he now had no superior, and scarce any equal, for the skill of treating a troubled soul. (Mather 1853, I, 334)

Through the ministrations of Dod, Hooker, and the notable young John Preston (1587-1628) among others, Mrs. Drake was converted[2] and died contented in 1625. Other than the fact that Hooker was one of a dozen or so ministers[3] who feverishly sought to bring

---

[1] The Trodden Down Strength narrative seems to place Hooker as a seventh worthy divine to minister to Mrs. Drake. Dod was followed by none other than James Ussher, later Primate of the Anglican Church of Ireland; the Scot John Forbes, later co-laborer with Hooker in the Netherlands; a certain Dr. Gibson; John Rogers of Dedham; Robert Bruce of Edinburgh, who was followed by Hooker. After Hooker's departure, Mrs. Drake was ministered unto by the likes of a Mr. Witherall and Dr. John Preston.

[2] The ecstatic conversion of Mrs. Drake is recorded in Trodden Down Strength (1647) which was republished in 1654 as The Firebrand. Mather's own account was probably written independently of these, with Mrs. Hooker possibly serving as a source for Mather (Williams 1976, 5-6).

[3] For the most detailed critical accounts of the Drake incident, see Williams 1968, 11-128, 278-303 and Pettit 1966a, 59-63. Denholm (1961, 35) is confused regarding the origin of Trodden Down Strength which he in one statement attributes to Joan Drake herself.

relief to Joan Drake, these were tranquil times for the young pastor. Skills as a "physician to the soul" were sharpened as Hooker "grew famous for his ministerial abilities, but especially for his notable faculty at the wise and fit management of wounded spirits" (Mather 1853, I, 334). Though the parish at Esher was tiny, the position there, with Drake as patron, required no approbation from the Anglican authorities. Indeed, these Esher years proved to be among the happiest of Hooker's life. From within the Drake household a wife was found as Hooker married Mrs. Drake's woman-in-waiting, Susannah Garbrand. Their first child, to the delight of the Drakes, was named after Mrs. Drake.[1] In this pastoral environment, Hooker became a specialist in "cases of conscience." His gentleness is seen in this description from The Firebrand.

> This man Hooker, being a good, acute, smart preacher, when he listed, besides that information Mr. Dod had given him, was so wise, first to try her spirit, to find her disposition, using her with much mildness and love, ere he would venture to meddle with her spirit, choosing rather that way made from her might usher the way unto his discourse, than that at first he should enforce anything upon her. (Denholm 1961, 36).

Though it would become obvious that Hooker never shied away from prodding the complacent, a distinguishing feature of his ministry would be the

---

Following the seventeenth-century bibliographer George Thomason, Catalogue I, 490, Denholm contradicts himself by identifying the author as John Hart. Denholm also beclouds the relationship between the pseudonymous Trodden Down Strength with its anonymous reissue in 1654 under the title Firebrand Taken Out of the Fire.

[1]Francis Drake expressed his appreciation by including Joan Hooker, later of Hartford, in his will. The will is dated March 13, 1634 and includes a bequest

peace that he sought to bring to discomforted "poor doubters." Without sacrificing his Puritan predestinarianism, the Drake incident, formative as it was, would remain a model for Hooker's theology of preparation for grace (Williams et al. 1975, 5). George Williams, after summarizing the contents of Hooker's Poor Doubting Christian, his preface to John Rogers' The Doctrine of Faith, and his Farewell Sermon, all works which antedate Hooker's 1631 departure for Holland, writes that these provide "the clearest evidence of Hooker's abiding concern with the problem of Joan Drake" (Williams 1968, 291). He further hypothesizes that Joan Drake may be viewed as a comparable factor in the development of Hooker's theology as was Anne Hutchinson in that of John Cotton (Ibid., 298).

THE CHELMSFORD PERIOD

The peaceful death of Mrs. Joan Drake in April of 1625 would close the Esher chapter of Hooker's life. Indeed, Hooker may already have left his Esher responsibilities by that time though he was at Mrs. Drake's bedside at the end. It appears that Hooker's fame was increasing steadily as the pastoral success in Esher became well known and by reason of Mr. Hooker's occasional preaching opportunities in and around London. Seven years earlier he had left Emmanuel a scholar; now he had grown "famous for his ministerial abilities" (Mather 1853, I, 334).

Another sign of growing fame was an incident with some trans-Atlantic importance. William Bradford's Of Plymouth Plantation notes that Hooker was called upon to help settle a dispute which involved the Plymouth colony and its backers. Edward Winslow had returned to

---

to "Johanna Hooker who is now in New England L30 to be paid her the day of her marriage." Johanna Hooker would marry the Rev. Thomas Shepard (Walker 1891, 38).

London with complaints about a certain John Lyford who had been sent to the colony by the London backers. Two "eminent men for moderators" were to be chosen, one by each faction (Bradford 1952, 167-168). That Hooker was chosen by the Plymouth Colony's supporters in London is indicative of his reputation. It probably as well lends some hint to Hooker's toleration of the separatist position, a sentiment which would bring him serious difficulties in subsequent years (Shuffelton 1977, 72).

Just as Hooker's matriculation at Emmanuel nearly coincided with the ascendency of James to the English throne, so was this transitional period accompanied by the succession of a new monarch, Charles I in 1625. Though the ecclesiastical powers had not yet interfered with Hooker's activities, Charles' zeal for conformity and Hooker's scruples regarding church government and ceremony were on a collision course with each other.[1]

Despite Hooker's willingness, Mather records that the providence of God gave an "obstruction" to a ministry in Colchester.

> About this time it was that Mr. Hooker grew into a most intimate acquaintance with Mr. Rogers of Dedham; who so highly valued him for his multifarious abilities, that he used and gained many endeavors to get him settled at Colchester; whereto Mr. Hooker did very much incline because of being so near unto Dedham, where he might enjoy the labours and lectures of Mr. Rogers, whom he would sometimes call 'The prince of all the preachers in England.' (Mather 1853, I, 334)

Hooker would later say,

> That the providence of God often diverted him from employment in such places as he himself desired,

---

[1] See the anonymous "Epistle To The Reader," in Hooker's The Danger of Desertion (1641) for an early indication of Hooker's non-conformity.

THE LIFE AND WORK OF THOMAS HOOKER

and still directed him to such places as he had no thought of. (Ibid.)

So it was that the church of St. Mary in Chelmsford, Essex, issued a call for Hooker to "break the bread of life" to them as their lecturer. George Leon Walker has noted that it was during the Emmanuel years as lecturer and catechist that Hooker was able to systematize his foundational thoughts as to experiential religion (Walker 1891, 30). But now, in his exceedingly popular lectures at Chelmsford, the application of doctrine and the unfolding of cases of conscience would evoke such glowing approbations as, "He was the best at an use that ever he heard" (Mather 1853, I, 335). The scholar of practical theology had become the practitioner of the same.

Not only did the devout travel long distances to hear Mr. Hooker, but the very environs of Chelmsford were transformed. After describing the "profaneness" of the town, especially in its desecration of the Sabbath, Mather notes, "But by the power of his ministry in public, and by the prudence of his carriage in private, he quickly cleared the streets of this disorder, and the Sabbath came to be very visibly sanctified among the people" (Ibid.). Hooker clearly also gained the respect and admiration of the other ministers in the Chelmsford area. On one occasion it was his voice as "an acute disputant" that turned the tide in a monthly meeting of Puritan ministers deliberating the proposed establishment of a lectureship at Cogshall (Colonial Society of Massachusetts 1932, 365-366; Shuffelton 1977, 74-75).

Mather records what has become an often quoted anecdote which he attributes to Clarke.

A profane person, designing therein only an ungodly diversion and merriment, said unto his companions, 'Come, let us go hear what that bawling Hooker will say to us;' and thereupon, with an attention to make sport, unto Chelmsford lecture they came. The man had not been long in the church, before the quick and powerful word of God, in the mouth of his faithful Hooker, pierced the soul of him; he came out with an awakened and distressed soul, and by the further blessing of God upon Mr. Hooker's ministry, he arrived unto a true conversion; for which cause he would not afterwards leave that blessed ministry, but went a thousand leagues to attend it and enjoy it. (Mather 1853, I, 337)

Here the physician of the soul was prodding the complacent, just as he would as frequently be called upon to reassure the distressed poor doubter.

Hooker was held in especially high esteem by the younger ministers in and around Chelmsford "to whom he was an oracle and their principal library."[1] Many would often take recourse to him "to be directed and resolved in their difficult cases" (Mather 1853, I, 336). Even when Laudian pressures were brought to bear against Hooker, some forty-seven conforming ministers petitioned the Bishop of London, seeking to assure him that Hooker's ministry was not injurious or offensive to them. As Mather records it they testified "that they esteem and know the said Mr. Thomas Hooker to be for doctrine, orthodox; for life and conversation, honest; for disposition, peaceable, and in no wise turbulent or factious" (Ibid.). As will be seen below, this petition for leniency served little to stifle Laudian pressures for conformity.

The writings of Roger Williams, who was destined to become a non-conformist in the extreme, preserve what may be a significant incident of Hooker's life from the Chelmsford period. It seems that in July of 1629, Williams came to Chelmsford and he and Hooker rode together to Boston in Lincolnshire in order to confer with John Cotton and the members and associates of the Bay Company (Williams 1975, 17; Winslow 1957, 90).

---

[1]Goodwin 1908, 1189-1190; This phrase has been traced to a letter of Samuel Collins, vicar in Braintree, to Dr. Arthur Duck, chancellor under Laud (Williams 1975, 12).

George Williams has described the scene as "pregnant with the future of New England," and the formation of their respective three colonies (Williams 1975, 17). Their musings together involved the problems of separation and the use of The Book of Common Prayer. Soon after coming to the Chelmsford area, the Hookers rejoiced in the baptism of their daughter Anne at Great Baddow in January, 1626. Towards the end of the Chelmsford period, on August 26, 1629, the Hookers' infant daughter Sarah was buried (Walker 1891, 39). Adding to the difficulty of this time, the Laudian pressures against non-conformity were now being intensified. Hooker's growing fame could not but draw official disfavor.

EPISCOPAL SCRUTINY

King Charles, as quickly and with greater determination than his father had shown, proved himself a formidable antagonist to the Puritan and Parliamentary cause. Given the productivity of Emmanuel College, preachers with Puritan proclivities were to be found in the pulpits of London, Cambridge, and in many more rural parishes. This was the case even well before Laud came to power. Many like Hooker, took donative positions such as the one he held in Esher. In these situations benefices were given to donors (in this case a Mr. Francis Drake), who maintained the privilege of choosing rectors. Because the donors were not required to present their appointees to the bishop, many recipients were able to go about their pastoral duties while ignoring the statutes of conformity when conscience did not allow consent.

Like his father, Charles had a deep respect for his own position. "He believed that kings were directly responsible to God alone for their actions, and that prerogatives of the Crown could not be taken away by human means" (Lockyer 1964, 244). Immediate changes were made in public life and the relative moral laxity of the reign of James gave way to a measure of rigidity. With this inclination to rule by personal prerogative,

Charles heightened tensions between the crown and Parliament. On the continent, the Thirty Years war was dragging on with little encouragement to the Protestant side. With the ever present Spanish threat, and given the decadent state of the English forces, military subsidies from Parliament became all important. James had only half-heartedly acted upon the Spanish threat, all the more raising the ire of the Commons as they petitioned him to take more seriously the Protestant cause. The King being offended at such an attack upon his royal prerogative and at such "lecturing," Parliament was dissolved and James went about the Spanish problem according to his own agenda. As the throne passed to Charles, the sentiments in Parliament favored a naval campaign against Spain on the Elizabethan model (Ibid., 236-244).

As a result of dissatisfaction with Charles, Parliament voted only two military subsidies and eventually took the bold step of cutting the King's ordinary revenue. Breaking precedent, they voted the King the customs duties "Tonnage and Poundage," for only one year, not the customary life-time appropriation. Parliament continued to air grievances and to withhold funds until the dissolution of 1629. Charles' insistence on his own prerogative in foreign matters was mirrored in his actions regarding the church. Indeed, Parliament itself was filled with Puritan protagonists.

Increasingly, the members of the Puritan movement sensed a looming crisis which would separate Englishmen into the loyal and the faithless. William Laud in 1627 was made a Privy Councillor and in 1628, the Bishop of London. In 1633 he was to become the Archbishop of Canterbury. With Thomas Wentworth and his policy of "Thorough," Laud provided a second prong in Charles' insistence on conformity to his dictates. So "thorough" were their policies that Laud presented to Charles an exacting list of clerical names with symbols attached indicating the level of the man's orthodoxy or puritanism (Shuffelton 1977, 29). Laud and Wentworth became the "champions" of the personal rule of Charles. For Laud, not wishing to look into the souls of men, an outwardly conforming, comprehensive and national church, was the ideal. Conformity was seen as a sine qua non of unity.

> Unity cannot not long continue on the Church when uniformity is shut out at the church door. No external action in the world can be uniform without some ceremonies. . . . Ceremonies are the hedge that fences the substance of religion from all the indignities which profaneness and sacrilege too commonly put upon it. (Quoted in Lockyer 1964, 255)

With these sentiments, Laud set about to remove Puritan irregularities. He correctly surmised that the greatest flow of Puritan agitation was springing from the preachers who held Lectureships, which in reality had become Puritan foundations (Denholm 1961, 40-41).

Given Hooker's growing fame as a preacher and his influential monthly ministerial conferences, he became a natural and prime target of Laudian pressure. The inevitable came in 1629 as Hooker was summoned to London to appear before Bishop Laud. In sermons like "The Church's Deliverances" and "The Carnal Hypocrite," both probably preached in 1626, Hooker put forth what he viewed as signs that God is losing patience with England. Along with many other Puritan preachers, Hooker used Leviticus 26 to put forth the options of blessing or curses before the people. He announced, "The famine hath been threatened, the plague inflicted, and the sword is coming" (in Williams et al. 1975, 80). The apocalyptic theme of imminent danger is sounded as Hooker notes that sin is on the increase and that the nation faces the peril of God's judgment. By these sermons, which brought him trouble from the authorities, Hooker sought to "recover our country and times out of those dangers that are threatened against us" (in Williams et al. 1975, 92).

Contemporaneously with the dissolution of Parliament, Laud began to suspend Puritan ministers and lecturers. Hooker's friend and mentor, John Rogers of Dedham, was one of the first targets. Though Hooker's fame was no doubt already known to Laud, a letter from

Samuel Collins, Vicar of Braintree, written to Laud's chancellor Dr. Arthur Duck, flamed with urgency and must have moved Laud's hand. Hooker's departure from the diocese was urged as,

> His private conference . . . hath already more impeached the peace of our church than his publique ministry. . . . there be divers young ministers about us that spend their time in conference with him. . . . Our people's pallats grow so out of tast, that noe food contents them but of Mr. Hooker's dressing. (in Davids 1863, 150-151)

This was indeed a time of growing anticlericalism of the Episcopal sort as the unpopularity of the prelates was aggravated by their association with the personal rule of Charles. Laud was now convinced that stricter policies against the Puritan agitators were necessary.

In late May of 1629 Hooker was called to London to appear before Laud's High Commission. Across the country and especially at Cambridge, the news of the summons was spread. Collins wrote that Hooker's predicament had the effect of even drowning "the noise of the greater question of Tonnage and Poundage" (Ibid., 152; cf. Trevor-Roper 1962, 16). Perhaps as a result of Collins' cautions to deal carefully with Hooker given his great popularity, rather than being banished from the diocese, Hooker was simply stripped of his lectureship and was required to post bond, guaranteeing upon request his reappearance.

So it was that by the middle of 1629 Thomas Hooker was officially silenced. Returning to his home at Cuckoos Farm in Little Baddow, just outside of Chelmsford, Hooker opened a grammar school, being assisted by John Eliot (Shuffelton 1977, 128; Winslow 1968, 19-20). Despite the official silencing, Hooker's preaching activities seem to have been little curtailed. Davids' chronicle reports the complaints to Laud of a Mr. Browning who laments Hooker's continued practices (Davids 1863, 152-153). Laud also received a petition of support for Hooker from forty-nine ministers of Essex. Curiously, the timid Rev. Collins, who had asked for anonymity in his reports to Dr. Duck, signed the petition of support for Hooker. The divisiveness that was being caused in the diocese became all too evident when Laud, only a week after receiving the petition in support of Hooker, received a counter petition of complaint against Hooker from forty-one conforming clergymen. In July of 1630 Hooker was called to appear again in London. Laud's zeal would no doubt fall more harshly against Hooker this time. It is of little surprise then that "Mr. Hooker's friends advised him to forfeit his bonds, rather than to throw himself any further into the hands of his enemies" (Mather 1853, I, 338). A certain Mr. Nash had been bound in the sum of fifty pounds for Hooker's reappearance. With Hooker's assent the sum was forfeited to the court with Nash's surety being reimbursed "by several good people in and near Chelmsford" (Ibid.) Exile appeared now to be the only plausible course given Hooker's fame. Shuffelton, relating the soul-searching importance of the decision that now lay before Hooker, suggests that he most likely consulted with men like John Rogers, Thomas Welde, and possibly with Richard Sibbes, with whose sermons a draft of Hooker's "The Poor Doubting Christian" had been published in 1629. (Shuffelton 1977, 132-133). By the spring of 1631 the difficult decision had been made and Hooker secretly set sail for the Netherlands.

Most likely, just prior to this departure, Hooker preached his so-called farewell sermon, "The Danger of Desertion." Traditionally this sermon has been thought to be Hooker's "farewell" to England in 1633 as he departed for New England with other Puritan luminaries, among them John Cotton and Samuel Stone. George H. Williams has recently argued convincingly that Hooker preached this sermon during Holy Week of 1631 (Williams 1975, 221-227). It served as a farewell even to his own family who would be left behind in England as Hooker explored the possibilities of a less hindered ministry in the Low Countries. The tone of the sermon is ominous, with its mood of desperation colored by apocalyptic themes. Following the present dearth of gospel truth in England, she will feel the sword of

God's judgment unless the sincere prayers of the church are able to turn such away. In the face of the devastation then being worked on the continent, Hooker urges England to awake from her slumber of self-assured safety. Hooker declares that God may indeed remove His love from a people and also the tokens of His love, His Word and sacraments, the means of salvation.

> . . . glory is departed from England; for England has seen her best days, and the reward of sin is coming on apace; for God is packing up his gospel, because none will buy his wares (not come to his price). . . . Oh, therefore my brethren, lay hold on God, and let him not go out of your coasts. (He is going!) Look about you, I say, and stop him at the town's end, and let not thy God depart! Oh England, lay siege about him by humble and hearty closing with him, and although he is going, he is not gone yet! (in Williams et al. 1975, 246)

Thus in what will be seen to be a typical Hookerian fashion, he pleads with his complacent hearers to "do something;" in this case to close with God by repentance and pleading. Some time in late April of 1631 Hooker secretly sailed for the Netherlands, most likely traveling alone. Shuffelton probably errs in saying that Hooker's family accompanied him as he embarked on this pilgrim exploratory journey (Shuffelton 1977, 133). By the summer of 1631, Hooker's name had been inscribed in the record of the Amsterdam English church and his short-lived Dutch career had begun (Carter 1964, 192: Sprunger 1973, 18).

THE NETHERLANDS EXPERIMENT

Prior to Keith Sprunger's 1973 article "The Dutch Career of Thomas Hooker," students of the period labored with a paucity of information concerning Hooker's sojourn in the Netherlands during the years of 1631-1633. Walker's 1891 biography, until recently the standard such work, went little beyond Mather's *Magnalia* in its scant report of the Dutch period of Hooker's career. Yet this short span of time proved to be most formative in Hooker's ministerial development. Of greatest importance is the flowering of Hooker's ecclesiastical principles which in time would become known as "Congregationalism." Because Hooker was leaving England with non-conformist principles, an evolution would take place from within a crucible of conflict with a certain Rev. John Paget and the Dutch Classis at Amsterdam. A decade and a half later, the final fruit of this formative period would come to light with the publication of Hooker's A Survey Of The Summe Of Church Discipline.

This interim Dutch career lasted at least twenty months, but no longer than twenty-three months (Sprunger 1973, 18-19). By no calculations can Denholm's mention of a "three year sojourn" be correct (Denholm 1961, 50). Above all, this interim career served as a troubled experiment in congregational polity. In the end it gave way, as with so many of the Puritans who had sojourned in the Netherlands, to a voyage to the New World.

Because of the two dozen or so English churches in the Netherlands, the prospects for ministry there were good. Hooker received an invitation from certain members of the English Reformed Church at Amsterdam. As it would turn out, this invitation from "interested persons" was issued in less than a regular fashion. An inn keeper, a Mr. Stephen Offwood, wrote on behalf of a faction in the church seeking to find a replacement for the recently deceased Rev. Thomas Potts. Potts had served for fourteen years at Amsterdam as co-pastor with the senior minister, the Rev. John Paget (Sprunger 1973, 18-19). In a demonstration of propriety, Hooker let it be known that he would indeed minister at Amsterdam, but only if he were to receive an official call from the church. In the meanwhile, he would proceed to Rotterdam, "expecting the call from hence" (Ibid.). While awaiting the call, Hooker most likely visited with Hugh Peter (1598-1660) the English preacher in Rotterdam.

Having left England's turmoil behind, Hooker

must have anticipated with excitement the new opportunities to minister. The Offwood correspondence had offered nothing but encouragement. Little did Hooker know that the church was racked with bitter factionalism. Offwood, formerly a separatist, had joined the English Reformed Church only in 1629. Several others of the same faction had formerly been separatists. Hooker, by reason of their outreach, was now aligned, at least by perception, with this radical faction which was opposed by a group led by the Rev. Paget himself. Paget himself had a clear non-conformist record, having left Cheshire rather than to conform. He now labored in a church which received support from the city government and was united to the Dutch Reformed Church. Paget and Potts had taken session with the Amsterdam Classis, marking the church and its ministers as fully in fellowship with the Dutch establishment. In fact, Paget had opposed the establishment of the separate English-speaking Classis. As the unfolding debate with Hooker would show, Paget's principles belong to what would soon be labeled as "Presbyterian." Indeed Walker, in describing the English Reformed Church at Amsterdam, gives it the premature designation "British Presbyterian" (Walker 1891, 52). Hooker was only one of several unhappy choices made by the independent minded faction as they sought to counter the views of their own pastor. At one time or another, such notables as Hugh Peter, Thomas Welde, William Ames, and John Forbes, were also put forth (unsuccessfully) as possible associates to Rev. Paget (Sprunger 1973, 21).

An official call had come in July of 1631 and though the Classis had not yet approved it, Hooker began his preaching duties at the church, seemingly to the liking of the majority of the members. But Paget was not satisfied and eventually announced to the Consistory that he would address a certain twenty questions to Mr. Hooker in order to try his suitability for the English Reformed ministry. At this point we need not chronicle the intricate judicatory process involving Paget, the Consistory, and the Classis. Hooker's answers to Paget's questions provided more than was needed to evoke a negative verdict from the Classis.

Paget's questions and Hooker's answers are now most accessible in Williams' Thomas Hooker: Writings In England And Holland.[1] To discover the salient and distinguishing points of Hooker's crystallizing ecclesiology, some attention must now be given to the document itself.

Considerable concurrence between the two ministers is obvious in at least seven of the propositions put forth. Paget and Hooker agree in one degree or another as to the legitimacy of such practices as set prayers that are sometimes read (Question #4), the use of the so-called "Lord's Prayer" (Q. #5), preaching at Christmastide, Easter, and Whitsuntide (Q. #7), the use of lay readers (Q. #8), discipline by the Elders (Q. #9), suspension from the Lord's Table as a form of lesser excommunication (Q. #16), and the proposition that one is justified by the active as well as passive obedience of Christ (Q. #20).

Nevertheless, the seriousness of their divergent views on such matters as relations with the Brownists, the baptism of children of non-church members, and the powers of the individual congregations becomes quite obvious in this document. Once committed to writing, "John Paget's XX Questions and Thomas Hooker's Answers" explicated Hooker's opposition to the views of both Paget and the Dutch Reformed churches. Paget appears as the relative "high churchman" in allowing for baptism of infants of those who are not members of the church "according to the manner of these Reformed Churches" (Q. #6). Hooker responds that such a practice is foreign to his thinking. In response to Paget's proposition that church members be received without public examination, Hooker seemed to concur, but no doubt

---

[1] Hooker had been requested by Paget to prepare four copies of his answers. Some variants have appeared as one copy was transcribed in the "Boswell Papers" and has been reproduced in full in Stearns 1940, 105-113. The Consistory Register transcribed another copy which has been reproduced in Carter 1964, 189-200. Williams presents what constitutes a composite edition.

raised some questions by remarking that others cannot be accepted unless they are publicly examined (Q. #10). The eventual outworking of Hooker's view on this matter would be the less stringent "visible saint" requirement practiced in Connecticut as relative to that in the Bay Colony.
Two other answers of Hooker not only set him at odds with Paget, but also would be mirrored in his New England ministry. Question #11 concerned the necessity of Classis approval of a minister called by an individual congregation.

> Touching this query, then, my opinion is this, a particular congregation hath complete power by Christ's institution to give a complete call unto a minister without any derived power from a Classis. . . . If the Classis should not approve, they may lawfully and without sin choose without or against the approbation of the Classis if they saw good reason, by the convenient fitness of the party to induce them thereunto. And so I judge of the eleventh query. (in Williams 1975, 284-285)

Of course such sentiments would become the hallmark of Hooker's congregationalism as finally codified in his A *Survey* of the *Summe* of *Church Discipline* (1648).
Question #17 constitutes that which ominously foreshadows the New England Hutchinsonian controversy, the settlement of which would find Hooker serving as one of the moderators. At this early time, Hooker sought to maintain the authority of the offices of the church, yet, invoking the view of William Ames, he concluded,

> If it be a Christian duty thus allowed by Scripture and practiced by the saints to interpret the gospel unto all, as opportunity calls or invites, occasionally thereunto, the same Christians, still keeping the proportion of their gift, not crossing their places, employment, and finding other expedients for the action, they may at set times and in set places do it ordinarily. (in Williams

1976, 288-289)

After noting that severe abuses are quite possible, Hooker says,

> The like failings issue from the folly of men's minds and corruption of men's hearts but are not caused by the practice of this duty, the cautions of expedience, order, and such like being attended therein. (Ibid., 289)

It is therefore clear that while Hooker desired to maintain a high view of the church offices, he nevertheless was careful not to attribute to the clergy an exclusive right to interpret the Holy Scripture.

Before leaving this overview of Paget's "Twenty Questions," Hooker's answer to Question #19 must receive some detailed attention, for it touches upon his morphology of conversion, seen in this present work as the most last legacy of Thomas Hooker. Question #19, which Paget answers in the negative, asks whether true repentance or any saving work precedes true faith in those who are regenerate. Hooker responds:

> There is a double repentance. The first is of preparation, wrought by the almighty and irresistible power of the Spirit, causing the sinner to go out of himself (and sin) in humiliation before he can go to God in Christ by faith in vocation; and this goes before faith and I conceive it to be nothing but the stroke of the Spirit in the very first work of conversion wherein the soul makes itself merely passive as our divines used to speak, and in the true nature of it, cannot be in any reprobate. Second, there is a repentance in sanctification, that word being strictly so taken; and it comes after faith. So Mr. Rogers of Dedham in his treatise; so Mr. Chibal in his treatise of the 'Trial of Faith' (Ibid., 290).

Here is an early indication of Hooker's preparationism, including the chronological aspects of his morphology.

Note the constituent parts mentioned: "preparation," "humiliation," "vocation," and "sanctification." Yet Hooker's monergism is clear in the answer as he takes pains to show himself, in this land of Dort, to be with the high Calvinists. Of particular importance is the recognition of "almighty and irresistible power of the Spirit," the "stroke of the Spirit," and the passivity of the soul.

The mention of Mr. John Rogers is a reference to the author of *The Doctrine of Faith* (1627) which was prefaced by Hooker's own "Epistle To The Reader," the first Hookerian piece to be published. Even then, a doctrine of a double repentance can be found in Hooker,

> Though therefore we must have faith before we can be in Christ, the soul must be contrite before it can have faith . . . the one is a sorrow of preparation, the other a sorrow of sanctification, and yet both are saving. The one is wrought upon us, wherein we are patients of the work of the Holy Spirit bringing us unto Christ; the other is wrought through the Spirit given to us and dwelling in us when we have received Christ. (in Williams et al. 1975, 147-151)

So it was that some four years before his interroga-tion by John Paget, Hooker had gone to print with his version of Calvinism, newly conjoined with a nascent form of preparationism. It was now evident that Hooker differed from Paget not only in ecclesiology, but also as to some of the finer points of soteriology.

As Hooker completed his twenty answers to Paget, he concluded with words that express his foresight of the inevitable.

> And because I do apprehend your opinion and affections to be so far settled . . . . I am resolved contentedly to sit down and suddenly as I see my opportunity to depart, wishing that the God of Peace would provide so comfortable an assistant as might suit with you in all truth and godliness for your mutual comfort and the building up of the

body of Christ. (in Williams 1975, 291)

The Amsterdam Classis, with its copy of the twenty questions and answers translated into Latin in hand, then rendered its judgment. No minister with such opinions was to be admitted into the Classis nor could such a one serve the English Reformed Church at Amsterdam (Walker 1891, 53-54; Burrage 1912, I, 296, 309-312). Paget was vindicated and thanked for his conscientious work while the Consistory in question was warned concerning Hooker "not to bring him in the future into the pulpit" ("Acts of Classis" in Sprunger 1973, 27).

Cotton Mather's verdict was that the whole affair had a foregone conclusion seeing that "the old man (Paget) being secretly willing that Mr. Hooker should not accept of this invitation, he contrived many ways to render him suspected unto the classis" (Mather 1853, I, 339). It is the view of this writer that Mather's attribution to Paget of personal jealously toward Hooker is to be rejected. Given the succession of congregationalist ministers rejected for the Amsterdam post, it appears rather that Paget's opposition to Hooker was genuinely based on divergent views, especially in the realm of ecclesiology. On their respective sojourns following their departures from England, Paget was consciously moving in the direction of a continental Reformed and Presbyterian model, while Hooker was in a painfully formative stage of his Congregational persuasion.

Though the Classis had rendered its verdict, the defiance of the Hookerian faction in Amsterdam refused to be silenced. In late October of 1631 this pro-Hooker group asked the Consistory to allow Hooker to preach for several Wednesdays "as in former tyme hee had done." With a sympathetic disposition the Consistory approved the suggestion, an act which constituted a clear defiance of the Classis. Hooker himself prevented any open rupture by declining the honor. The offended Classis dispatched a delegation to censure the elders of the English church for their anti-Classis invitation (Sprunger 1973, 31).

Before the month of November was over Hooker had departed Amsterdam for the hopefully more friendly confines of Delft, leaving behind the havoc wrought by his Amsterdam candidacy. This may have been the occasion for the famous "reconciliation sermon" of William Ames, preached at the Amsterdam Church (Sprunger 1973, 34). At Delft, Hooker was received by the aged Scottish minister, the Reverend John Forbes, to whom Hooker became the assistant at the Prisenhof Church. Forbes had resided in the Netherlands for over two decades, having been forced to flee his native Scotland as a consequence of his participation in the Aberdeen Assembly of 1605. Not only did Hooker and Forbes share common sentiments as to synods and assemblies, but their affinity with one another was also strengthened by the fact that both had ministered to the needs of Mrs. Joan Drake while in England (Williams 1975, 27). Mather's description of their close fellowship together is well known as he likened Forbes and Hooker to "Basil and Nazianzen . . . one soul in two bodies" (Mather 1853, I, 339).

Forbes was one of the most prominent English preachers in the Netherlands and he served as the President of the English Classis or Synod. This English Classis to which Forbes' church belonged, differed significantly from the Dutch Classes in that it functioned only in an advisory manner, according to the tenets of congregational ecclesiology. Though desiring this increased independence, the English churches were still generally dependent upon the respective municipalities for financial assistance. Nevertheless, especially within the English-Scottish community in the Netherlands, there is clear evidence of a growing congregationalism in this period, with only Amsterdam and Utrecht having joined the Dutch Classes.

Hooker spent some sixteen months in Delft during which time services without the Prayer Book were characterized by increasing spontaneity and improvisation. In addition, departing from the continental Reformed model, Hooker refused to baptize the children of non-church members (Williams 1975, 28; Sprunger 1973, 40-41; Stearns 1940, 31-40). With such sentiments, the formative nature of this sojourn in the Netherlands marks it as a foretaste of the "New England Way."

During this period, in October of 1632, Hooker's *The Soules Preparation For Christ, Or, A Treatise of Contrition*, was anonymously published in London. In this preliminary preparationist work, to be examined here in a later chapter, Hooker calls upon his hearers to recognize their sin and to prepare their frame of heart for the reception of God's grace. "If I could finde my soule grieving within mee for my rebellions and sins, I should not doubt of mercy" (Hooker 1632, 239). The series of sermons collected in this 1632 volume had probably been first preached during the Chelmsford period (Walker 1891, 185). Preparationism and the estimate of the minister as a physician to all the ills of the soul were themes that were being nurtured during this Netherlandish sojourn of Thomas Hooker.

Very few details of this Delft period are extant given that church records do not survive. Because of the lack of connection with the Dutch Classis, the records thereof contain little mention of the English Church at Delft. Nonconformity had reached such an extreme that it was recorded of Hooker in this period that he never used the Lord's Prayer ("Boswell Papers," in Sprunger 1973, 41). These English ministers, having left behind Laudian scrutiny, were in the Netherlands conforming neither to English nor to Dutch practice.

Mather stands as a solitary voice in reporting that Hooker was called to serve in the English church at Rotterdam alongside none other than the "invaluable Dr. Ames" (Mather 1853, 339). But Mather not only mistakes the length of Hooker's stay in Delft, but also fails to note that Ames himself did not come to Rotterdam as Hugh Peter's assistant until late summer or fall of 1633. By this time Hooker had nearly reached New England. Perhaps Mather was attempting a reasonable reconstruction of the events given Dr. Ames' well known approbation of Hooker's ministry. Ames remarked that "he had never met Mr. Hooker's equal, either for preaching or for disputing." In reciprocity, Hooker noted that if a scholar was to study Ames' *Medulla*

Theologia and *De Conscientia*, he would become "a good divine, though he had no more books in the world" (Ibid.).
The precise occasion of this mutual respect remains unknown. Yet the publication of Dr. Ames' *Fresh Suite Against Human Ceremonies* (1633) contained a lengthy preface written by Hooker. At this stage in the development of his thought, Hooker assumes that the only legitimate polity is that which binds together experientially covenanted Christians under the reign of Christ. For Hooker, the question of ceremony was wed to that of polity in that no bishop was to impose from above humanly devised ceremonies. As to further inspection here, this "Preface," and Hooker's last work *The Survey of the Summe of Church Discipline* (published posthumously in 1648) provide the major expositions of Hookerian congregationalism. None other than Stephen Offwood, who had originally invited Hooker to Amsterdam, was the publisher of this Ames-Hooker work. The Amesian legacy of covenant theology and congregational polity would eventually be carried to New England by Thomas Hooker. In a summary statement that might seem to disparage the importance of the likes of John Cotton, Denholm remarks, "Ames was the chief formulator of the system and Hooker was its chief New England exponent" (Denholm 1961, 61).

Despite his accomplishments and growing renown in the Netherlands, Hooker was growing restless. Williams wonders if Hooker may not have secretly visited London following the Delft period, in order to confer with John Cotton and John Davenport (Williams 1975, 30-31). What is firmly established is that sometime in early 1633 Hooker wrote from Rotterdam to Cotton in England. The letter fragment has been preserved only in Mather. Hooker laments that the Dutch seem to "content themselves with very forms, though much blemished." Hooker goes on to express his own recent introspections and evaluations of his life as he has wrestled to understand God's providence which has been "wonderful in miseries, and more than wonderful in mercies to me and mine" (Mather 1853, I, 340; Williams 1975, 295-296).

Already, while he sojourned in the Netherlands,

many of Hooker's Essex disciples had set sail for New England bearing the name of their mentor, being known as "Mr. Hooker's company." Early in 1633 Hooker quietly slipped from the Netherlands back into England and began to make preparations for his own trans-Atlantic voyage.

ON TO NEW ENGLAND

Tempered and matured, Thomas Hooker left behind a two year experiment in order to face a much greater frontier. Perhaps he could find space in New England. Perhaps the new shores would provide a haven for heart religion of the Amesian-Hookerian type, far from the long arm of Laud which had even reached into Holland (Walker 1891, 60).

In the meanwhile, "Mr. Hooker's Company" in New England busied themselves with preparations for the arrival of their mentor. Though no correspondence between Hooker and his "company" has survived, the somewhat orderly preparations, along with Mather's report of communication, indicate that the lines of communication were open and that Hooker's eventual arrival in New England was a foregone conclusion. Hooker's company, after a short stay at Mount Wollaston, near Boston, had settled by order of the Court, in Newtowne. There they longingly awaited a fully equipped ministry, both Pastor and Teacher of the church. Thus a co-worker was sought for Mr. Hooker. William Ames, harboring some designs about following Hooker, had died soon after Hooker's departure from Rotterdam. Given the previous correspondence with John Cotton, that worthy appeared a logical choice were he willing. But after those plans were abandoned, the New Englanders turned to the consideration of three younger ministers, Thomas Shepard, John Norton, and Samuel Stone (Walker 1891, 61; Shuffelton 1977, 159). The choice fell finally upon Rev. Stone, lecturer at Towcester in Northamptonshire. Stone, originally from Hertford, had taken his B.A. from Emmanuel in 1624 and his M.A. in 1627. Four years the elder to Thomas Shepard, it was by Shepard's recommendation that Stone became the lecturer at the considerable town of Towcester. Indeed it was with Stone that the fugitive Hooker was housed briefly upon his return to England before the trans-Atlantic journey in 1633.

Mather records a somewhat humorous incident involving the pipe-puffing and Rahab-like Mr. Stone. During the period when Stone was housing Hooker, one of his pursuers approached the dwelling behind whose walls Hooker and Stone were at that moment discoursing with one another.

> The officer demanded whether Mr. Hooker were not there? Mr. Stone replied with a braving sort of confidence, 'What Hooker? Do you mean Hooker that once lived at Chelmsford!' The officer answered 'Yes he!' Mr. Stone immediately, with a diversion like that which once helped Athanasius, made this true answer, 'If it be he you look for, I saw him about an hour ago, at such an house in the town; you had best hasten thither after him.' (Mather 1853, I, 340)

And so Hooker escaped the captor's snare and set his sights resolutely towards New England.

In this context Mather places the preaching of the farewell sermon, based on Jeremiah 14:9, "We are called by Thy name, leave us not." In this moving sermon, entitled "The Danger of Desertion," Hooker almost apocalyptically announces the imminent removal of God's favor from England. Williams, dating this sermon to April 17, 1631 (Hooker's departure for Holland) has almost certainly corrected the traditional view as set forth by Mather (Williams et al., 1975, 221-227).

From Downs in July of 1633, Hooker, Stone, and Cotton set sail for New England upon "The Griffin." Cotton and Hooker, sensing the danger of their being pursued, boarded the ship in disguise and unobtrusively joined the two hundred or so other passengers. Laud, desiring in no way to strengthen the "heretics" in New England, was having the ports watched in an effort to stem the hemorrhaging flow of preachers to the distant shores. Only Stone, the youngest and least known of the triumvirate, dared to disclose his ministerial status before the ship reached the open sea (Mather 1853, I, 341; Williams 1975, 34). Mather, in his biography of his venerable namesake, provides this summary of the crossing.

But by one or other of these three divines in the ship, there was a sermon preached every day, all while they were aboard; yea they had three sermons or expositions, for the most part every day: of Mr. Cotton in the morning, Mr. Hooker in the afternoon, Mr. Stone after supper in the evening. And after they had been a month upon the seas, Mr. Cotton received a mercy, which God had now for twenty years denied unto him, in the birth of his eldest son, who he called 'Sea-born,' in the remembrance of the never-to-be-forgotten blessings which he thus enjoyed upon the seas. But at the end of seven weeks they arrived at New England, September 3, in the year 1633; where he put a shore at New Boston. (Mather 1853, I, 265)

The passage no doubt was marked by much theological discussion between the three worthy ministers. Foreshadowing their immersion into the "congregational way," Cotton's new-born infant was not baptized on board, for it was felt that the group did not represent a duly gathered church. Perhaps more strikingly and distinctively "congregational," neither did the three consider themselves proper ministers while in transit since they had no oversight of a particular congregation (Winthrop 1908, I, 107).

Differences in sentiment between Hooker and Cotton, later to become obvious most notably in the Antinomian controversy, may have surfaced during the passage. Previously, for unknown reasons, Cotton had declined the invitation of Mr. Hooker's company as their first choice as co-worker with Hooker. Whether owing to known differences or not, in October Hooker and Stone settled in Newtown as pastor and teacher respectively, leaving Cotton behind to minister in Boston (Winthrop 1908, I, 137).

Walker, writing before the significant works of Burrage and Miller, and the further refinements by Morgan, mistakenly describes the fluidity of ecclesiology in New England as a gradual assumption of congregationalism in the Bay from the neighbors in Plymouth (Walker 1891, 66). Hooker's <u>Answers</u> <u>To</u> <u>The</u> <u>Twenty</u> <u>Questions</u> <u>of</u> <u>John</u> <u>Paget</u> and the afore-mentioned actions aboard the Griffin, provide evidence enough that for these men a congregational view of the church was not received from Plymouth but rather had English, Dutch, and Amesian roots. Ever present seemed to be the tension that existed between proto-Presbyterianism and the perceived anarchy of Separatism, sometimes viewed as the logical extension of the congregational way. The eventual appearance of synodical assemblies, though admittedly only in an advisory capacity, served to build perceived bridges to Presbyterianism while all real debt to Brownism was denied. Stephen Foster has shown that as immigration continued in the mid 1630's (after Hooker's passage) it became characterized by radical and more stringent sentiments as the prospects of conscientious compromise became increasingly difficult under the now overtly Arminian and conformist strictures of Laud and Wren (Foster 1984, 3-37). As Hooker arrived in 1633 he stood in the mainstream of moderate but evolving congregationalism. In a sermon on "Selfe-Tryal," the second of <u>The</u> <u>Christian's</u> <u>Two</u> <u>Chiefe</u> <u>Lessons</u> (1640), Hooker maintained,

> For the confuting of those sectaries among us who do reject the ministry of the Church of England, together with the Ministers, as no Ministry nor Ministers, in regard of some defects accidental, not substantial in the same. We for our justification refer ourselves unto the whole armies of Converts, which are the glory and crown of many godly teachers among us.
> (Hooker 1640a, 204)

Leaving Cotton behind in Boston, Hooker and Stone proceeded to what had fast become the second most powerful town in the colony. Yet the very existence of

Newtown represented a troublesome reminder of the civil differences which could be found in the colony. The pair were received by the Deputy Governor of the colony, Thomas Dudley, for whom the rise of Newtown was something of a special project. Dudley and Governor Winthrop had earlier disagreements concerning the proper settlement site in 1630 after Salem was found to be overcrowded. On the heels of some measure of bickering and the resultant random formation of towns, colony leaders decided on the need for a central fortified town. Dudley was no doubt gratified when the site choice became Newtown, which he had favored from the beginning. But to Dudley's frustration, early on, few were attracted to Newtown and no magistrates rushed to move their towns to the site. Just as it appeared that the plans for Newtown were destined to become a failure, new life was injected into the town with the arrival of "Mr. Hooker's company," assigned to Newtown by the order of the General Court (Shuffelton 1977, 161-164; Rutman 1965, 25).

Denholm notes that Hooker and Stone, by reason of geography, were now perceived as being aligned with Dudley and the freemen, as opposed to the more oligarchical magistracy as represented by Winthrop. Inadvertently, they were thrust into this contest of strength. Denholm wonders, even while admitting that there is no evidence in this direction, whether or not these early differences contributed to the eventual removal to Connecticut (Denholm 1961, 85-87). Denholm's remarks must be assigned to the whole host of suppositions lacking evidence as to the factors which finally resulted in the westward removal. This follows, especially on the lack of any evidence of anything but seemingly cordial and sincere agreement between Hooker and Winthrop prior to the removal when Hooker suggested that towns in the colony were set too close to one another. Surely such a sentiment in itself represented no basic difference of political ideology between the clergyman and the governor.

It was to a town of about a hundred families that Hooker and Stone came in the fall of 1633. Already the work of establishing a gathered church was under way among those who had preceded Hooker by some fourteen months. A meetinghouse had been erected and William Goodwin chosen as ruling elder. Hooker and Stone were ordained on October 11, 1633, in the same congregational manner as Cotton had been the day before in Boston (Winthrop 1908, I, 106, 110-111). That first winter for the Hooker family was marked by the need for adjustment to the new surroundings and the task of church organization. Thomas and Susannah had arrived in New England with three daughters and two sons, and were given another son within a few months of coming to Newtown. It is likely that it was the latter son whose death Winthrop reports in December of 1634 (Winthrop 1943, III, 177; Shuffelton 1977, 162n). Newtown, no longer languishing, was a pleasant and orderly place. Writing in the year of Hooker's arrival there, William Wood gave this description of the town:

> This is one of the neatest and best compacted Townes in New England, having many faire structures with many handsome contrived streets. The inhabitants most of them are very rich. well stored with cattle of all sorts; having many hundred Acres of ground paled in with one generall fence, which is about a mile and a halfe long, which secures all the weaker Cattle from the wilde beasts. (Young 1846, 402)

The town's sense of community and aesthetics became obvious when, in the first town meeting in the new meeting house, it was agreed that all roofs would be of slate or board rather than thatch and that for uniformity, all houses were to stand in a row, six feet from the road (Paige 1877, 18). Shuffelton summarizes the ambitious nature of the Newtown residents as being frustrated at being denied political centrality, but still determined to become the most imposing town in the Bay (Shuffelton 1977, 165). Hooker took up his pastoral duties no doubt with zeal. More than a decade later, in his <u>Survey</u>, he would codify his own conception of the pastoral office.

> The scope of his Office is to work upon the will and the affections, and by savoury, powerfull, and affectionate application of the truth delivered, to chafe it into the heart, to wooe and win the soul to the love and liking, the approbation and practice of the doctrine which is according to godlinesse . . . his labor is to lay open the lothsome nature of sinne, and to let in the terrour of the Lord upon the conscience, that the careless and rebellious sinner may come to a parley of peace, and be content to take up the profession of the truth. (Hooker 1648, II, 19)

The psychological nomenclature is characteristic of Hooker's view of the ministry and his own pastoral career. Whether writing a technical treatise as here, or in actual pastoral ractice in one's parlor, Hooker showed himself a careful and probing "physician to the soul."

Leaving aside a discussion of possible tensions between Newtown and Boston, or Dudley and Winthrop, and any possible differences in polity at this early stage, it remains clear that the arrival of Cotton and Hooker brought stability to the incipient congregationalism in the Bay. Hubbard writes that the two "did clear up the order and method of church government, according as they apprehended was most consonant to the word of God" (Hubbard 1878, 181). Students of the period are not often enough reminded that Thomas Hooker was the first settler with prior experience in administering a congregationalist church owing to his experiences at Delft and Rotterdam (Shuffelton 1977, 167).

Apart from Hooker's joy at being there, Mather reports nothing of the thirty-two month ministry at Newtown. Reunited with many former friends, Hooker declared, "Now I live, if you stand fast in the Lord" (Mather 1853, I, 342). To nurture such "heart religion" was Hooker's lifelong driving motivation. The most significant episode of this Newtown phase of Hooker's career is one that worked havoc in the whole colony, the case of Roger Williams. An examination of these events is instructive not only as it reveals Hooker's own sentiments but also as it sheds light on the synodical form of congregationalism that was then emerging.

THE CASE OF MR. ROGER WILLIAMS

As early as 1631 the celebrated Mr. Williams had had a disquieting influence in the Bay Colony from within the Salem fellowship. This restive spirit subsequently wandered to the Plymouth colony where he proved to be just as disquieting. Commending him back to Salem in 1633, the brethren at Plymouth did so "with some caution to them concerning him, and what care they ought to have of him" (Walker 1891, 77). Along with Rev. Skelton, the minister at Salem, Williams early on opposed any consociation of ministers, fearing in such a form of proto-Presbyterianism (Ibid, 74). Without entering too fully into any litany of complaints as put forth by Roger Williams (cf. Winslow 1957; Morgan 1967), a brief rehearsal of Williams' more radical tendencies will suffice. Williams' subsequent expulsion was not brought about by any divergent doctrinal views in the strict sense. Rather, his downfall was a result of his judgments against the congregational polity of the Bay and his views of the Church of England.
Williams had refused to join the Boston church in 1631 because of that body's refusal to renounce fellowship with the churches of England. When Williams proceeded on to Salem in 1631, the Boston authorities managed to stifle the process whereby Williams would be called as a teacher to the flock there (Winthrop 1908, I, 61-61). This resulted in the above mentioned and short-lived sojourn to Plymouth. Returning to Salem in 1633, Williams showed himself a subversive by questioning the colony's title to the land which he viewed as the proper property of the Indians alone (Ibid., 116). Eyebrows were no doubt raised and fears of English reprisal warmed, when Williams charged that King James had committed blasphemy by calling Europe "Christendome, or the Christian world" (Ibid., 117). With the death of Skelton in 1634 Williams became the

teacher in Salem.

        The judgments of Mr. Williams came in rapid fire succession, most being viewed as seditious, being dangerous to the safety of the colony especially in view of careful trans-Atlantic scrutiny. Williams opposed all oaths taken by the unregenerate, feeling that such involved the abuse of the Lord's name. He announced that worship in any church that had not renounced the churches of England was no worship at all. For this reason, given the non-separating sentiments in the Bay (cf. Morgan 1963, 54-56,82-83), he urged the Salem church to withdraw from fellowship with the others of the Bay. When this advice was not heeded, he himself withdrew, denouncing his own wife who did not (Winthrop 1908, I, 149, 154, 157).

        Perhaps the incident which aroused the greatest perceived threat to the public order was that which was brought before the Court of Assistants on November 5, 1634. Williams' opinions had infected the Salem magistrate John Endicott. At Williams' urging, Endicott had defaced the English ensign by cutting out the "superstitious" cross. Winthrop notes that "much matter was made of this, as fearing it would be taken as an act of rebellion, or of like nature, in defacing the king's colors" (Winthrop 1908, I, 137). The propriety of the use of the cross in an ensign was referred to the ministers and Williams was formally summoned to appear at the court. His appearance would not take place until October of 1635. In the intervening time the problem of the Salem magistrate John Endicott would be handled.

        All of this was for Hooker a distraction from his real desire, which was to nurture sainthood in the inhabitants at Newtown. Particularly painful must have been his duty, acting in conjunction with Cotton and Weld, to deal with his old friend John Eliot who had railed against the magistracy for making peace with the Pequots without the consent of the people. Williams' boldness had evidently shattered the peace of the colony and the submissiveness of some of its inhabitants.

        The question of the cross in the ensign was taken up in March of 1635 in a meeting held at Newtown. Hooker preached the opening sermon of which no transcript is extant (Winthrop 1908, I, 147). The various ills of the colony were discussed though no agreement was reached on either how to deal with Mr. Endicott or with the ensign controversy. In May the Court met again, this time censuring Mr. Endicott, leaving him out of office for a year for "taking upon himself more authority than he had and not seeking the advice of the court." The ministers, while disapproving of Endicott's rash excision of the cross from the ensign, nevertheless expressed their own uncertainties about the propriety of its presence. Hooker's personal verdict, was expressed in his tract "Touching the Crosse in the Banner."

> Not that I am a friend to the crosse as an idoll, or to any idollatry in it; or that any carnall fear takes me asyde and makes me unwilling to give way to the evidence of the truth, because of the sad consequences that may be suspected to flowe from it. I bless the Lord, my conscience accuseth me of no such thing; but as yet I am not able to see the sinfulness of this banner in a civil use. (Massachusetts Historical Society 1909, 274)

Shuffelton suggests that this "soft answer" of Hooker's would not have found agreement from Cotton who probably sided with Endicott in this matter (Shuffelton 1977, 191n). If this was the case, we may have another small example of the differences of viewpoint between Hooker and Cotton. As noted briefly above, these two "giants" were also paired with magistrates, Dudley and Winthrop, who clearly maintained divergent opinions. Curiously, it was the Newtownian Dudley and the Bostonian Cotton who maintained the more stringent views while Hooker and Winthrop patently sought to exercise judgments of charity.

Though the Court met in March, May, and again in July of 1635, all their proceedings were tangential to the persisting problem of the how to handle Mr. Williams himself. In these earlier proceedings, the General Court had already endorsed the declaration of the Court of Assistants that Williams' views were "erroneous, and very dangerous" (Winthrop 1908, I, 154). By the time the Court met in October of 1635, Williams was alienated from his own congregants in Salem. Hooker, famous for his disputation skills since his days in Esher, was called upon to deliver the final blow against Williams. Ola Winslow captures the confidence of the Bay leaders in appointing Hooker to the task. "If anyone could convince him (Williams), Thomas Hooker was the man" (Winslow 1957, 119). Hooker, representing the mainstream within the Bay, was seeking to preserve the unity of the colony while trying to work out their evolving congregational principles. It should be noted that these principles still gave some place to the synodical concept. Pragmatically speaking, the mainstream could see no value whatsoever, in lobbing across the ocean inflammatory statements regarding the state of church in England. For Williams, the avowed separatist, purity and consistency were everything. His desire was for an immediate explication of Puritan beliefs regardless of how importunate this proved.

Mr. Williams could not be persuaded from any of his errors and the inevitable banishment followed (Winthrop 1908, I, 162-163). No doubt the Court took into consideration Laudian watchfulness (cf Winthrop 1908, I, 145; Shuffelton 1977, 202) when the Salem minister was ordered to depart from the Bay within the six weeks ensuing. Hooker, notwithstanding his official role in the banishment, had still revealed his conciliatory spirit and his ever abiding concern for peace. Charitable judgment did not necessitate complacency in the face of real and dangerous error. In this sense, Hooker's pastoral practice is mirrored in his official and public activities.

This chapter in the Bay's history had come to an official conclusion. Perhaps the sentiments were that real serenity might now rest upon the colony. It would not be so, for in the midst of these contentions, "Mr. Hooker's company" had not so quietly resolved to remove from Newtown.

SERMONIC AND LITERARY ACTIVITY IN THE NEWTOWN PERIOD

This is an opportune place to consider Hooker's literary production in this period. The multiple Hookerian publications that came forth from the London presses in 1637 and 1638 might seem to indicate a furious writing, or at least preaching, schedule for this phase of Hooker's career. The major works which explicated Hooker's morphology of conversion, though later to be reworked in The Application of Redemption (1656), were all published first in 1637 or 1638. These include, The Soules Humiliation, The Soules Ingrafting, The Soules Vocation or Effectual Calling To Christ, The Soules Implantation, Foure Learned and Godly Treatises, The Properties of an Honest Heart, The Sinners Salvation, The Soules Exaltation, The Soules Possession of Christ, Spiritual Thirst, The Stay of the Faithful, Three Godly Sermons, The Unbeleevers Preparing For Christ. Another, The Soules Preparation for Christ, was published in 1632, prior to Hooker's departure for New England. Despite the distractions caused by Williams and Endicott, and notwithstanding the sometimes squabbling Dudley and Winthrop, Hooker no doubt was preaching the constituent parts of his morphology, with its preparationism, to his Newtown parishioners. Thomas Goodwin and Philip Nye, in their preface to The Application of Redemption (Books I-VIII, 1656), make note that previous editions were the result of the transcriptions of several hands. Though these hands were "pious," imperfections nevertheless abounded. They were therewith presenting an "authorized version" of Hooker's morphology. In their preface they give a history of the contents of the work.

> He preached more briefly on this Subject first, whilst he was Fellow and Catechist in Emmanuel Colledg in Cambridg. The Notes of which, were then so esteemed, that many Copies thereof, were by many that heard not the Sermons, written out, and are extant by them. And then again, a Second time, many years after, more largely at Great Chelmsford in Essex; the Product of which, was those Books of

Sermons that have gone under his Name. And Last of all ; now in New England, and that in, to a settled Church of Saints. (Hooker, 1656a, "To The Reader")

These words identify the 1637-1638 publications as belonging to the Chelmsford period, but also imply that Hooker was rehearsing these themes with his Newtown congregation. Mather notes that his New England parishioners, having been his old Essex hearers, "desired him once more again to go over the points of God's regenerating works upon the soul of his elect" (Mather 1853, I, 347).

THE REMOVAL TO CONNECTICUT

In the midst of domestic problems of the magnitude of the Roger Williams incident, and while jealously guarding against trans-Atlantic alarm, the "Masters of the Bay sagged under the strain" (Battis 1962, 82) of the Newtown congregation's resolve to depart for the Connecticut Valley. The list of supposed reasons for the westward migration is long indeed. Some of these provide the "springboard" for the attributions to Hooker of an incipient "democratic spirit."
For the present, it will suffice to present the sentiments of the would-be immigrants themselves as they sought approval from General Court for their westward adventure. For this record, the nearest we can approach to "hard facts," indebtedness is almost entirely to Winthrop in his *Journal*.
By New England's standards, Newtown seemed to be flourishing. Yet an uneasiness persisted that is not easy to trace. As early as May of 1634 the residents of Newtown had requested either "enlargement or removal," citing "straitness for want of land, especially meadow." With the approval of the Court scouts were sent to examine Agawam and Merimack, and in July others headed to the Connecticut River (Winthrop 1908, I, 124,128). In September of the same year, this desire of the Newtown residents became the main business of the Court in that session which met at Newtown.

> And now they moved, that they might have leave to remove to Connecticut. This matter was debated divers days, and many reasons alleged pro and con. The principal reasons for their removal were, 1. Their want of accommodation for their cattle, so as they were not able to maintain their ministers, nor could receive any more of their friends to help them; and here it was alleged by Mr. Hooker, as a fundamental error, that towns were set so near each to other. 2. The fruitfulness and commodiousness of Connecticut, and the danger of having it possessed by others, Dutch or English. 3. The strong bent of their spirits to remove thither. (Ibid., I, 132)

No underlying reasons are given of this "strong bent" and one wonders whether any disputative spirit is therein harbored.

The reasons put forth against the removal included the debilitating effect the move would have upon the already weak Bay Colony. In particular, the departure of Mr. Hooker, "would not only draw many from us, but also divert other friends that would come to us." Also mentioned as a reason against the removal was the danger to be expected in such a wilderness. It was felt that "some enlargement which other towns offered," or a removal "within the patent," were much better solutions. Finally, this apocalyptic sounding sentiment was offered, "The removing of a candlestick is a great judgment, which is to be avoided" (Ibid., I, 133).

After the disputation, the question was put to a vote. The deputies, having been elected as representatives of their own towns, were participating in their first session as part of the colony's lawmaking body. They voted in favor of the motion. Winthrop led the opposition among the assistants, with newly elected Governor Dudley only able to muster two affirmative votes from the other assistants. When the secretary did not vote, no record of the vote was entered, for the patent required that there be six assistants in the vote. Foreshadowing a long-standing troublesome reality, Winthrop notes that this issue created "a great difference between the governor and assistants, and the deputies" (Ibid., I, 133).

Following the rendered decision in which the upper house overruled the deputies, Thomas Hooker as the host minister was asked to preach. He declined claiming "unfitness for that occasion" (Ibid.). Though one wonders whether Hooker's "unfitness" here is the result of personal frustration or even animosity toward the court, at least one later incident is known in which Hooker the preacher found himself at a loss for words (Mather 1853, I, 342-343). Winthrop's chronicle goes on calmly to report that Mr. Cotton preached a fine sermon after which an enlargement was offered Newtown from Watertown and Boston. As if he wished to finally close the book on this difficult chapter in the Bay's history, Winthrop optimistically wrote, "and so the fear of their removal to Connecticut was removed" (Winthrop 1908, I, 134).

Not only was the removal controversy far from being settled, but another harbinger of trouble came to the Bay before the month's end as the "Griffin" arrived, bearing some two hundred passengers, including Mrs. Anne Hutchinson. With the latest action of the Court the residents of Newtown were disheartened indeed. The enlargement was unsatisfactory in that the Watertown grant consisted of land already in use by grazers from Newtown. This was no relief to their "straitness." Boston's "gift" lay south of the Charles River and was accessible only by boat. The "strong bent of their spirits to remove" persisted.

The following summer (1635) was marred by the Williams affair, the ensign controversy, and within Newtown itself, John Pratt's whiney and ill-advised letter to friends in England in which he suggested that New England had been "over praised" as to its prosperity and piety (Denholm 1961, 76-77; Winthrop 1908, I, 165). Amid these disquieting factors, in what must have been taken by the Newtownians as an affront to them, the Court granted permission for removal to certain parties from both Watertown and Dorchester. Amazingly, their desire for removal was based on their being "much straitened by their own nearness to one another, and their cattle being so much increased" (Winthrop 1908, I, 151). The "covenant bonds," which were used to retain Newtown the year before, had loosened to the point of breakage. By the end of the summer of 1635 the Newtown emigration had begun.

At the high point of the Williams disputations, which so involved Mr. Hooker, about sixty men, women, and children, together with their cattle, safely made the journey from Newtown to the Connecticut River (Winthrop 1908, I, 163). Those who temporarily stayed behind in Newtown were soon heartened by the arrival of new settlers being led by Mr. Thomas Shepard. The Newtownians were eager to sell their houses and lands and the newcomers were quick to receive such a blessing at the hands of Providence. In February of 1636 the Shepard group, with the participation of the neighboring churches' elders, was constituted a covenanted church (Winthrop 1908, I, 173). In May of 1636 Winthrop made the following entry into his journal.

> Mr. Hooker, pastor of the church of Newtown and the most of his congregation, went to Connecticut. His wife was carried in a horse litter; and they drove one hundred and sixty cattle, and fed of their milk by the way. (Ibid., I, 180-181)

This bare outline of the removal to Connecticut, gleaned mainly from Winthrop's Journal, sounds objective enough. But the supposed underlying reasons for the removal have engendered a large amount of controversy.

For this biographical sketch, little more than an historiographical survey of the ongoing debate is necessary. Walker's biography (1891) was peppered with statements attributing a democratic bent to Thomas Hooker. As to the removal, Walker gave as a partial reason, that Hooker "inwardly disapproved" of the "distinctively theocratic society" of the Bay (Walker 1891, 87-88). Walker seems to have mistakenly taken an oligarchical system and labeled it "theocratic." It was only in New Haven at a later date, that a distinctively theocratic experiment was conducted. James Hosmer, in his 1908 edition of Winthrop's Journal, in a comparison with John Cotton, assigns to Hooker a "more democratic spirit" (Winthrop 1908, I, 132n). This critical trend was followed and elaborated upon by James Truslow Adams in his The Founding of New England (1921). These writers, all evaluating Hooker in light of the events which were subsequent to the migration, especially focus upon a famous sermon of Hooker's preached on May 31, 1638. The text of the sermon is lost but some notes taken by a hearer have survived. From his Biblical text (Deuteronomy 1:13) Hooker presents three doctrines.

> I. That the choice of public magistrates belongs unto the people by Gods own allowance.
> II. The privilege of election, which belongs to the people, therefore must not be exercised according to their humors, but according to the blessed will and law of God.
> III. They who have the power to appoint officers and magistrates, it is in their power also, to set the bounds and limitations of the power and place unto which they call them.

Also of importance is "Reason 1."

> Because the foundation of authority is laid, firstly, in the free consent of the people. (Connecticut Historical Society 1850, I, 20,21)

Adams gives this surprising and unsubstantiated evaluation.

> Neither to Hooker, nor to his fellow colonists of Connecticut, was this last principle new, either in theory or in practice. He was arguing, not for a democratic government, which they already possessed, but for a fixed code of laws to rule the magistrates in their actions. (Adams 1921, 192)

Curiously Adams goes on to note that the Fundamental Orders of 1639 had little that could not already be found, either in custom or in legislation, in the Bay. Nevertheless, in speaking about this document, he spots a "democratic tendency" (Ibid., 193). In concluding his discussion of Hooker, Adams is bold enough to compare and align him with Roger Williams (and against John Winthrop) as the trailblazers of the American tradition (Ibid., 195). One wonders if Adams has forgotten who was the main disputant for the Court in its proceedings against Williams. That Hooker continued to view Connecticut as a Bible Commonwealth is also clearly seen from his second doctrine, a fact nowhere mentioned by Adams.

The apogee of this view of "Hooker the democrat" came with the 1927 publication of Vernon Parrington's The Colonial Mind 1620-1800. Parrington had little sympathy with the Puritans nor did he manifest signs that he had carefully read them for himself. Throughout he vents his low view of the theological endeavor. For Parrington, Hooker and Williams were men of creative ability and idealism. Echoing Adams, Parrington concludes that from these able men, and from their respective colonies, democratic principles arose. To his credit Parrington distances Hooker from the leveling radicalism of Williams but nevertheless he grossly overstates that Hooker was "busily erecting the democracy of Hartford" (Parrington 1927, 53).

Scant evidence had been presented, but the views of Adams and Parrington held sway and can still be found proliferated in cursory comments by many authors. Perry Miller stemmed the tide with his voice of dissent. In 1931 Miller wrote,

> There may in practice have been a greater leniency in Connecticut. One gets the impression from the records that the Bible Commonwealth notion was not quite so insistent as in Massachusetts. But the Connecticut records are meager, and to some extent the difference may have resulted from the character of the population. Furthermore, New England's battles against heresy were fought in the Bay, and the banished heretics did not come to Connecticut. But if the practice was less stringent, the theory was still the same. (Miller 1931, 663-712; reprt. Miller 1936, 34)

As to the views of Adams and Parrington, Miller noted,

> In relatively recent times a few persons, inspired by the argument that Hooker was the pioneer democrat, have been moved to read his publications. In them they have discovered, as they should, a magnificent stylist, whereupon they become content to leave Cotton unread. They pounce upon this or that passage to prove that Hooker's exposition of the theology carries a democratic implication antipathetic to Cotton's. . . . Some of the more extravagant claims that have been advanced for Hooker's democracy come from secularists no longer capable of grasping this Protestant paradox. And then, it is true that by translating this position into an organized polity, Congregationalists inadvertently opened a bit wider, wider than they ever intended, a door for the democratic propulsion. But in this historical process, Cotton and Hooker were so closely in step that they are not to be distinguished, one against the other, into such opposing camps as are presumed in the modern usage of theocrat and democrat. (Miller 1956, 46-47)

In his *Orthodoxy In Massachusetts* (1933) Miller continued to combat what he saw as the democratic "myth" being perpetuated by the likes of Adams and Parrington. If an element of democracy was found in the New England Way, it remained only one element in the total makeup. This mixture represented a Calvinistic ideal (Miller 1933, 172). Both Cotton and Hooker had been schooled in Amesian thought which maintained:

> The forme of this polity is altogether monarchicall in respect of Christ, the head and King; but as touching the visible and vicarious administration, it is of a mixt nature, partly as it were aristocraticall, and partly as it were democraticall. (Ames 1643, 145)

For Hooker, Christ the Monarch had laid down His

law and it was to be exercised through two prerogatives, that of the elders and that of the people. Each owes it existence and authority to the Head, not to one another. The essential call of the minister comes from Christ, though outwardly by the people.

> A Pastors power, or power of Office, is an united power from many. The peoples is a divided power, lying in many combined, and therefore not the same. . . . The Elders are superior to the Fraternity in regard of Office, Rule, Act, and Exercise; which is proper only to them, and not to the Fraternity. The people or Church are superior to the Elders in point of censure; each have their full scope in their own sphere and compass, without the prejudice of the other. (Hooker 1648, I, 191)

It is mutual covenanting which creates a visible church. But such sentiments nowhere approach a direct democracy. This covenant is taken up "in a Church Way and for Spiritual ends" (Ibid., I, 47).

> The Sum in short is this. By mutuall ingagement each to the other, such persons stand bound in such a state and condition to Answer the terms of it, and to walk in such waies, as may attain the end thereof. (Ibid., I, 46)

Hooker, like the other New England ministers, had a high view of his own authority. Once the people had given an outward call to a minister or to elders, congregational liberties were to be expressed by subjection and obedience to the office holders. The following words, representing the advanced stage of Hooker's own thinking, hardly provide evidence that he labored to erect a democracy in Hartford.

> The Officer may by a superior united right, call them together, they cannot refuse. He may injoin them to hear, they may not withdraw. He may injoin them silence if they shall speak disorderly or

impertinently, he may dissolve the congregation, and they must give way while he delivers the mind of Christ out of the Gospel, and acts all the affairs of his Kingdome, according to his rule; and as suits his mind; he is thus above the whole Church: but in case he erre and transgresse a rule, and becomes a Delinquent, he is then liable to censure, and they may proceed against him though not by any power of office, for they are not officers, but by the power of judgement which they do possess. (Hooker 1648, I, 192)

For Hooker as with Cotton, church authority rests not with the people but with the Elders. Yet by the people's liberty and judgment, tyranny is prevented. These sentiments were codified in the Cambridge Platform of 1648, which incorporated the congregational ideals of Hooker, Cotton, Shepard, and Richard Mather (Miller 1953, 6).

To continue this historiographical survey, when Miller reviewed the ongoing controversy twenty-five years after he first entered it, his verdict was firm. "Parrington simply did not know what he was talking about" (Miller 1956, 17). Miller also reminds the reader of that which is almost too obvious, that which Miller himself had failed properly to regard in 1931, that being the fact that Hooker was the author of the most learned and most complete presentation of the orthodox New England way of church discipline (Ibid., 18). Hooker's Survey sounded a voice for all of New England. More recently Sacvan Bercovitch has noted the "myth" which continues to portray Hooker as some sort of "John the Baptist to Thomas Jefferson" (Bercovitch 1975, 151, 236n).

In 1952 Clinton Rossiter had argued for a mediate position between those views of Parrington and Miller (Rossiter 1952, 459-488). For Rossiter, Hooker was no democrat in the modern sense but the seeds for the same were present. He stands as an indication that the New England way contained the means of its own liberation (Ibid., 488). While correctly reminding us that the Parrington-Miller debate misses the "essence" of Hooker's career, Rossiter leans heavily toward Miller in noting that "we must remember that the only society that made sense to Hooker was one in which church and state were not merely united but one" (Ibid., and Rossiter 1953, 159-178). It is also clear that Hooker's brand of Congregationalism was of a mixed sort for he had not completed divested himself of English societal structures. Notwithstanding his earlier divergence from the views of Reverend Paget, Hooker retained elements common to Presbyterianism in his developing Congregational thought. Rossiter wrote very cautiously, yet the adamant Miller insisted, "On this matter there is no middle ground" (Miller 1956, 17). By and large, Miller's views have now been largely accepted, and properly so (Ahlstrom 1962, 415-431). Parrington's account must now be judged a superficial one which has attracted much more attention than it ever deserved.

Because the storm is much quieter outside the Parrington-Miller debate, very little has yet been put forth as to the positive reasons for the Hookerian removal to Connecticut. As it has been shown, Winthrop only mentions the need for more land and the "strong bent of their spirits" (Winthrop 1908, I, 132). Keeping in mind that Cotton had declined the original offer by Newtown to become Hooker's colleague there, the probable disagreement of the two in the ensign controversy, and the loyalties Hooker and Cotton were manifesting to Dudley and Winthrop respectively, Hubbard's supposition of a personal rivalry between the two has been adopted by later historians.

> Two such eminent stars, such as were Mr. Cotton and Mr. Hooker, both of first magnitude, though of differ-ing influence, could not well continue in one and the same orb. (Hubbard 1878, 173)

One need not be condemnatory to see the reasonableness of such a judgment. Mather could bring himself to say nothing negative about the "Luther and Melancthon of New England," as he noted that each became the "oracle of their several colonies" (Mather 1853, I,

342). Miller, in his reintroduction to the essay directed against the Parrington thesis, noted that he was "now fully persuaded that the purely personal rivalry between Hooker and Cotton was much more a factor in this removal than I had naively supposed" (Miller 1956, 17). By reason of its strong denial, Winthop's 1635 letter to Sir Simonds D'Ewes may indicate that problems did indeed exist.

> Not for any difference between Mr. Cotton and him, for they do hould a most sweet and brotherly communion together (thoughe their judgment doe somewhat differ about the lawfullnesses of the Crosse in the ensign) but that the people and cattle are so increased as the place will not suffice them. (quoted in Miller 1956, 25)

Miller remarks that "there could hardly be so much smoke without some fire" (Miller 1956, 25).

The economic ingredient may have been as real as the personal rivalry, but it appears to this writer that the most important reason for the removal was Hooker's desire for a serene pastoral environment in which to nurture the faith of his flock (Miller 1956, 17; Shuffelton 1977, 204-210).

Hooker had not found peace in his native land nor during his Dutch sojourn. With his new Ramistic "answering method," Hooker had become known for his expertise in dealing with cases of conscience. Early on, at Emmanuel and then at Chelmsford, he had begun to develop the points of his morphology of conversion to the great benefit of his "company" of hearers. In 1633 he had viewed the shores of New England as a haven, far from Laudian pressures, where real heart religion might be nurtured. Though he had been held in high esteem in the Bay, his stay thus far had been marked by controversies.

Taking the complaint of 1634 at face value, the "straitness of land" presented more than just an economic problem. The cattle lacked space and the minister could not be properly supported. But these were more than just economic difficulties. These were problems that could easily serve as distractions from one's communion with God. While some no doubt had their eyes set on wealth, prosperity with its ancillary ease might also be used to serve pious purposes. Hooker did not urge the removal to Connecticut so as to establish a democracy but rather to find peace amiable to the nurture of obedient faith. Christ was to be king in all matters. Hooker was no political theorist as was Winthrop. As has now been repeatedly stated, minutely to examine Hooker in order to glean some political theory is to miss his enduring significance. Redemption displayed itself in a regenerating and renewing fashion in individual lives. With a pastoral motivation, Hooker took his "company" to Connecticut that genuine faith and heart religion might be nurtured, and still others brought to see the soul's need for humiliation and contrition that they might be called and effectually ingrafted into Christ. The greatest controversy of the period loomed large and this too would draw in Mr. Hooker. Yet the physician to the soul, at the age of fifty, was now better situated to carry out his pastoral duties than at any previous period of his life.

THE ANTINOMIAN CONTROVERSY

The Antinomian crisis, more so than any controversy heretofore discussed, not only involved Hooker but concerned that for which he is most significant, his preparationist morphology of conversion. The literature concerning the controversy is extensive, with Emery Battis providing the most important modern evaluation (Battis 1962). David D. Hall's The Antinomian Controversy, 1636-1638: A Documentary History (1968), provides the most pertinent primary sources as well as an excellent and compact overview of the controversy. As Perry Miller has shown, Hooker's preparationism, which eventually became part and parcel of the New England Way, lies at the center of the Antinomian storm (Miller 1943, 253-286; 1953, 57). So significant were the questions of amendment of life, preparationism, and saving merit, that Sydney Ahlstrom called the Antinomian Controversy the "opening chapter in American intellectual history" (Ahlstrom 1972, 152). To detail the events of the controversy as it unfolded from October of 1636 to March of 1638 would serve little purpose in this present work. The developing crisis is easily followed in Winthrop's *Journal* (Winthrop 1908, I, 195-265) and more minutely in his *A Short Story of the Rise, Reign, and Ruine of the Antinomians* (in Hall 1968, 199-310). Throughout the difficult months as the controversy raged, the very social order of New England was being threatened. Anne Hutchinson, the Puritan admirer of the Rev. John Cotton in England had come to New England in May of 1634. She soon became well known for her home meetings in which the Sabbath day sermons were discussed. Before very long, her attacks were directed against the ministers of the colony, excepting Mr. Cotton and her brother-in-law, Mr. Wheelwright. As early as the spring of 1636 Cotton had been warned of the tumult which might be caused by such a dissenter. In October of 1636 a private conference was held as several ministers met with Hutchinson, Cotton, and Wheelwright. At this early stage of the controversy, both Cotton and Wheelwright were willing to agree that sanctification could be a possible evidence of justification (Winthrop 1908, I, 195-196). At the time, Hooker was just settling in upon the Connecticut River and therefore had a limited involvement in these Bostonian struggles. But he could not long avoid the pressing questions of the day since by and large his patent "judgment of charity" found its basis in some show of apparent sanctification.

The following months saw continued unrest as Hutchinson continued to accuse the majority of ministers in the Bay of preaching a "covenant of works." Hutchinson's subversion was not that she considered morality to be irrelevant, but rather that a real danger of that implication might be drawn from her teaching. A Hutchinsonian faction of the Boston Church attempted, evidently as a display of their dissatisfaction with their Pastor, John Wilson, to have Wheelwright become a second teacher along with Cotton. Winthrop recorded the unrest caused by these proceedings including the points made by a certain "brother" who rose to speak against the appointment of Wheelwright. Wheelwright, as had Hutchinson before, was thought to hold an erroneous opinion regarding the indwelling of the Holy Spirit in the believer, one which stressed union to a perceived mystical extreme. The extent of the unrest is described by Winthrop as "divers of the brethren took offence at the said speech against Mr. Wheelwright" (Ibid., I, 198). Little resolution came the next day as the "brother" tried to explain himself but "how this was taken by the congregation, did not appear, for no man spake to it" (Ibid., I, 199).

In December of 1636 Winthrop made this entry.

> Mr. Wilson made a very sad speech of the condition of our churches, and the inevitable danger of separation, if these differences and alienations among brethren were not speedily remedied; and laid blame upon these new opinions risen up amongst us, which all the magistrates, except the governor and two others, did confirm, and all the ministers but two. (Ibid., I, 204)

The governor here referred to was Henry Vane, of outspoken Hutchinsonian sentiments. Neither Cotton nor Wheelwright shared Wilson's evaluation of the state of the churches in the Bay (Murray 1978, 18).

That the controversy was predominating the affairs of the Bay is clear from this January 20, 1637, entry by Winthrop.

> The differences in the said points of religion increased more and more, and the ministers of both sides (there being only Mr. Cotton of one party) did publicly declare their judgments in some of them, so as all men's mouths were full of them. (Ibid., I, 208)

Unrest was further inflamed by Wheelwright's fast day sermon of January 19, 1637, which seemed to have an effect of launching a crusade as the "legal preachers" were labeled "antichrists" (Hall 1968, 7). Wheelwright was bold to declare,

> True, I must confesse and acknowledge the saynts of God are few, but they are but a little flocke, and those that are the enemyes to the Lord, not only Pagonish, but Antichristian, and those that run under a covenant of works are very strong. . . . Brethren, those under a covenant of works, the more holy they are, the greater enimyes they are to Christ. (in Hall 1968, 163-164)

Even the fast itself, called by the "legal preachers," was criticized as being superstitious.

In March a General Court met again. Winthrop reported that the majority present were "sound" in their views but Wheelwright refused to repent and was found guilty of contempt and sedition, notwithstanding Bostonian protestations (Winthrop 1908, I, 210-211).

That the very social order of the colony was being threatened by the ongoing wranglings was made clear in April of 1637. Mr. Jones and Mr. Peter Bulkeley were to be installed in Concord as Pastor and Teacher respectively. Winthrop reports this "boycott" of the event.

> The governor, and Mr. Cotton, and Mr. Wheelwright, and two ruling elders of Boston, and the rest of that church, which were of any note, did none of them come to this meeting. The reason was conceived to be, because they accounted these as legal preachers, and therefore would not give approbation to their ordination. (Ibid., I, 212-213)

At the next General Court, held in May at Newtown, Vane was deposed as Winthrop was elected governor. A special synod was decided upon to be held at Cambridge and to commence on August 30, 1637. On August 5, 1637, Thomas Hooker, taken once again from his own flock and his pressing pastoral concerns, arrived at Boston. Much of the month was taken up in private meetings with Cotton, Wheelwright, and Wilson.

The synod officially convened on August 30 and did not adjourn until September 22. It accomplished its design in dealing with the errors of the Antinomian party and also took up certain questions of church order, such as the legitimacy of Hutchinson-like private meetings. Winthrop's compact summary of the almost month long synod is worth quoting here.

> The assembly began with prayer, made by Mr. Shepard, the pastor of Newtown. Then the erroneous opinions, which were spread in the country, were read, (being eighty in all;) next the unwholesome expressions; then the scriptures abused. Then they chose two moderators for the next day, viz., Mr. Bulkeley and Mr. Hooker, and these were continued in that place all the time of the assembly. There were about eighty opinions, some blasphemous, others erroneous, and all unsafe, condemned by the whole assembly; whereto near all the elders, and others sent by the church, subscribed their names; but some few liked not subscription, though they consented to the condemning of them. (Winthrop 1908, I, 232)

That Hooker, previously called upon to deliver the "final blow" against Roger Williams, was now called upon to be a moderator, is a reflection upon his abilities as a theological polemicist. One might also wonder if the choice was at all a studied one, based upon previous differences between Hooker and Cotton. After the adjournment of the court, it soon became obvious that even more stern measures were necessary as Wheelwright and his sympathizers refused to be persuaded of their errors. The General Court of November 2, 1637, ordered the banishment of the leaders of the Antinomian party. Hutchinson herself remained to be examined. Answering to the worst fears of those who wondered at the Antinomian emphasis on the personal indwelling of the Holy Spirit, Hutchinson "vented her revelations" (Winthrop 1908, I, 240), and thereby sealed her own banishment. The winter saw church after church cleansing themselves of Antinomian sentiments.

At the Boston church, Hutchinson was formally found guilty and excommunicated on March 22, 1638. Within a week she was en route to Rhode Island and would eventually be slaughtered in an Indian raid in August of 1643 near present day Rye, New York. Following the General Court of September, 1637, for which he served as co-moderator, Hooker returned to Connecticut. Though he did not therefore attend Hutchinson's actual trial, his well known opinions were no doubt sounded many times in the months leading up to her banishment in March of 1638.

Because this controversy had such a decided effect upon New England society, some evaluation of Hooker's part in it and its effect upon his ministry is called for at this point. It will be subsequently shown that Frank Shuffelton somewhat overstated the case when he wrote that the controversy affected the content of nearly all of Hooker's preaching after 1637 (Shuffelton 1977, 238).

Until the winter of 1637-1638, John Cotton seemingly failed to see how very destructive to all of New England society were the views being perpetrated by Wheelwright and Hutchinson. He came to realize the problem very late, after his name had granted a measure of credibility to the dissidents (Murray 1978, 55). Hutchinson's "revelations" not only necessitated his siding with the mainstream leaving her standing virtually alone, but also presented a greater problem. John Cotton was too prestigious to be banished, especially in consideration of the dangerous ramifications such would have as to the maintenance of the Colony's charter. But it was not this inter-ministerium debate alone which threatened the stability of the Bay. Hutchinson had dared to lash out at the whole authoritative body of ministers, with Cotton alone finding her support. The Hutchinsonian proponents of "free grace" had to be shown to be a dangerous and disreputable element. The clerical mainstream likewise prided themselves as being preachers of "free grace," standing in the flowing stream of the Reformation of the previous century. The rejection of their orthodoxy as a "covenant of works" could not be countenanced.

These considerations have produced the modern scholarly trend which diverges from the traditional view of the Antinomian controversy as one which revolved around Anne Hutchinson. Perry Miller (Miller 1967, 50-77) and now David Hall have suggested that John Cotton himself is to be considered the major figure in the crisis and that "his differences of opinion with the other ministers in Massachusetts were at the heart of the controversy" (Hall 1968, 4). Hutchinson came to New England to follow Cotton. She pronounced that only Cotton and her brother-in-law John Wheelwright had remained faithful. Because Cotton did little to dissuade such sentiments, Miller could write that "Hooker triumphed in New England, for the good and sufficient reason that Cotton's doctrine fathered the awful heresy of Antinomianism" (Miller 1967, 61-62). Antinomianism constituted not only a theological threat, but a social and political one as well. Had Cotton not acquiesced, the very authority structure of New England society might have toppled. That he did indeed come to at least outward compliance highlights the significance of Thomas Hooker.

Winthrop's earliest summary of the then incipient controversy conflated it under two heads, "from which grow many branches."

> 1. that the person of the Holy Ghost dwells in a justified person. 2. That no sanctification can help to evidence to us our justification. (Winthrop 1908, I, 195)

The first question virtually disappeared amid finely tuned distinctions between "indwelling" and "union" with the Holy Spirit as "personal union" (Winthrop 1908, I, 196, 198; Hall 1968, 34-42). Quite recently the novelist John Irving, while commenting on the banishment of John Wheelwright, has euphemistically described his downfall in terms of "some heterodox opinions regarding the location of the Holy Spirit" (Irving 1989, 19).

But the second "head" figured as a major issue of contention in the debate between Cotton and the ministers in the Bay. As noted above, at an initial private meeting in October of 1636, both Cotton and Wheelwright had given assurances that they held that sanctification might give some basis of assurance of justification (Winthrop 1908, I, 195-196). But Cotton continued to preach sermons which seem to counter his admission. In December several ministers drew up "Sixteen Questions of Serious and Necessary Consequence" that were presented to Cotton for his reply. In his answers Cotton maintained that to look to sanctification as evidence of justification may indeed (but not necessarily) constitute a "building of Justification upon Sanctification" and a "going aside to a Covenant of Workes" (Hall 1968, 43-59).

By reason of the evidence drawn from such primary sources, the Antinomian controversy has rightly been summarized as concerning the place of moral amendment in the lives of the justified. But given Hooker's prestige in both the Bay and subsequently in Connecticut, his developing morphology, and growing fame in the difficult cases of conscience, preparationism should now be seen as being an important ingredient in the crisis as well (Habeggar 1969, 346). The Antinomian controversy involved both prospective and retrospective considerations as to the place of moral amendment of life and its relation to justification. One should not fail to note that the two "legal preachers" who were made moderators were also among the most preeminent "preparationists."

We can confidently surmise that even before Hooker's removal to Connecticut preparationism was a mark of his ministry. Back in Essex his "company" had benefited from his earlier sermons concerning contrition and humiliation. Coming to New England, many had prevailed upon him to "resume that pleasant subject" (Mather 1853, I, 347). In 1637, as the Antinomian controversy raged, Hooker's early morphological formulations, already being reworked in New England, were going to press in London. Relatively little of the extant sermonic material of Hooker's concerns itself with post-justification matters. His preparationism was sufficient cause for the Hutchinsonians to view him as one of the "legal" preachers. John Cotton made only what Ahlstrom has described as an "ambiguous peace" (Ahlstrom 1973, 153), as to the question of whether sanctification can properly evidence justification. But on the question of preparationism, Cotton seems to have remained at odds with its chief New England architect, Thomas Hooker. Add to this Hooker's fame and prestige, and it is little wonder that he was called from Connecticut to play a leading role in the Antinomian controversy.

Cotton insisted that "to works of creation there needeth no preparation" (Hall 1968, 177). Antithetically, Hooker maintained that the soul could not receive Christ unless it had been prepared, principally by being brought to the depths of contrition and humiliation. Hutchinson denied that any such stages of conversion existed, maintaining as she did with Cotton that man is "passive in his regeneration, as in his first generation" (in Miller 1953, 58). So it was that the uncompromisable lines were drawn.

Because Cotton remained the apostle of the sudden and violent conversion even to the "surprise" of the will, there could be no room for a time of preparation (Cotton 1659, 39). The teachings of his enthusiastic admirer Hutchinson have been summarized by Miller as amounting to one thing, "a denial of preparation" (Miller 1953, 59). It thus appears that preparationism with its prospective considerations of the place of human strivings, was not only a hidden issue in the 1637 crisis, but in reality was a very basic one.

Concerning the crisis, Iain Murray has insisted that preparationism was not an issue but that the question of assurance was the central concern (Murray 1978, 46). A reading of the primary materials does indeed show how crucial the question of assurance was in the controversy. Yet with a consensus developing as to a morphology of conversion, assurance might plausibly be built upon prospective as well as retrospective considerations (as relative to the act of faith in conversion). But John Cotton denied both in favor of the "witness of the Spirit" (Hall 1968, 7, 80, 141). Whether justly or not he was therefore perceived to be closely aligned with Anne Hutchinson (Winthrop 1908, I, 75, 138). Contrary to the verdict of most interpreters of the crisis, Iain Murray has denied that Cotton should be aligned with Hutchinson and has even attempted to portray the former as a preparationist himself (Murray 1978, 24, 38-45). Murray's thesis, running as it does against the views of Miller, Pettit, Hall, Ziff, and Morgan, has yet to be thoroughly evaluated.

The "Augustinian strain of piety" (Miller 1939, 3) tenaciously maintained that orthodoxy as to predestination and human depravity must not be allowed to undermine the conception of man as a responsible moral agent. But how the justified might have assurance of their salvation from above was another key question in the Antinomian controversy. Could external amendment of one's life provide a sign of justification? Hutchinson, Wheelwright, and less emphatically Cotton, denied that such could provide assurance. Their emphasis on direct knowledge of Christ, though it seemed to echo the view of Calvin himself in his Institutes (III, xxiv, 5), raised the specter of the possibility of visions and direct revelations, the latter of course providing the ground for Hutchinson's banishment. The mainstream, labeled by the Hutchinsonian party as "legal" preachers were likewise advocates of the then evolving preparationism. Again concerned with the practice of piety, the question was being posed whether or not the one in covenant only externally, as marked by baptism, might respond to God's promises. The preparationist triumvirate of Hooker, Shepard, and Bulkeley, answered with a qualified "yes," while Cotton resounded with a firm negative voice, noting that "if ever the Lord mean to save you . . . he will pluck away all the confidence that you have built upon" (Cotton 1659, 144-145).

Hooker's grace-ladened preparationism provided an answer to the question of how one might be enabled to respond to God's promises. For Hooker preparationism was a requisite saving work resulting from God's special grace (Emerson 1955, 177). This prevailing position carefully insisted that sorrow in preparation was a work wrought upon the sinner. With this presupposition the

Synod of 1637 announced to the Hutchinsonians that "in the ordinary constant course of his dispensation, the more wee indevour, the more assistance and help wee find from him" (in Miller 1953, 56). It was understood that only the elect would "labor" and these do so with Christ's help (Emerson 1955, 155). The voluntarist appeals would continue to be sounded by New England Calvinists, now with a synodical imprimatur.

The essence of the Puritan spirit was the nurture of experiential piety flowing from a revealed theology. This was the life's work of not only Cotton, but Hooker as well. Cotton's emphasis on the freeness of grace was saved from degenerating into lawlessness and hedonism by his particular view of how regeneration takes place. As relative to Hooker, regeneration for Cotton was more arbitrary. Grace often suddenly seized upon its "target." But if the conversion experience could not thereby lend itself to systematization, it was no less real. Indeed, while stressing the inner experience of grace, this for Cotton should consequently be able to be articulated in a "narrative of conversion" which demonstrated inward signs. Hooker likewise gave himself to the nurture of experiential piety and heart religion, but he was quicker to give encouragement as to its presence when outward signs were evidenced. In the sense that he saw a larger place for the Old Testament Law in the conversion experience, the appellation "legal preacher" is not altogether inappropriate. Coupled with this acceptance of an outward amendment, Hooker's "judgment of charity" provided a less restrictive view of church membership than that which was practiced in Cotton's Boston. Stepping back from the details of the Antinomian Controversy, we see that the "legal preacher" Hooker had a more gratuitous view of when grace was truly present, than did even the scrutinizing arch-defender of "free grace."

The subsequent portions of this book will largely focus on the significance of the Law in Hooker's morphology, the significance of the Amesian view of the covenant for preparationist theology, and the impact of the Antinomian Controversy on Hooker's sermonic material. It remains here only briefly to bring to a conclusion this biographical portion of this work.

THE FINAL YEARS

The remaining decade of Hooker's life, those years following the Antinomian controversy, were the most settled of his whole life. According to Mather, Hooker felt himself committed to "two great reserves of enquiry for this age of the world."

The first, wherein the spiritual rule of our Lord's kingdom does consist, and after what manner it is internally revealed, managed and maintained in the souls of his people? The second, after what order the government of our Lord's kingdom is to be externally managed and maintained in his churches? (Mather 1853, I, 348)

The former of these two "reserves" was officially disposed of in the Antinomian controversy. Hooker's last years are best known today for his production of his definitive treatise on congregational polity, The Survey of the Summe of Church Discipline, which went to press the year after Hooker's death.
These were years in which "the way" of the congregational churches was taking shape. The recent controversies had demonstrated, at least for many, the need for some form of a consociation of churches. In England in the early 1640's, English Puritanism was tending heavily toward Presbyterianism. When Parliament in 1643, without the King's consent, called for an assembly of ministers, those of New England were not forgotten.

There came letters from divers Lords of the upper house and some thirty of the house of commons, and others from the ministers there, who stood for the independency of churches, to Mr. Cotton of Boston, Mr. Hooker of Hartford, and Mr. Davenport of New Haven, to call them, or some of them, if all could not, to England, to assist in the synod there appointed, to consider and advise about the settling of church government. (Winthrop 1908, II, 71)

Hooker quickly let it be known that he "liked not the business, nor thought it any sufficient call for them to go 3,000 miles to agree with three men" (Ibid.). Though Cotton and Davenport were more inclined to accept the invitation, the matter was put in abeyance when relations between King and Parliament so deteriorated as to render the long trip inexpedient (Bush 1972, 291-300).

Presbyterian sentiments, which dominated in England, were also making an appearance in New England. In Newbury, Pastor Thomas Parker and Teacher James Noyes began openly to advocate a Presbyterian polity. This unsettling presence gave rise, in September of 1643, to a meeting in Cambridge for which Hooker and Cotton were chosen as moderators. The assembly came to no concrete conclusions but it was now clear that a definitive exposition of the church polity in the colonies was necessary. The following year saw a flurry of writing on the subject, most notable being Cotton's *Way of the Churches Of Christ in New England* (1644). Samuel Rutherford ably wrote for the Presbyterian side with his *Due Right of Presbyteries* (1644). John Ball, in *A Tryall of the New-Church Way in New England* (1644) bluntly reminded the Calvinists of New England that their polity was unlike any of the Reformed tradition (Ball 1644, 88). Cotton's *Keyes of the Kingdom of Heaven* (1644) was prefaced by Goodwin and Nye who remarked that the work presented "a very Middle-way between that which is called Brownisme and the Presbyteriall-government" (Cotton 1644, "Prefatory Letter").

Cotton's *Keyes* appeared contemporaneously with Rutherford's tome which was so highly esteemed that it was deemed worthy of a formal and direct answer. The assignment seems to have fallen to Hooker who presented a work for the approval of an assembly at Cambridge in July of 1645. Meeting with the approval of the ministers there assembled, and following some further work by Hooker, the answer to Rutherford was entrusted upon a ship sailing from New Haven in January of 1646. This copy was lost when the ship perished at sea. Hooker, bound by the restraints of Rutherford's governing form, very reluctantly began to rewrite his defense of the New England way. The work was still unfinished at Hooker's death and was subsequently printed in London in 1648. The Survey of the Summe of Church Discipline carried the unofficial imprimatur of all of New England. The autonomy of the church congregational in matters of discipline is insisted upon, as is the legitimacy of the "visible saint" requirement. Consociations of churches, or synods, are presented as beneficial to the church but are for the purposes of advisement and admonishment only.

The literature on the development of New England congregationalism is quite extensive. The best summaries are in Miller's Orthodoxy In Massachusetts (1933) and more recently, in Hall's The Faithful Shepherd (1972) and Morgan's Visible Saints: The History of a Puritan Idea (1963). Contrary to earlier thought, it is now clear that Plymouth and John Robinson were not the direct sources of New England congregationalism. The "New England Way" was an unfolding of certain sentiments existent in Europe and promoted by the likes of William Ames. That New Englanders went beyond Ames is evidenced by the lack of any requisite "narrative" in Ames' own developing thoughts on polity.

Hooker's convictions as to the place of synods had been put into practice in New England in May of 1646 when the Court of Massachusetts called for a General Synod. Representatives of Plymouth, Connecticut, and New Haven were to be given the same voice as those from the Bay (Winthrop 1908, II,280). Winthrop records a smattering of opposition, primarily from the Boston, Salem, and Hingham congregations, but these voices of dissent were little heard (Winthrop 1908, II, 280-282) as the Cambridge Synod convened on September 1, 1646. By reason of his failing health, Hooker was unable to make the trip to Boston. He wrote to his son-in-law Thomas Shepard.

My yeares and infirmityes grow so fast upon me, that they wholly disenable me to so long a journey; and because I cannot come myself, I provoke as many elders as I can to lend their help and presence. The Lord Christ be in the midst among you by his guidance and blessing. (Albro 1853, cliii)

While the synod was in adjournment, Hooker wrote to Shepard, defending as he would do in his Survey the full power of the magistrate in calling a synod. According to Mather, Hooker was ever a "hearty friend" to the consociation of churches (Mather 1853, I, 349). Once again Hooker stops short of the philosophical consequences of a thorough-going Congregationalism. He gives place not only to a synodical concept but also to the power of the magistrate to call such a meeting. The letter to Shepard shows that extent of these sentiments as Hooker exceeds the view even of Rutherford the Presbyterian.

I fynd Mr. Rutherford and Apollonius to give somewhat sparingly to the place of the magistrate, to putt forth power in the calling of synods, wherein I perceive they goe crosse to some of our most serious and judicious writers. (in Walker 1891, 148)

In June of 1647 the Cambridge Synod reassembled but was decimated by the "epidemical sickness" then prevailing over the colonies (Mather 1853, I, 350; Winthrop 1908, II, 326). The synod having dispersed, Samuel Stone arrived home to find Hooker upon his death bed. Almost two weeks after Hooker's death, Stone wrote to Shepherd.

Dearest brother, God brought us safely to Hartford, but when I came hither God presented me a sad spectacle. Mr. Hooker looked like a dying man. God refused to hear our prayers for him, but tooke him from us July 7 a little before sunne-set. Our sunne is set, our light is eclipsed, our joy is darkened, we remember now in the day of our calamitie the pleasant things which we enjoyed in former times. His spirits and head were so oppressed with the disease that he was not able to expresse much to us in his sicknesse, but had exprest to Mr. Goodwin before my returne that his peace was made in heaven and had continued 30 years without alteration, he was above Satan. Marke the upright man for the end of that man is peace! He lived a most blameless life. I thinke his greatest enemies cannot charge him. He hath done much work for Christ, and now rests from his labours and his workes follow him, but our losse is great and bitter. (Massachusetts Historical Society 1868, 544-546)

One who anticipated this loss came to Hooker as he lay dying. This would-be comforter said to Mr. Hooker, "You are going to receive the reward of your labors." To this, the ever careful theologian replied, "Brother, I am going to receive mercy!" (Mather 1853, I, 350). To the end, Hooker shunned any Arminianizing tendency. It remains to be demonstrated below what lies behind these death bed words of Hooker, that he steadfastly remained, amid his preparationist theology, an orthodox Calvinist.

CHAPTER TWO:
HOOKER'S MORPHOLOGY OF CONVERSION, CONTEXTUAL CONSIDERATIONS

Before an analysis of Hooker's morphology of conversion can be presented certain contextual considerations must receive some treatment. The present chapter evaluates how Hooker's preparationism relates to the more pristine form of Calvinism. This will set the stage for the demonstration of Hooker's faithfulness to his Calvinistic theology before, during, and after the Antinomian crisis.

Hooker is here presented as a rightful heir to the "Calvinistic" designation. Developing federalism provided a seed-bed for the voluntarism that so marked Hooker's theology. It is therefore necessary that some verdict be given as to the place of the covenant concept in Calvin's own theology.

In addition, this chapter in its third section presents an overview of Hooker's works from which his morphology has been gleaned. The various works will be identified as to their date of composition. This is crucial given the unfolding temporal schema of interpretation, pivoting on the Antinomian crisis, which is here to be employed.

In the final section of this chapter Hooker's voluntarism will be examined in the context of the faculty psychology. Hooker's psychology will be compared retrospectively and prospectively with the views of John Calvin and Jonathan Edwards. Though clear differences can be seen between these representatives of Reformed theology, the basic Calvinistic framework of the two Connecticut River Puritans cannot be denied.

PREPARATIONISM IN CONTEXT, THE COVENANTAL MILIEU

The preparationism which became a part of the New England way after the Antinomian controversy raised basic theological and psychological questions. Marked by voluntarism and a seeking to bring the sinner low, a larger use of the moral law was employed. Questions would arise regarding human ability and whether the movings of preparation could properly be conceived as graces of God. More than any other New England divine, Thomas Hooker would strive to expose the windings of the human heart so as to ascertain what a person can and cannot do without the aid of the Holy Spirit.

In 1979 R.T. Kendall's <u>Calvin and English Calvinism</u> <u>to</u> <u>1649</u> brought a renewed interest in the relationship between the views of the Genevan reformer and those of his followers who constituted English Puritanism. Kendall among others, has maintained that Puritan theology, streaming from Beza and not Calvin himself, departed significantly from Calvin. Of the issues raised by Kendall, those most germane to this study include voluntarism and the function of the Law in preparationist theology.

This is no place for any lengthy evaluation of Kendall's work. His superficial readings and faulty conclusions have been briefly demonstrated by Paul Helm (Helm 1982). Nevertheless, that such a debate has been opened provides justification for a cursory portrayal of the milieu of covenant and preparationist theology in order that Thomas Hooker's place in the same might be determined. This follows, given this author's thesis that Hooker steadfastly remained an orthodox Calvinist. This fresh look is necessary given Kendall's view that the developing voluntarism of the English and American Puritans represented an incipient form of Arminianism. Concluding his chapter on Hooker, Kendall's verdict is:

> It seems then that Hooker's doctrine of faith is voluntaristic from start to finish. All his pleadings about an 'effectual' calling of God are rendered meaningless by his appeal- indeed, his urgent and impassioned counsel- directly to man's

will. (Kendall 1979, 138)
Kendall is correct in regard to Hooker's voluntaristic emphasis. Yet he fails to see that, for Hooker, sovereign grace is maintained from the very first stirrings of preparation. In a more recent work, John Morgan, who makes occasional reference to Kendall, even wonders whether Hooker is some sort of "sophisticated Arminian" (J. Morgan 1986, 29n). Thus it is imperative to ask, "Does the type of ministry as Hooker's, which has sometimes been summarized in the one word 'preparationism,' have a rightful claim to the Calvinistic tradition?" (Kendall 1979, 128). Any attempted answer will have to take into consideration the larger constructs of Reformed theology. Because preparationism and voluntarism as expounded by the Puritan divines flowered in the soil of federal theology, a tracing of the place of the covenant scheme in Calvinistic theology is here appropriate. While acknowledging the evolutionary nature of Puritan thought, it is here maintained that the likes of Hooker, Bulkeley, and Shepard had every right to identify themselves with the teachings of the Genevan reformer. Indeed, though they tailored it, they wore Calvin's mantle well.
  Federal theology has a long pre-Puritan history. Calvin himself, in his __Institutes__ (II, x, 1-2) provides some of the roots of federalism which would be further developed by Bullinger and through him, the English divines. Peter Alan Lillback has recently provided the first comprehensive evaluation of the plethora of opinions as to Calvin and the covenant concept. Lillback insists that Calvin made extensive use of the covenant concept (Lillback 1986, 488). While extracting any Medieval notions of merit in the fulfillment of convenantal stipulations, Calvin is seen as an "historical bridge between the Medieval Schoolmen's covenant doctrine and that of the later Calvinistic federal theologians" (Lillback 1985, 490).
  Heinrich Bullinger was one of the first systematizers of the covenant scheme. By reason of writings like his __Decades__, and his hospitality to the

Marian exiles, Bullinger became in England one of the most influential of the continental reformers. His covenantal thinking molded those "especially like Preston, who were the fount of New England covenant thought" (Baker 1980, 166). In his study of Bullinger, J. Wayne Baker sees a divergence from Calvin as regards the covenant concept. But Baker takes Bullinger in an Amyraldian direction and contrasts his views with Calvin's strict double predestinarianism. Baker fails to notice the conditional element in Calvin's view of the covenant. For Baker, a conditional covenant must exclude any notion of double predestination. These matters are crucial to this paper's thesis that the preparationism and voluntarism of Puritans like Hooker were clearly non-meritorious in nature.

Lillback has now provided convincing evidence that no divide existed between the "Rhineland Reformers" and Calvin over the matter of the mutuality and conditionality of the covenant (Lillback 1985, 268-285). Lillback's thesis that Calvin's covenant terminology is also that of Bullinger's provides an important corrective to the views of J. Wayne Baker.

A codified acceptance of the covenant scheme came at the Westminster Assembly, and for New Englanders, at the Cambridge Synod of 1648. It is granted that in the century following Calvin, his pristine view of the unity of God's gracious covenant with the seed of Abraham was systematized, dichotomized, and given "new clothes." Yet the heart of federalism, that God deals with man by way of covenant, remained (Emerson 1956, 136-144).

From within a developing federalism with its bilateral contractual conditions, Puritan voluntarism arose.

It has pleased the great God to enter into a treaty and covenant of agreement with us his poor creatures, the articles of which agreement are here comprised. God, for his part, undertakes to convey all that concerns our happiness, upon our receiving of them, by believing on him. Every one in particular that recites these articles from a spirit of faith makes good this condition. (Sibbes 1864, I,civ)

Developing preparationism was concerned to chronicle the "windings" of the soul which preceded its going out to God in faith. Calvin himself, while explicitly denying that man could prepare himself, indicates that God may so work in the sinner before his conversion, especially by the piercing of the sinner's conscience with his Law (Institutes II, ii, 27; II, vii, 3-10). Commenting on St. Luke 19:1-10 (the Zacchaeus pericope), Calvin attributes to God the very desire Zacchaeus felt to see Jesus.

Now though faith was not yet formed in Zacchaeus, yet this was a sort of preparation for it; for it was not without a heavenly inspiration that he so earnestly desired to get a sight of Christ. (Calvin 1843, III, 433-434)

Voluntarism receives treatment by Calvin as he discusses the place of the will in conversion (Institutes II, iii, 6-14). In these concepts of covenant, preparation, and voluntarism, notwithstanding the systematization that took place, there is commonality between Calvin[1] and those Puritans like Hooker who consciously stood in the Reformed tradition.

In England the genealogical line of influence is easy to trace through the "fathers and sons" of the Reformed faith. It runs from Perkins (d.1605) through Baynes (d.1617), Sibbes (d.1635) and Ames (d.1633), Hooker (d.1647) and Cotton (d.1652), and to Preston (d.

---

[1] The present writer should not here be misunderstood as to think Calvin a "preparationist" in the Hookerian sense of the word. What is here maintained is that there is nothing in Hooker's preparationism that disqualifies him from the "school of Calvin." More positively, covenant theology, and the preparationist form of it, underwent an evolution the roots of which draw strength from Calvin's theology.

1628). As Cotton, Hooker and Shepard brought this covenant theology to New England, Perkins remained a "giant" in their thinking. For Perkins, the covenant of grace was God's "contract with man, concerning the obtaining of eternal life, upon a certaine condition" (in Miller 1956, 58). The conditionality of the covenant would be employed in order to prod the complacent to nurture any seeds of grace that they may have been granted.

Richard Sibbes, known as the "heavenly doctor," noticed a measure of uniformity in the working of God through the covenant.

> It is true God usually prepares those he means to convert, as we plough before we sow. We do not sow among the thorns; and we dig deep to lay a foundation; we purge before cordials. It is usual in nature and in grace preparations; therefore preparations are necessary. There is such a distance between the nature and corruption of man and grace, that there must be a great deal of preparation, many degrees to rise by before a man come to that condition he should be in. Therefore preparations we allow, and the necessity of them. But we allow this, that all preparations are from God. We cannot prepare ourselves, or deserve future things by our preparations; for the preparations themselves are of God. (Sibbes 1864, VI, 512)

As it will be shown, this is the same sort of clear preparationism, and yet high Calvinism that Hooker brought to New England.

Also in this Perkins-Baynes-Sibbes tradition was none other than John Cotton while in England. Kendall is able to document his statement that Cotton "comes the nearest of any figure examined so far in positing preparation on man's part before regeneration" (Kendall 1979, 110-117). This is an important and curious discovery given Cotton's subsequent and almost solitary refusal to adopt Hooker's preparationist theology in New England.

Clearly the most famous of the disciples of Perkins was William Ames. We have seen in the biographical sketch of Hooker that both he and Ames were forced to flee to Holland by reason of non-conformity. Though death prevented his migration to New England, in many ways Ames is mirrored on New England soil by Thomas Hooker. Perry Miller has presented Ames as the "father of New England church polity" (Miller 1933, 148-211). This of course is reflected in Hooker's final work. More pertinent to the present discussion is the clear voluntarism which flows from the covenant theology of both Ames and then Hooker. Ames' Medulla Sacrae Theologiae (1623) and De Conscientia (1630) became the standard theological textbooks in New England. Likewise, both Ames and Hooker were driven by a zeal to lead others to serve God, to "do something" with their faith, to practice godliness. This practical divinity became a hallmark of Hooker the pastor-theologian. In a section below on Hooker's "plain style" of preaching, it will be shown that this view of theology as the "art of living well" has Ramistic undergirding.

Pierre de la Ramee (1515-1572) had sought to rescue Christendom from the "errors" of scholasticism and Aristotelianism. Despite his well known categorical denial of Aristotle's teaching, his own ideas still borrowed from Aristotle. Ramus' significance is as a reorganizer of logic and rhetoric for pedagogical purposes. Employing a Platonic principle of dichotomy, utilitarianism was emphasized throughout his writings (Sprunger 1972, 107-109; Miller 1939, 142).

Ames was the chief proponent of Ramism at Franeker when none other than Cocceius studied under him and went on to become known as the "father of covenant theology." Because Laurence Chaderton was an early enthusiast for Ramism at Cambridge, and because Perkins employed Ramistic principles in his Arte of Prophesying, Hooker came from Emmanuel not only with a "new answering method," (having been one of the many students orbiting around the lecturer Alexander Richardson), but also with a desire to make the struggles of the interior life intelligible and usable (J. Morgan 1986, 296; Sprunger 1966, 133-151).

With this background, and especially with the Amesian emphasis on human will, Hooker could fully develop his preparationist theology, the natural outgrowth of his experimental predestinarian thinking. The quotation from Sibbes above indicates the impulse toward a morphology of conversion. What is evident is a very practical concern to observe the usual operations of God's Spirit. This might not only be desirable from a practical and ministerial point of view, but also may be deemed as comforting on cognitive grounds. The workings of God having been observed, can thereupon be expected in similar situations. Later in New England, displaced Puritans whose world had otherwise known great upheaval, found comfort in the reliability that a morphology of conversion could imply. Roger Clap of Dorchester wrote that many were so helped "to try their own hearts and to consider how it was with them, whether any work of God's Spirit were wrought in their own hearts or no" (in Young 1846, 355).

Since his days in Chelmsford Hooker had frequently encountered difficult cases of conscience among his troubled parishioners. Iain Murray has noted the commonality of opinion as to the general workings of God upon a soul.

> Hooker and his brethren did not discount the possibility that some true conversions may seem to occur swiftly and with little apparent trouble of soul, but they did deny that this was the Biblical norm. (Murray 1980, 18)

With this sort of developing consensus as to preparationism the morphology would be "fine tuned" so as to be a helpful instrument in the hands of the physician to the soul. Eventually in the Bay Colony especially, the morphology may also have provided a justification for the innovation of the "conversion narrative" as a requirement for church membership. This suggestion must remain a tentative one. Edmund Morgan had done the most work on the subject of the narrative requirement yet he has admittedly been unable to trace the practice to its precise origins (E. Morgan 1963,

64-112). Nevertheless this much is clear. Developing federalism with its conditional promises gave rise to the voluntarism and preparationism expounded by Puritan divines like Hooker. Having traced the development of federalism in Calvinistic theology, it is here maintained that Hooker's brand of voluntarism coupled as it was with the morphology, has a rightful claim with the Calvinistic tradition.

HOOKER'S ORTHODOXY AND THE DEVELOPING FEDERAL THEOLOGY

Because an analysis of Hooker's morphology will constitute the major remaining portion of this work, it remains here only to comment on Hooker's orthodoxy against the background of the developing federal theology. Hooker stood in the line, and drank deeply at the wellsprings of theological thought of the "giants" of his day, Perkins, Baynes, Sibbes, and Ames. With them he had been armed, while at Emmanuel, with the rhetoric and systematizing skills of Peter Ramus. The preoccupation of William Perkins with the Reformed conception of the "ordo salutis," is given new application in Hooker's pastoral theology and specifically his "conversion sermons." While standing on his own as an intellectual giant, Hooker employed well the spirit of Ramistic utilitarianism in his sermons. Giving expression to a certain reliability in God's dealings with sinners, Hooker's fame was magnified. His opponents recognized this early in his career. Laud's agent Samuel Collins, reported in 1629 that he had,

> lived in Essex to see many changes, and have seen the people idolizing many new ministers and lecturers; but this man (Hooker) surpasses them all for learning, and some other considerable parts, and . . . gains more and far greater followers than all before him. (in Miller 1956, 19)

Being well respected both in Europe and in New England

as one of the leading thinkers and writers of his day, it is no surprise that he was invited along with Cotton and Davenport to constitute a New England delegation to the Westminster Assembly (Winthrop 1908, II, 71). Hooker's extant works are voluminous, totalling some 5,000 pages. The great bulk consists of transcribed "conversion sermons," which best characterize the tenor of his entire ministry. The very titles of Hooker's published sermons betoken well his pastoral practicality. This sermonic material reveals Hooker to be not only the greatest psychologist of the Puritan era but also its most ardent preparationist.

To some, these callings for preparational gestures smelled of Arminianism. Indeed at the synod of 1637 in which the Hutchinson precipitated Antinomian crisis was settled, the "prophetess" contrasted the other ministers with Cotton, maintaining that they knew "no more than the apostles did before the resurrection of Christ" (Hall 1968, 320). More particularly she said of the preparationist Thomas Shepard, that he failed to preach clearly a covenant of grace (Hall 1968, 322). By banishing her, New England give itself to preparationism as a tenet of its orthodoxy. But Hooker's Calvinism for any who dip into his sermons, must go unchallenged. The chief events in the drama of redemption are all explicated in a most orthodox manner: the fall, the atonement, calling, justification, and sanctification of the elect. Consider Hooker's federalism: "Adam. . . represented all mankind (as a Parliament man doth for the whole country) for all that should be born of him; so that look what Adam did, all his posterity did" (Hooker 1651, 28). Because Adam had liberty, so did the race in him (Hooker 1640b, 137). With the fall the will of man is wholly tainted (Hooker 1656b, 315-317). Man is now unwilling to know the truth and "like bats, live most at ease when they have the least light." In addition, man is not only unwilling, he is unable to be willing. He "cannot be willing to be severed" from sin (Ibid., 307-319). As to the disposition of the will, corruption has taken the place of righteousness (Hooker 1638g, I,128).

Hooker's preparationism must not obscure his

rigorous tough-mindedness as to original sin. Commenting on the fifth chapter of Paul to the Romans, Hooker notes,

> Then for the sinne of Adam God may justly condemn all, though they never committ actual sin, is the judgment of all that are judicious. Death overspread all by Adam's sinne, and therefore wee see infants that dye, Adam's sin was actual; and let him shift what he can, the case is cleare, and the word condemns men for original sinne. (Hooker 1649, 28)

In one place Hooker quipped, "If we had dropped out of our mothers womb into hell and there had been roaring . . . it had been just (Hooker 1640b, 202).

The advanced state of Hooker's federalism in seen in his exposition of the divine tribunal in which the "covenant of redemption" was brought forth. The Son having agreed to put himself in the "roome of a sinner, " the Father then was to proceed against him with the Law and his own wrath, "revenging justice upon him" (Hooker 1638d, 175, 210-214). Particular redemption necessitated that the damned make payment for their own sin by suffering in hell.

Hooker's doctrine of justification is likewise typically orthodox. Counter imputations leave the sinner "accounted just, and so . . . acquitted before God as righteous" (Ibid., 132). New affections and new desires always result from, but are never the cause of justification. Saving faith, while necessary for salvation, is always a gift of God to the elect. God makes "all that belong to the election of grace willing to receive him" (Hooker 1638g, I, 126). For the reprobate, inability is always culpable and therefore leaves no room for complaint (Hooker 1656c, 308).

Hooker's voluntarism arose from the covenant schema. The great condition of the covenant is faith in Christ. Noting that covenantal language arises only occasionally in Hooker, Everett Emerson assumes he knows the reason.

> Since Hooker always made it clear that belief is God's gift and is limited to the elect, the covenant metaphor is not often found in Hooker's works. (Emerson 1967, 197)

This statement is correct in regard to Hooker's doctrine of faith, but is faulty in its assumption that the conditional nature of the covenant demands some sort of self engendered faith. As it stands, Emerson's statement constitutes an unjust indictment of most of the federalist school.

Thus it appears that in every major area of theological concern, Hooker is shown to be quite orthodox. As a "physician" to the soul Hooker viewed the fallen but elected creature of God, like all men, as a creature of desires. Therefore God offers Christ as a needful and to be desired gift. To all the faculties of man God makes appeal; to the understanding, will, and affections. This sets the stage for Hooker's preparationism. It is only to the mind which understands, and to the will which longs for relief, that God grants his grace of salvation (Hooker 1637a, 283-284). God's appealing to the mind is a necessary preparation for salvation (Hooker 1638g, II, 20-24). But the intellectual grasp is not enough. The will is the "commander of the soul," and it must likewise be prepared" (Hooker 1637a, 283).

With Hooker's orthodoxy established, and with his voluntarism seen as placing him squarely in the stream of the then developing federalism, it now is necessary to make a systematic examination of Hooker's morphology in three different stages. As it has been noted above, Hooker's conversion formulations were born during his days at Cambridge, were preached at Chelmsford, resumed at Newtown and Hartford, published in the 1630's, and brought to final form in the incomplete <u>Application</u> <u>of</u> <u>Redemption</u> series of sermons. The Antinomian controversy had threatened to shatter the very foundations of New England society and Hooker's brand of preaching had at least partially given rise to the Hutchinsonian objections. It remains to be shown what effect the controversy of 1637 had on Hooker's morphology which will next be examined as it first came to print, then in any sermons that can be traced to the crisis period itself, and finally as it appeared in its final form in the publications of 1656.

ESTABLISHING HOOKER'S MORPHOLOGY FROM HIS PUBLISHED WORKS

From the corpus of Hooker's writings published before and during 1638, a broad outline of his morphology of conversion can be gleaned. It should be remembered that all of these sermonic formulations reflect a pre-New England environment, and would receive some revision in later works. Nowhere does Hooker neatly list some sort of ordo salutis. Rather the following inventory must be garnered from the various sermons since death prevented fuller systematization beyond the ten books of the Application of Redemption volumes (1656) and the Comment Upon Christs Last Prayer (1656). Hooker's ordo" is typical apart from the additional preparationist components that were his special concern. The stages are: contrition, humiliation, vocation, faith, justification, adoption, sanctification, and glorification. For analytical purposes, if these stages were set out, and an overlay of the titles of Hooker's works was placed upon them, one would easily see that the great bulk of Hooker's interest and efforts was directed towards the initiatory and preparatory stages. The Application of Redemption series is representative of this. The very titles of the major works in Hooker's corpus at large also bears this out. Sanctification finds but scant treatment in Hooker and casuistry is hardly noticeable. Emerson has remarked, "Although Hooker's works are full of exhortation to good works, one is surprised at how seldom Hooker gives his reader any idea of what constitutes the good life" (Emerson 1955, 120). In the main corpus of Hooker's writings, that is those published in 1638 or before, only the 170 page The Soules Possession (1638) is a work on sanctification. Later would be published a supplementary work, The

Saints Dignitie and Duty (1651).
All dates given in this work are dates of publication. It should be noted that these do not always reflect the chronology of composition. Yet it does appear that the chronology of composition generally reflects Hooker's actual ordo, meaning that the preacher very deliberately and systematically sought to nurture his parishioners along their respective spiritual sojourns. Intending to examine Hooker's morphology in three different stages of his career: pre-Antinomian crisis, sermons and works from the crisis period, and final forms, the following early major works express Hooker's morphology in that first period of his career.

1) The Unbeleevers Preparing For Christ (1638)
2) The Soules Preparation For Christ or A Treatise of
    Contrition (1632)
3) The Soules Humiliation (1637)
4) The Soules Ingrafting (1637); The Soules Implantation
    (1637); The Soules Implantation Into The Natural Olive Tree (1640)
5) The Soules Vocation or Effectual Calling (1637)
6) The Soules Exaltation (1638)
7) The Soules Possession of Christ (1638)

Though these early works, totalling some 2,572 pages, amply reflect Hooker's morphology, several of the more supplementary works will also be included in the following analysis.[1] Leaving aside for now any discussion of works from the Antinomian period, Hooker's morphology took its final form in the posthumously

---

[1] Regarding the Hooker canon, see Bush in Williams et al. 1975, 378-389. Bush overviews the present state of knowledge regarding the Hooker canon and makes important comments regarding newly discovered editions and works of doubtful Hookerian authorship. Cf. also Emerson's "Notes On The Hooker Canon," (Emerson 1956b, 555).

published The Application of Redemption volumes (1656). Much of the thematic material from The Unbeleevers Preparing For Christ was revised in The Application of Redemption (Books IV, 1, VII, VIII). The Soules Preparation was revised in The Application of Redemption (Books IX-X). The Soules Humiliation, which along with The Soules Preparation are clearly the two most important early works, would no doubt have found revision in the furthering of the Application of Redemption series if Hooker's death had not ended his labors. A Comment Upon Christs Last Prayer (1656) deals with the final stage in Hooker's morphology, glorification. This latter work is identified on its title page as being Hooker's "Seventeenth Book, made in New England." In an advertisement in The Application of Redemption (Books I-VIII), the following notation appears:

> Eleven Books made in New-England, by Mr. Thomas Hooker, and printed from his Papers, written with his own Hand; are now published in three volumns, two in Quarto, and one in Octavo, viz . . .

Then follows a listing of the ten books of The Application of Redemption series. The advertisement continues,

> The Last, viz. Christ's Prayer for Beleevers, on John 17. There are Six more Books of Mr. Hookers, printing in two Volums. (prefacing Hooker 1656b)

Clearly we are to understand that Comment On Christ's Last Prayer was to be considered as "Book XVII" in the Application of Redemption series. This follows given its subject matter which is glorification. The other six books were never published and indeed probably never existed. Peter Cole the publisher, wishfully exaggerated by saying that the intervening six books were in "printing." Perhaps this reflects a degree of competition among printers for Hooker's sermons (Herget 1972, 231-239). Nevertheless, the possibility does exist that Cole did have some additional Hooker papers in his possession. The possible existence of such manuscripts implants a sense of mystery into the discussion of the Hooker canon.

HOOKER'S VOLUNTARISM IN THE CONTEXT OF THE FACULTY PSYCHOLOGY

    This writer purposes here to look back a century to the views of Calvin, to look forward a century to the views of Edwards, and to compare them accordingly with Hooker's psychology. This will serve to test Hooker's Calvinism against the touchstone of its namesake, and to compare Hooker's place in the development of Puritan psychology to Edwards.
    Calvin of course would hear of no "faculty" of man which might independently aspire to good.

> Those who attribute to God's first grace that fact that we effectually will, seem to imply, on the other hand, that there is a faculty in the soule voluntarily to aspire to good. . . . Yet if we hold the view that men have, apart from grace, some impulses (however puny) toward good, what shall we reply to the apostle who even denies that we are capable of conceiving anything (2 Cor. 3:5)? (<u>Institutes</u> II, ii, 27)

Calvin was very careful to maintain the inability of the will to choose the good without the Holy Spirit. Speaking of the conversion of the will and its very first stirrings, Calvin insisted that God moves the affections, "arousing love and desire and zeal for righteousness in our hearts." Everything good in the will is attributed to "the work of grace alone" (<u>Institutes</u> II, iii, 6). As will be shown in the discussion of <u>The Soules Effectual Calling</u>, Hooker concurred with this, even in the first moving of the affections, Hooker's "wheels" of faith.
    Calvin adopted with approval the teaching of Bernard.

To will is in us: but to will good is gain; to will evil, loss. Therefore simply to will is of man; to will ill, of a corrupt nature; to will well, of grace. (Institutes II, iii, 5)

This is standard monergism, with which Hooker fully concurred. But the understanding of Calvin, as to the then reigning psychological views, should also be noticed. As it is well known, Calvin the Renaissance humanist made wide use of secular authors, especially of Platonic thought. God's promises are presented in a body of propositions to which God must open our eyes of understanding. From his intellectual heritage, Calvin inherited the conception of the human being as a hierarchy of faculties, with the mind as the chief commander (Bouwsma 1986, 98-101). Yet curiously, faith is not operative somewhere "down the line" of the faculties, but often is by Calvin located, not so much in the will, as in an intellectual assent which has effects. Calvin notes the Biblical synonyms for faith as being "recognition" (agnitio) and "knowledge" (scientia) (Institutes III, ii, 14). The intellectual aspect of faith, being rooted in the revealed promises of God, is prominent in his understanding.

But Calvin balks at any view of faith seen as "nothing deeper than a common consent to gospel history" (Institutes III, ii, 1). Though it remains true, "take away the Word and no faith will then remain" (Institutes III, ii, 6), faith is more then bare intellectual assent. For Calvin, as for his spiritual descendants, faith involved the affections as it is "more of the heart than of the brain, and more of the disposition than the understanding" (Institutes III, ii, 8). Given the tenor of the whole of Calvin's work, clearly he in no way deprecates the intellectual aspect of faith. Nevertheless, his brand of psychology is not so patently hierarchical.

And here again we ought to observe that we are called to a knowledge of God: not that knowledge which content with empty speculation, merely flits in the brain, but that which will be sound and fruitful if we duly perceive it, and if it takes root in the heart. (<u>Institutes</u> I, v, 9; cf. Dowey 1952, 24-28)

Calvin does not systematize his understanding of the faculties. But given the prevailing psychological constructs of the day, his view seems to be that once knowledge is gained, whether located in the <u>cerebrum</u> or <u>cor</u>, the other faculties will follow into love and obedience (Wallace 1959, 218).

The purpose of this overview is to compare and contrast the understanding of Calvin and Hooker, and later Edwards, with one another. As with Calvin, the intellectual assent to Biblical propositions is of great importance to Hooker. Both recoiled at the enthusiasts or familists of their respective periods. Both maintained the utter necessity of conjunction of the Spirit with the Word.

Hooker manifestly had the greater voluntaristic emphasis in his ever present calls for his hearers to labor for contrition and humiliation. Sinners were exhorted to go out and "fetch" Christ. But Calvin's more "quiet assent" of the mind is not terribly unlike Hooker's portrayal of the actual exercise of faith as the will finally says "Amen to the promise, and saith O that mercie I will have, and thus the soul is come home to God by vocation" (Hooker 1637a, 668).

Both Calvin and Hooker became heirs of the "faculty psychology." They each modified the prevailing view, yet in different ways. Hooker followed the schema more closely than did Calvin, its hierarchical nature being well suited to his unfolding morphology. Yet, though Hooker followed its constructs, his departure from its most basic tenet is more radical than any departure on the part of Calvin. For Hooker, the volition, not the intellect, was given the place of the chief commander. Hooker maintained that "all the affections come to the will, the great commander" (Ibid., 152-153, 296; also Hooker 1640a, 11). It is important here to take direct notice of his understanding of the relationship between cognition and volition. Against the prevailing system of psychology, Hooker maintained that "understanding and reason are but underlings of the will, they are servants and subjects to it" (Hooker 1632, 116; Hooker 1656c, 279). It thus appears that Perry Miller errs in assuming that Hooker employed a faculty psychology without modification (Miller 1939, 248, 253). On the contrary Hooker followed the thought of Ames who had maintained both the Calvinian concepts of faith as an act of the understanding, and the insistence that it involved much more.

> To believe signifies ordinarily an act of the under-standing as it gives assent to evidence. But since the will is wont to be moved and reach out to embrace the good thus proved, faith may rightly designate this act of the will itself . . . it is an act of choice, an act of the whole man which is by no means a mere act of the intellect. (Ames 1968, 80)

These statements reflect the inherited faculty psychology with an added monistic emphasis, the latter providing a foreshadowing of the views of Edwards.

But a statement by Ames in the second part of his Marrow reveals more clearly his voluntarism which was inherited by Hooker.

> Those who place faith in the understanding confess that there must be some action of the will to secure that assent . . . so if faith depends upon the will, it must be that the first beginning of faith lies in the will. (Ames 1968, 242)

Ames thus appears to hold forth a "volition emphasis" (Cherry 1974, 13). But an "intellectual emphasis" is also sometimes seen in Ames. Indeed Miller presents Ames as a champion of the faculty psychology (Miller 1939, 248-249). Ames' own statements do appear to be eclectic, possibly being indicative of a more monistic view of human psychology.

As it has been shown, Hooker goes well beyond Calvin and also the cautious modifications of Ames, to declare the will to be the "great commander" of the soul (Hooker 1632, 116).

Jonathan Edwards, especially with his respective studies of the affections and the will, becomes another touchstone within the Reformed tradition by which to evaluate the views of Hooker as to cognition and volition. It has been shown that Hooker, whose morphology in some ways paralleled the outlines of faculty psychology, nevertheless radically departed from that understanding at its very fountainhead. It now remains to be seen what Jonathan Edwards did with the faculty psychology which still prevailed in his day.

Edwards developed his view of human psychology most fully in his <u>Treatise</u> <u>Concerning</u> <u>Religious</u> <u>Affections</u> (1746). Hooker, concerned as he was more with preparatory graces than with the consequential effects of faith, had portrayed the "affections" of hope, desire, love, and joy, as "wheels" that carry faith. Edwards was more concerned to show that true religion consists of holy affections, which are themselves divine and supernatural. Thus, their respective concerns regarding the "affections" were on different planes. What is more pertinent here is their use, modification, or abandonment of the faculty psychology.

On a superficial level, a paradigm of Edwards' psychology might seem to demonstrate affiance in the faculty psychology in that the affections, chief of which is love, flow from the inclinations and understanding. But Edwards had a more monistic understanding of the human soul than this, maintaining an essential unity between the understanding and affections (Miller 1949, 180-181). Edwards' departure from the faculty psychology is clearly seen in <u>The</u> <u>Freedom</u> <u>of</u> <u>The</u> <u>Will</u>(1754).

> The will itself is not an agent that has a will: the power of choosing, itself, has not a power of choosing. That which has the power of volition or

choice is that man or the soul, and not the power of volition itself. (Edwards 1957, 163)

Edwards, careful not to sharply delineate the faculties or "offices," presents no hierarchy of powers in the act of faith (Hoopes 1988, 207). Conrad Cherry offers this summary of Edwards psychology of conversion.

> In faith the power of intellect and will tend to merge into one; strictly speaking, the various movements of the self in the act of faith are not distinct acts but are different modes of the same act. (Cherry 1974, 17)

That the current state of Edwardsean studies on this question is not settled is reflected by Cherry's objection to Winslow's understanding of Edwards' subordination of one power to another (Cherry 1974, 17; Winslow 1940, 216). Miller maintained that Edwards was not quite able to completely break from the faculty psychology (Miller 1949, 177-190). Miller's view that Edwards, with his more monistic understanding was following Locke in his rebellion against the faculty psychology, has now been seriously challenged. James Hoopes has maintained that Edwards' understanding provided a defense against Locke's own psychological empiricism (Hoopes 1988, 205-210).

More importantly, Norman Fiering has investigated the sources of Edwards's thought and has concluded contrary to Perry Miller, that Edwards was influenced less by Locke than by intellectual principles which long antedated Locke. Fiering's acclaimed work has restored a proper recognition of the fundamental place that must be given to theological considerations in Edwardsean thought. As to the matter of faculty psychology, Fiering has shown that neither Locke nor Edwards were in outright rebellion against the faculty psychology but rather were concerned for a more monistic understanding of human motivation (Fiering 1981a, 262-271). By arguing that in the act of faith the common distinction between human powers breaks down, Edwards, more so than did Hooker, drew upon themes found in

Calvin and then in Ames (Ames 1968, 83).
    Clear differences can thus be seen between these three representatives of different eras in the development of Reformed theology. Thomas Hooker clearly had the greatest voluntaristic emphasis, and this reflects the place afforded to volition in his understanding of human psychology. Calvin, and later Edwards, emphasized the assent of the mind, though they both insisted upon a unitary concept of man. Edwards, in the years following the "reign" of Solomon Stoddard, restored experimental religion to the central position it had found in Hooker's preaching, indeed going beyond Hooker in his requirements as to a "conversion narrative." Hooker's biographer notes,

> The tradition which Hooker left behind of evangelical preaching and experimental religion flourished on the river. Edwards was simultaneously its last great exponent and the initiator of a new spiritual era. (Shuffelton 1977, 303)

    No linear path of development can be traced from Calvin to Edwards through Hooker. These American Puritans, sometimes using the same sources, were nevertheless original thinkers. Yet amid shades of differences as to psychology, voluntarism, and assurance, once must not lose sight of the obvious, the basic Calvinistic framework of these two Connecticut River Puritans.

CHAPTER THREE:
HOOKER'S MORPHOLOGY OF CONVERSION, EARLY FORMULATIONS

THE EARLIEST STAGES OF THE MORPHOLOGY AS EXPLICATED BY HOOKER DURING THE CHELMSFORD PERIOD 1626-1630

Goodwin and Nye, noting that Hooker had first developed his morphology while at Cambridge, report that he went over the same themes,

again a Second time, many years after, more largely at Great Chelmsford in Essex; the Product of which, was those Books of Sermons that have gone under his Name. ("To The Reader," in Hooker 1656b)

As evidenced by the publications in 1638 of material Hooker had preached before his departure from England, it is clear that a complete morphology had been formulated and preached by Hooker before he fled to the Netherlands.

The year 1627 brought the first publication of a Hooker document, his preface "To The Reader," in the second edition of John Rogers' The Doctrine of Faith. This was the same John Rogers who was respected by Hooker to such an extent that upon leaving Esher, Hooker had hoped to settle in Colchester in Essex that he might be near the great preacher considered by Hooker to be "the prince of all the preachers in England" (Mather 1853, I, 334). Instead, circumstances had led Hooker to Chelmsford where his own preaching was finding great popularity. The work of Rogers, who would in 1629 be silenced for non-conformity, clearly echoes the same themes that Hooker must have been contemporaneously sounding in Chelmsford. Hooker's brief preface is marked by obvious warmth and agreement between the two ministers. During this period Hooker preached before the Dedham congregation the sermon which would later be published as The Faithful Covenanter (1644). Given Hooker's approval of the work of Rogers, the content of The Doctrine of Faith is as revealing as Hooker's preface is, as to his current understanding of faith and conversion.[1] Rogers defined faith as,

> The mighty work of the Holy Ghost, whereby a sinner is humbled by the laws, and quite driven out of himself, by or upon the gracious and sweet voice of the Gospel, and the free and unpartial offer of mercy from God in Christ, comes in time to cast himself upon Christ, and to trust to Him as the all-sufficient and only means of his salvation, and withal is willing to be subject to Him all his days. (Rogers 1627, A6-A6v)

Hooker, in his "To The Reader," similarly defined faith.

> Faith being nothing else but the going out of the soul to God through Christ to fetch a principle of life which in Adam we lost and now need. And hence it is that there is such an extraordinary worth in this precious grace, Eph. 1:19, and such an extraordinary virtue, even the mighty working of the exceeding great power of the outstretched arm of the Lord put forth to bring the soul to himself by believing. (in Williams et al. 1975, 140-144)

In both definitions of faith one should note that while a degree of voluntarism is present, yet neither writer hesitates to posit this alongside what is clear soteriological monergism. The seemingly logical inconsistency is allowed to stand in tension. The sinner must "cast himself upon Christ," and the soul must "go out to God through Christ and fetch a principle of life," yet this can be done only by "the mighty work of the Holy Ghost." Remaining firmly committed to his

---

[1] For background concerning Rogers, see Williams et al. 1975, 140-142. Shuffelton (Shuffelton 1977, 133) seems to be unaware that Hooker's preface made its first appearance in the 1627 second edition of Rogers' work. He views the 1629 edition as first carrying Hooker's preface.

Calvinism, Hooker would allow this tension to stand. He refused to allow any diminishing of the sola gratia principle. His activist calls reflect his desire for "heart religion," the practical and Ramistic "art of living to God." In Rogers' definition especially, there is a foretaste of Hooker's published treatises on contrition and humiliation. Hooker's approval of a preparationist theology, in this his first published piece, is clear.

In the Rogers quotation above, the typical preparationist use of the Law of God is employed as the means to humble the sinner. John Rogers went on to note that to neglect to preach the Law would be to "make folks licentious Christians, and to look for salvation by Christ ere ever they know what need they have of him" (Rogers 1627, 68). As Larzer Ziff has noted, the reality of churches filled with hardened people shaped predestinarian doctrine, leading it towards preparationism rather than sudden and seizing grace (Ziff, 1973, 55). Yet this preparationism, coupled as it was with high Calvinism, could still speak of a "holy kind of violence" whereby the sinner is "prepared," being drawn from sin and unto Christ (Hooker 1638g, 3,18, passim).

In the preface under discussion, Hooker is especially pleased to notice how Rogers makes "a saving contrition to go before faith" (in Williams 1975, 144). But Hooker is quick to make a technical qualification, noting that "every saving work is not a sanctifying work" (Ibid., 145). Though godly sorrow and hatred of sin cannot truly be in the reprobate, these may be found in those already enjoying the fruits of faith, as well as in those who are being brought low in contrition. This leads Hooker to explain.

> The one is a sorrow of preparation, the other a sorrow of sanctification, and yet both are saving. The one is wrought upon us, wherein we are patients of the work of the Spirit bringing of us unto Christ; the other is wrought by us through the Spirit given to us and dwelling in us when we have received Christ. (Ibid.)

Four years later, in much less congenial circumstances, Hooker would again defend his conviction of this "double sorrow" as he would contradict John Paget in their respective answers to the nineteenth of the <u>Twenty Questions</u> designed to test Hooker's qualifications for the ministry in Holland. Here in his preface to Rogers' work Hooker is emphasizing monergism in the preparation process. In the eyes of some critics this emphasis did not always shine so brightly.[1]

Hooker shows his pastoral side as he directs the reader to a particular passage in Rogers' work as to the "coming of faith." Rogers indicates that it is hard to ascertain at what instant faith is wrought. Hooker insists that weak faith is still true faith, being "the spawn of faith not yet brought to full perfection. The soul is coming toward God but not yet come to him to rest so fully and wholly on him as hereafter it will" (in Williams 1975, 146). Hooker is here being sensitive to the psychological realities of the soul which is striving towards God. Statements like these from Rogers and Hooker are used by Kendall to drive a wedge between the views of Calvin and the Puritans. Though Calvin did indeed labor to show that true faith is far from being <u>fides implicita</u>, but rather it is knowledgeable and exuded assurance (<u>Institutes</u>, III, ii, 7-10), even he acknowledged that the believer comes more and more to full faith. Hooker's prefatory epistle holds many clues as to the marks of his own career about to be popularized through his many published works.

A second published work which preceded the formal series of "conversion sermons," must here receive

---

[1] Kendall is one such critic. He writes (Kendall 1979, 128n) that in <u>The Unbeleevers Preparing</u> Hooker "explicitly imputes an enormous responsibility to the natural man." This criticism fails, when one realizes that for Hooker "responsibility," which is ever maintained, does not imply "ability." On the basis of his thesis, Kendall no doubt thinks Hooker attributes great ability to natural man.

some notice. The Poor Doubting Sinner Drawne Unto Christ (1629) was a work of immense popularity. This, the earliest of Hooker's published sermon texts, has a tangled publication history that seems to reflect different underlying manuscripts. The issues involved in the publication history are still open to debate and lay outside the scope of this dissertation (Cf. Williams 1975, 147-151; Bush 1973, 3-20; Shuffelton 1971, 68-75). All references made here will be to the text published by Robert Dawlman in 1629 as reproduced by George H. Williams (Williams 1975, 152-186). This represents the most pristine text of the work, suiting best the desire here for an examination of the earliest views of Hooker. The Biblical text for the sermon is John 6:45, "Every man therefore that hath heard, and learned of the Father, cometh unto me."

In typical fashion Hooker begins his sermon with the utter necessity of being brought low in contrition. This is demonstrated by means of the explication of "such hindrances as really keep men from coming to take hold of Christ at all." These obstacles include an assumed safety, an attempted reformation of life, a faith which rests but does not work, and a self determined effort to "hammer out a faith of his own making (in Williams 1975, 152). But these maladies which "fasten" one tightly to his sin do not provide the major points of discussion in the work. Hooker is concerned to uncover those "hindrances which do not indeed deprive a man of title from Christ, but make the way more tedious" (Ibid., 153). Probing the interior life, Hooker finds the basis for these hindrances.

> When men out of carnal reason contrive another way to come to Christ than ever he ordained or revealed, when we set up a standard by God's standard, and out of our own imagination we make another condition of believing than ever Christ required or ordained. Thus we make bars in the way, and manacle our hands, and fetter our feet, and then we complain that we cannot go; thus it is with you poor Christians, and the fault is your

own. (Ibid.)

It becomes obvious very early in the work that Hooker has a goal to reassure the doubter, to point to Christ, and to issue a charitable judgment to the one who has been brought low. The work is largely formed by an imagined dialogue as the "windings" of the soul are investigated by means of various questions and answers. Characteristic here is not the complacent drunkard, but the one who has seen the holiness of God yet can not dare to think that mercy may belong to him (Ibid.), the one who wants to believe but fears he may have "hoodwinked" himself (Ibid., 154), and the one who "looks upon his own sinfulness and worthlessness, and therefore dares not venture upon mercy" (Ibid.). Hooker has a ready answer of comfort. "Observe the folly of this plea: what Scripture ever said that the greatness of man's sins hinders the greatness of God's mercy?" (Ibid)

As the sermon unfolds, Hooker anticipates the same sort of objections in various forms. Indeed one objection seems to lead to another as the soul which wants to believe and be comforted and is weary of its own sin, somehow finds reason to think it must ever remain in misery. One is brought forth who is very conscious of his sin but fears that it is not sufficiently "burdened with them." This one has a heart that "cannot break and mourn for the dishonor of God." True to his expressed desire not to promulgate standards for coming to Christ that demand more than God does, Hooker reassures this "doubter" that such a condition does not hinder,

> provided that thy heart is weary of itself, that it cannot be weary of sin. The Lord shows mercy because he will show mercy. It is not because thou canst please him, but because mercy pleases him. (Ibid., 157)

It is good that one who cannot be weary of his sin should at least be weary of such a frame of heart. Similarly, the one who feels that the ordinances only harden his heart is encouraged that such knowledge itself is a ground of hope. The psychologist prods the struggling one to cease resting on self and to go to God. In a prescription that sounds very much like it could have come from Calvin himself, Hooker urges, "rest not in thy performances, but look beyond all duties to God, and desire him to give thee success above them (Ibid., 159).

It is in dialogue with one who seeks assurance but can not seem to "sense" or "feel" the presence of grace, that Hooker reveals his deep commitment to the place of the Bible in experimental theology. The objection too is rooted in Biblical revelation as the doubter wonders why he doesn't sense God's grace when the Bible reveals that "they who believe shall be filled with joy unspeakable and glorious." Hooker answers:

> Thou must not think to have joy and refreshing before thou go to the promise, but thou must look for it when thou dost chew and feed upon the promise. . . . This joy is a fruit that proceeds from faith and much wrestling; it doth not follow from faith at the first. First believe, and then joy; for the heart is not filled with joy before believing, but afterwards. (Ibid., 160)

For Hooker, if a man's faith be real, it may even be somewhat strong though it lacks the sense or feeling of joy and comfort. His prescription is "away with your sense and feeling, and go to the promise" (Ibid., 166). Evidencing his modified faculty psychology, Hooker says that both heart and conscience must be informed by the Word of God. This involves the reason which tends to object, the conscience which accuses, and the will which refuses to submit (Ibid., 171). To wander after sense and feeling is to be led astray. "Hold to the Word, and the devil will be tired and go away" (Ibid., 175). As accusers appear, the "poor doubter" is to let the Scriptures speak and is to refuse to hear any accusers who bring not the Word (Ibid., 174).

Near the mid-point of his sermon, Hooker issues a reminder as to his "target audience."

> All this while I speak to brokenhearted Christians.
> You profane ones, you have your portion already,
> and shall have more afterwards; but stand you by,
> and let the children come to their share. (Ibid.,
> 163)

This holds a key to that which may seem paradoxical in Hooker's words. His was a ministry characterized in a large measure by efforts to bring men and women to contrition and humiliation by a proper sight of their own sin. But in the present work, speaking to those whom he feels have already received the grace of faith, he urges,

> We must not look too long, nor pore too much or
> unwarrantably upon our own corruptions, so far as
> to be feared or disheartened from coming to the
> riches of God's grace. (Ibid., 161)

These ones, already brought to Christ, are likewise urged to avoid doubts regarding such questions as sovereign election. They are not to meddle in God's secrets nor let their own lack of understanding becloud their hope (Ibid., 165-166).
    As it shall be shown, Hooker's ministry was one in which a "charitable judgment" was to be practiced whenever even but the seeds of grace were perceived. In the <u>Poor Doubting Christian</u>, Hooker's hearers are urged to practice such a judgment upon themselves. Were it not that Hooker assumes grace has been bestowed, the words could hardly fall from his Calvinistic lips: "Be sure to take thy soul at the best" (Ibid., 168). Because the Lord rushes to be gracious, those recipients of grace must also be gracious to themselves. If one finds himself grieved with sin, that is reason for encouragement, for this is a form a faith as the soul turns to its "right side" in order to take the promise (Ibid., 169). It is a sign of a humble heart to take what God offers.
    Indeed the Law has a function of bringing the sinner low. But for the Christian constantly to condemn

himself contrary to the received Word of grace is extreme pride and self willed rebellion. Thus the physician of the soul turns the charge of sinfulness back upon the overly introspective. There is obvious tension here between the dangers of complacency on the one hand, and almost frantic self inspection on the other. Hooker never fully sorts out this difficulty but rather, as a physician who knows well his patients, he gives the varied remedies in accordance to the perceived need.

If the optimism of such a "positive psychology" as is found in the Poor Doubting Christian should cause any to doubt Hooker's orthodoxy, the doubts should be dashed by his concluding section entitled "Means To Obtain Grace and Faith." Faith itself is God's gift and therefore He must be waited upon. The means are to be attended unto for these are "conduits" for the gift of faith. All other props are to be removed for by nature "we would trust to our own strength and rely upon something of our own" (Ibid., 177). Voluntarism from within a covenantal scheme is evident as the doubter is urged not to attempt to bring good to the promise but rather to go to the promise for good (Ibid., 182).

> Buy without money. This is the condition that God offers mercy upon. Buy wine and milk; that is, grace and salvation without money; that is, without sufficiency of your own. (Ibid., 183)

Free grace is offered and no condition is be made other than that God makes by means of covenant. God's commodities are to be made "no dearer than God himself makes them" (Ibid.).

Elsewhere in Hooker's corpus the complacent are warned that to enter the realm of grace is no easy thing. But in this work, Hooker turns to the "poor doubter" who is quite agonized by his own unworthiness. These overly introspective ones are urged to stop looking within. Rather they are to go out of themselves to the gracious promise of convenantal grace.

Before moving to a discussion of Hooker's standard morphological works, another early sermon must receive notice. The Faithful Covenanter was preached in 1629 in the Dedham pulpit of John Rogers, the suppressed vicar of Dedham. Two years before Hooker had contributed the preface to Rogers' popular treatise on faith. The Faithful Covenanter was not published until 1644, at the height of competition for Hooker's works. Standing in sharp contrast with the work examined above, the sermon is a harsh one, which while using a covenantal scheme with its threats of cursing, addresses the lax conditions among the Christians of Dedham.

Throughout the sermon, promises and cursings, "Ebal and Gerizim," are put before the hearers, with the ominous warning that wickedness will bring the cursings and wrath of God. Like Hooker's "farewell sermon" of 1631, the present sermon contains an indictment of the entire English nation. In prodding the complacent to not rest in outward privileges, Hooker urges them,

> . . . not to depend upon our privileges, not to boast of them and rest in them, and go away and say, What the Spainards come into England! What the enemy overcome England! We have the gospel, the means of grace. No nation under heaven has so many in it that do fear the Lord as our nation hath. (in Williams 1975, 195)

To examine this sermon along with the most famous one of the same period, The Poor Doubting Christian, is instructive in that the two capsulize and represent the two characteristic marks of Hooker's brand of preparationism. Hooker seeks ever to bring low and to prod the complacent, and to encourage the doubting recipient of grace. The importance of God's Law is demonstrated on both counts.

> As in a covenant there are articles of agreements between party and party, so between God and his people. Here are the articles of agreement, the ten words which God Spake, the ten commandments (Ibid., 198).

The Law is to be viewed under two heads: First as a

legal absolute requirement, and second, as a means to guide and prod one to evangelical performance and obedience. Hooker here stands in the mainstream of Reformed thought with this use of the Law in the Christian's life. Quoting Romans 6:14 "We are not under law but under grace," Hooker will have no thought of the cessation of the Law's significance. Rather, Paul's meaning is that the Christian "is free from the rigor, and curse, and punishment of the law" (Ibid., 198-199). Departing from the more traditional terminology, Hooker posits a "covenant of being in God which is called the covenant of faith," and a "covenant of walking before or with God. . . answerable to grace bestowed. . . the covenant of his law, whereby we should be obedient unto him" (Ibid., 197).

Throughout, Hooker reminds that "we have no power of ourselves" to keep covenant with God and that every evangelical obedience is a relative performance which is graciously blessed. It is always an evidence which carries no worth by which to purchase salvation. The importance of the interior life is also characteristically stressed.

> The frame of an evangelical heart is to be in covenant: that is the spring of man's practice, the first mover, the weight that makes him strict in obedience to every commandment and approve inwardly of every commandment of God. (Ibid., 200)

Thus heart religion will outwardly manifest itself. As Hooker comes to the "uses," the importance of sincere introspective examination to "hunt out" hypocrisy is stressed. He warns of those who "play at religion" but remain no different (Ibid., 205, 207). An "honest heart" mourns for the shortcomings of its payment in obedience (Ibid., 209).

Though seeking in the main to warn those complacent ones who think little of breaking covenant, Hooker characteristically adds a word of consolation to those who do indeed "love and fear the Lord." Here again is his two-pronged emphasis. Finally, in an exhortation directed to all, and one that will be typical of the entire sequence of the morphology, Hooker would have his hearers determine "to labor for a good conscience and endeavor to walk with God" (Ibid., 220). In this early sermon, the importance of the interior life, voluntarism, evangelical obedience, and high Calvinism, all come together.

The ethic that is being uncovered here is one of evangelical obedience enabled by the grace of God and flowing from a grateful heart. But even this must remain a struggle due to the imperfections of the soul and the allurements of this world. Sargent Bush misses the mark when he describes Hooker's evangelical obedience ethic as meaning that "men must simply express the goodness in their hearts as best they can and God will accept the attempt despite its imperfection" (Bush 1980, 281). Hooker did not view it in such easy terms. Yes, man's performance is relative and this is nevertheless blessed. But everywhere in Hooker the upward striving for a gracious amendment is propounded, as is the soul's heaviness in view of its imperfect frame and obedience. Indeed it was Hooker's major concern to have the interior life, the heart of man, properly framed. Casuistical preaching played little part in Hooker's sermonic material because once the heart was properly framed and conscience was properly informed by the Word of God, the practice of faith would naturally follow.

THE MAJOR MORPHOLOGICAL WORKS: THE UNBELEEVERS PREPARING

Turning to The Unbeleevers Preparing For Christ (1638) one encounters the "pre-initial" stage in Hooker's morphology. Though published after the immensely popular Soules Preparation (1632) and Soules Humiliation (1637), the Unbeleevers Preparing concerns the natural state of man and his need for contrition and humiliation. It therefore logically precedes the two most popular of Hooker's morphological works. An advertisement page in the volume provides an ordo of Hookerian writings reflecting his morphology. The Unbeleevers Preparing is indeed placed first in this

paradigm. The work is of great importance despite the fact that it has not received as extensive treatment by scholars as have other Hookerian works. Important to the thesis of this study is the fact that it is in the Unbeleevers Preparing, according to Kendall, that Hooker "explicitly imputes an enormous responsibility to the natural man before regeneration" (Kendall 1979, 128n). Such is a curious charge in view of the fact that the volume contains six sermons all seemingly designed to show man's utter misery and helplessness apart from grace. Because the very nature of preparation as propounded by Hooker is so often misunderstood, and given the foundational nature of this initial volume despite the relative disinterest shown towards it by scholars, the work must here receive careful attention.
In the initial sermon on Revelation 22:17, "Whosoever will let him take of the water freely," Hooker immediately puts forth the utter necessity of preparation. It is significant to note the high esteem in which the pulpit was held by Hooker.

> A powerful Ministry is the ordinary means that the Lord hath appointed to prepare the soule of a poore sinner soundly for Christ. (Hooker 1638g, I,2)

Hooker goes on starkly to declare that he will explicate both "God's part" and "man's part" in the process. Such phrases as these perk the interest of those who would find an Arminian tendency in Hooker. Hooker must be allowed to speak for himself as to his meaning of "God's part" and "man's part."

> On God's part . . . first the freeness of the offer of his grace; secondly, the universality of this offer of grace to all, and thirdly, the easiness of the condition whereupon he offereth it, whosoever will may receive it and that freely. On man's part, two things are to be considered. First, he must consider that his own corruption doth oppose the grace of God. And secondly, he must consider that God hath appointed to work this grace in man. (Ibid.)

These words hardly represent a theology which optimistically attributes a great deal of ability to man in his natural state.
One may wonder, despite implications that may be drawn concerning man's inability, if preparationist theology must still remain one which, in the end, must attribute more ability to man than did the more pristine Calvinism of the century before. Hooker, after painting a mental picture of the building of Zerubbabels' temple, comments:

> And as it was thus in the material temple, so it is here in the building of the soule, a Temple for the Lord. The beginning of grace, the receiving of grace, the continuing of grace, all is grace, grace; from beginning of election to the end of glorification; from the beginning of conversion, to the end of salvation, all is grace and mercy; nothing but grace that doth all, workes all, prepares all for the good of God's people. (Ibid., I, 8)

Here is Hooker's theology of grace seen everywhere in this volume, which has somehow been viewed by some as the work in which Hooker most attributes to man an ability to contribute towards his own conversion!
Hooker shows himself to be the pastor-theologian as he takes this theology of grace, and emphasizing the freeness thereof, puts it forth to the wicked as,

> a ground of incouragement unto them to seeke after this mercy: they may thinke with themselves thus, why the offer of grace is free, and therefore why may not I come to have some of this mercy as well as another. (Ibid., I, 19)

Here the psychologist of the soul wants the wicked one to think of the possible reception of mercy and to "wait upon God in the ordinances" (Ibid., I, 21).
Though grace and mercy are free, Hooker also affirms that God is completely sovereign in the

distribution of grace. God may deny mercy as well as grant it. Yet since the granting thereof is possible, Hooker's exhortation is to "try all means possible to obtain it" (Ibid., I,22). Here is clear voluntarism even at this "pre-initial" stage of the morphology. Having affirmed that preparation itself is a work of grace, Hooker nevertheless calls for introspection.

Shut downe those proud hearts and lofty spirits of yours which think themselves too good to waite the Lord's leisure, and reason with your soules and say, why is my heart not humbled? (Ibid., I, 25-26)

Emphasizing the normal means by which preparation is wrought, Hooker notes that the preacher-messengers of God have offered mercy, so therefore "worke yet more upon your soules, and turn unto us a cheerful answer in this case" (Ibid., I, 79).

Though "Christ will not be a guest with us, unlesse he bee entertained by us" (Ibid., I, 41), real heart religion and contrition are no easy things.

What a wretch am I, doe I think that God will have mercy on mee, because I say and profess that I am a sinner, and because I say that I pray unto God for the forgiveness of my sinnes; no, no, those very words will condemne me, because my heart goes not with the words. (Ibid., I, 45)

Here is the typical Hookerian inspection of the windings of the soul which is ever in danger of being "hoodwinked" by itself.

As Kendall rightly notes, Hooker stresses human responsibility in this early work. But one must be careful not to confuse the concepts of responsibility and ability as Hooker understands them. The second sermon in the volume is one that treats the anthropological considerations directly. But in the first sermon, Hooker wants especially to proclaim to his listeners that grace is free and available to the soul who wills to receive. This freeness shows,

> the just and heavie condemnation of all such as perish, they are damned and go to hell and everlasting destruction, because they will be damned. (Ibid., I, 65)

But on the other hand,

> if any poore soule will take mercy offered and receive grace tendered unto him, hee shall have mercy, hee shall receive grace. (Ibid., I, 63)

Having affirmed that the offer of grace is free, the necessity of willing for Christ and grace, and that if any wills he will indeed receive grace and Christ, Hooker then maintains that no man by nature is able to will Christ and grace. Here is the safeguard for Hooker's Calvinism. Despite his exhortations to "be humbled," to "be prepared," to "go out and fetch Christ," Hooker's preparationist theology is one which includes an orthodox Calvinistic anthropology. For Hooker human inability is a recognized factor in the preparation process. The "natural man" is defined in accordance with Jude 19 as one who is devoid of the Spirit and Hooker goes on to express his conviction that there is "no way to be made partakers of these (graces) without the Spirit" (Ibid., I, 85-89).

The natural man actually opposes the work of salvation and must be overcome.

> As long as he continueth in that estate he is not capable of grace, but yet God can make him fit, and disposed thereunto, he may be wrought thereunto and God by his Spirit can make him able to entertaine grace, but he must first be disposed thereunto. Looke as it is with a vessel that is full of puddle, there is an unpossibility now in this vessel, as long as it is full of that pudly and filthy water, that it should receive cleane and pure water, but when it is emptied of that filthy water, then it is capable to receive pure water, but first the durty water must be put out, before it can receive the pure . . . so that God must

empty the soule of these lusts, and abominations, and prepare him for grace, before grace can be put into him. (Ibid., I, 94-95)

This statement is something of a classic statement of Hooker's preparationist theology. In it God Himself is portrayed as the author of preparation. Yet this is not to say that tension does not exist between Hooker's anthropology and his urgent and impassioned volunteristic pleadings. Natural man is "stripped of all holiness and righteousness . . . deprived of the image of God, and altogether overspread with wickedness and unrighteousness" (Ibid., I, 105). Natural man is in such a plight that he cannot turn to God yet Hooker's frequent exhortation is to "labour to get out of this natural condition." No sleep is to be given to the eyes until,

> you have studied all the means possible to recover yourselves out of your naturall condition, beginne speedily and persevere constantly in the means that God has appointed, that the Lord may bestow the power upon you whereby you may be enabled to receive grace and salvation offered you so that it will go well with you forever. . . . Away therefore from yourselves and look higher, flie unto God for strength and sufficiencie. (Ibid., I, 119)

For Hooker, man is incapable, by reason of sin, of coming to God. Yet he must do so. He therefore must be brought. Tension is obvious in Hooker's teachings that man is unable to amend his own life yet he must labor nevertheless to be enabled. Ames' textbook of theology was presented in two "books," putting forth faith in God and then observance toward God. Hooker seeks to bring this Ramistic and Amesian emphasis on practicality even to his anthropological considerations.

Man's inability to obey in no way lessens his own responsibility or God's right to command. But the student of Hooker will eventually ask, "What can man do?" An answer comes, though it is not one which allows room for any celebration of man's goodness or ability.

Man can become "thoroughly convinced of the misery he is in and informed of his own insufficiencie," he can recognize that his heart is "stout," he can acknowledge his lack of response to gracious promises, and he can convince his own heart "that there is an All-sufficiencie in the promise that the Spirit is able to doe good unto your souls" (Ibid., I, 121). But the same sermon, almost as if Hooker cannot stand to dwell too long on what man can do, ends in a doxology-like attribution of all power to God.

> Though I be a dead man thou canst put life in me, though I can doe nothing, yet thou canst doe all things, I am a blackamore, but thou canst make me a white hew, I am a leaper. but thou canst take away my spots; I am naturall and carnal, in me there is no good thing, but Lord thou canst make me entertaine spiritual things. (Ibid., I, 123)

Similarly, the final words of the sermon leave no room for boasting.

> It is not in your power to doe good unto your soules, or receive good, and therefore beginne betimes and wait upon God in the meanes, that you may have grace and salvation thereby. (Ibid., I, 125)

A third sermon continues these basic anthropological themes. The sermon is based on Ezekiel 11:19.

> And I wil give them one heart, and I wil put a new spirit within you: and I will take the stonie heart out of their flesh, and will give them a heart of flesh.

The sermon is important not only for its reinforcement of the themes of grace sounded in the previous sermons, but also for its positing of formal definitions of terms as used by Hooker. The "heart" is defined as the "will of man, or that ability which is a reasonable soul, whereby he willeth or rejecteth a thing" (Ibid., I, 127). Repeatedly in his sermons, Hooker, the sane churchman, urges his hearers "to use the meanes." This reflects his high view of the sermon as a means of grace. Yet, so that use of the means might not provide a false sense of security he notes:

> Now all the meanes as the Word and the like is outward, and can doe no good in this kind, they cannot break the union betweene a man's heart and his corruptions, unless God give a blessing to these meanes, unlesse the Lord by his Almighty power and infinite wisdome make a separation between sinne and the soule, and dissolve the union. (Hooker 1638g, I, 153)

But this is no cause for complacency. Having put forth the sovereignty of God's grace, Hooker is unbothered by the paradoxical command, which he issues anew, to practice evangelism, taking the message of Ezekiel 11:19.111

This preliminary volume also provides a summary of the entire conversion process. The quotation below gives a feel not only for Hooker's monergism, his view of the difficulty of the conversion process, but also reveals a bit of the warm piety of a typical Hooker sermon.

> This great worke of conversion, the fitting and preparing of a poore sinner to entertaine the Lord Jesus, it is a worke of great weight, it is a worke not of ordinary, but of marvellous and admirable difficulty; if it be the worke of the Lord only, if nothing else can doe this worke but it lieth upon God's alone Almightie power, if all meanes faile, nay if the wisedome of men and Angels stand aghast and amazed at this work, then I must conclude it is the Lords worke, and it ought to be marvellous in our eyes. (Ibid., I, 149)

The final sermons in Part I of The Unbeleevers

<u>Preparing</u> <u>For</u> <u>Christ</u> are joined together in a fifty page section on Luke 19:42 and Matthew 20:3-6. These sermons are significant because of their different nature. In them Hooker seeks to describe the timing and circumstances of conversion, always being careful to note the necessity of a continued attendance to the appointed means if "God will, if ever, fit us and prepare us for mercy" (Ibid., I, 149). Again the formal ministry is stressed as Hooker says that in God's own time he sends his faithful ministers to discover to the people life and salvation (Ibid., I, 162). This happens for the elect either sooner or later in their lives, but very "few are called when they are old" (Ibid., I, 155). Yet that this is the normal way of God's providence, can be used as a prod to exhort the younger but it ought not to be the basis for a rash judgment.

> For we know that God can call at the eleventh houre, and therefore be not too rash in censuring this way, but receive the exhortation of the Apostle, 1Cor. 4:5, there saith the text: Judge nothing before the time, untill the Lord come, who doth bring to light the hidden things of darkenesse, and will make manifest the counsels of the hearts. (Ibid., I, 188)

We see here a hint of the type of sentiment from Hooker which would lead him in New England to be a proponent of a charitable judgment of others whenever he could find good grounds, especially as it related to the question of conversion narratives for church membership.

The second part of <u>The</u> <u>Unbeleevers</u> <u>Preparing</u> is an extended 119 page sermon on John 6:44. Clearly the theme throughout is the necessity of preparation set against the backdrop of the text which provides the emphasis upon human inability. Only after the soul is prepared will the Lord "come suddenly into his temple" (Ibid., II, 2). Hooker notes that "preparation," as he uses the word, involves two things.

> First the dispensation of God's gracious work upon the soule of a poore sinner. Secondly, the frame

and disposition that God works upon the soule, in converting it to himselfe. (Ibid.)

The sermon on the whole does not dwell on any particular aspects of preparation. These were taken up by Hooker in the subsequent sermons which are preserved in the major morphological volumes. Here, his interest continues to be anthropological.

> Every man in his natural condition is fastened and settled in the state of sinne and corruption. Secondly, that the Lord by a holy kind of violence plucks off the soule from sin, and draweth it to himself. (Ibid., II,3)

But before he describes the drawing process Hooker lingers still over the plight of man who is "stuck fast and glued to our corruptions." Reflecting Augustinian sentiments Hooker bemoans the fact that mankind is "rooted in the rebellions of Adam . . . riveted unto corruptions, which have been convaied thereunto and drived from our first parents" (Ibid., II, 3-4). So complete and rigorous is this plight that Hooker, in vivid style portrayed it as follows.

> If a theefe, or a Traytor, were apprehended and convicted, and imprisoned, and had bolts and fetters upon him; and further, if he were condemned, and hang'd drawne, and quarter'd. . . . Men might say, now he is sure enough, now he will steale no more, nor plot treason any more; just so it is with the soule of a poore sinner, every man naturally is so farre forth under the power of sinne and Satan, that he is not only surprised and taken by Satan, but his sinnes are as many bolts and fetters about him, nay he is shut up in prison, nay further sinne has slain him out right. (Ibid., II, 5)

But God graciously uses "cords of mercy" to draw and unfetter such as he desires to do so. The Lord gives light showing to man his lost condition and that he, the

Lord, is ready to give pardon for sins. The Lord is not only willing but calls and commands poor sinners to come. The Lord actually pursues his elect, following him and "sendeth another cord after him, and pursueth him with mercy and kindness" (Ibid., II,34). These cords, which work on men's consciences, have "hookes" which draw one away from sin. These "hookes" are the voice of an informed conscience which "comes to be an accuser of him and a witness against him before God" (Ibid., II,47).

The reasons that the Lord must use this "holy sort of violence" include the fact that there is a natural union between the soul and corruption and the "strong man" must first be cast out. Such language provides a foretaste to Hooker's subsequent callings for the necessity of contrition and humiliation in the conversion process. In view of the voices today that are being sounded suggesting that the Puritans greatly departed from more pristine Calvinism, Hooker's own claim ought to be heard. While discussing these "cords" of mercy by which one is prepared, Hooker claims to stand squarely in the Reformed tradition saying,

> This is the interpretation of Divines in this case: they say, that the Lord doth take away that deadness, and stupity of heart, whereby it may lay hold on grace, if it resist not the good motions of the Spirit. (Ibid., II, 64)

And again,

> There is an old phrase, which Saint Austin propounded in his time and Divines take it up with one consent in this case, and that is this, that God of an unwilling will, doth make a willing will. (Ibid., II, 68)

Everywhere in the volume the prerogatives of God are safeguarded. One wonders how it can be, that by any reading of Hooker's sermons, he can be charged with betraying his Calvinism by attributing greater power to man than does the Bible. In this introductory work,

concerned as it is with anthropological issues, Hooker's vigorously seeks to show that man can do nothing by himself to contribute to his salvation. While developing a profound analysis of conversion with a decided zeal for the practice of the same, Hooker proves himself a high Calvinist who is quite aware of the dangers of Arminianism (Emerson 1956c, xiv).
In The Unbeleevers Preparing For Christ, the pre-initial stage of Hooker's morphology is unveiled as anthropological factors such as inherent depravity and inability are considered in a rather straightforward fashion. Hooker, holding to the absolute necessity of preparatory activity, places the disposition of the heart at the center of this necessity stage of the conversion process.

THE MAJOR MORPHOLOGICAL WORKS:
THE SOULES PREPARATION

Seeking to establish Hooker's morphology in its logical sequence, the next volume to come under consideration is The Soules Preparation For Christ: A Treatise of Contrition (1632). As with the volume just discussed, the sermonic material herein contained dates from its earliest formulation at Cambridge as refined during the Chelmsford years. Formally speaking, the volume concerns itself with the first or earliest stage in Hooker's morphology, contrition.
The book first appeared during the difficult days while Hooker was in the Netherlands. Indeed something of a disclaimer is found preceding the first page of this work.

Christian Reader, thou hast here some sermons brought to light, which by reason of the Authors absence, are presented to thy view, both with some letter escapes, and in more homely termes, than his judicious eye would have suffered. (Hooker 1632, verso opposite Table)

This immensely popular work has received, as

relative to the previously discussed one, much more scholarly attention. Misunderstandings of Hooker, particularly those that view him as moving in an Arminian direction, can be partially attributed to a neglect of the anthropological considerations while great attention is focused upon his calls for preparation. In consequence of this, stereotypical views and superficial readings refuse to be reconciled to Hooker's actual statements.

In his customary fashion Hooker early in the work is careful to define his terms.

> This contrition (as I conceive) is nothing else but namely, when a sinner by the sight of sinne, and vilenesse of it, and the punishment due to the same, is made sensible of sinne, and is made to hate it, and hath his heart separated from the same and the sight of sinne makes itselfe knowne in three particulars: First, when the soule is sensible of sinne. Secondly, when it hath a hearty and sound sorrow for the same, and an earnest detestation of it. Thirdly, when he hath his heart separated from his corruptions. All this is not wrought, so much by any power that is in us, as by the Almighty power of God working in us; for the sinner would not see his sinne, but the Lord forceth him. (Hooker 1632, 2)

For Hooker, contrition is the essence of preparation. The constituent parts are a realization of the vileness of sin, a hated and sorrow for the same, and a heart separated from these corruptions. It is this third ingredient of contrition that Hooker will expand upon in the closely related work, The Soules Humilition (1637). In the quotation above, the passive voice of the verbs ought to be noted as should the monergistic tones of the final words of the definition Hooker gives for "contrition." Paradoxically, Hooker notes in a related work, The Soules Ingrafting Into Christ (1637), that contrition and humiliation as to the disposition of the heart, involve "something on our part" (Hooker 1637d, 2). Nevertheless, such statements are not indicative of

a supposed meritorious or self-engendered cooperation in salvation, but rather betoken God's activity in making of an unwilling heart a willing one.
R.T. Kendall, while emphasizing Hooker's voluntarism, nevertheless attributes to Hooker a view which maintains "passivity" in the preparation process (Kendall 1979, 138). Though Hooker often employs the passive voice as shown above, this does not indicate man's passivity in the process, but rather that God is the "prime mover," the initiator and conductor of preparation. Kendall seems to be wrong in his suppositions of how Calvinistic sympathizers with Hooker might define his preparationist theology. No one, upon a fair reading of Hooker, could suppose that Hooker puts forth passivity as a central ingredient in his morphology. His is a "do something" theology, voluntaristic, while maintaining the doctrine of sovereign grace.

According to Kendall, Hooker imputes a significant "power and freedom to natural man" (Ibid., 131). Yet upon a reading of The Unbeleevers Preparing and The Soules Preparation, the works dealing most directly with man in his natural state, one is struck by the vigorous protection rendered to orthodox Calvinistic soteriology. Though A. T. Denholm might have glossed too quickly over Hooker's voluntarism, he is quite right about Hooker's view of natural man.

> It is an open question as to whose natural man makes the greater smell, Hooker's or Calvin's. There is no difference in their basic views. If there is a difference of emphasis, it is too nebulous to be measured or evaluated. (Denholm 1961, 238)

For Hooker, the fallen will could be renewed only by grace.

> It is possible, nay God doth it also, hee makes the soule of man feele the burthen of sinne because of the vileness of it, as well as of the plague and punishment of it. Whensoever the Lord will fasten

a man's sinne to his conscience, he is able to force the soule to apprehend the evill of sinne, as well as the torment and plague of sinne. (Hooker 1632, 148)

In their works cited throughout this study, Shuffelton, Emerson and Denholm, view Hooker as a "high Calvinist." Norman Pettit seems not so sure, and R.T. Kendall is unintelligible. Thus far much has been brought forth to defend Hooker's soteriological orthodoxy. Leaving that controversy aside once again, several other significant factors, component parts of Hooker's morphology, can now be noted from The Soules Preparation.

One mark of The Soules Preparation, when viewed in relation to The Unbeleevers Preparing, is the increased use of the Law of God as a tool to bring the sinner low. The sinner is admonished to "labour to acquaint your selves thoroughly with God and with his law, and to see the compass and the breath of it." Hooker notes how content the apostle Paul had been in his self-righteousness. Paul, says Hooker, was deceived as are many other otherwise "well learned who are ignorant of God's law" (Ibid., 36,37).

> Therefore looke your selves in this glasse of the Word, all you who say, how ever you are not able to talke so freely as others, yet you have as good a heart to God as the best, I tell you if you could but see the filthinesse of your hearts you would be out of love with yourselves forever. (Ibid.)

Hooker here addresses those who "are not able to talke so freely as others," that is, those who are not able to "narrate" their conversion. These cannot articulate how they were brought through the sorrow of sin and made to "fly" unto Christ for refuge. They have not been brought low, yet they claim to "be seated in the heavenlies" (Ephesians 2:6). The physician to the soul here seeks to prod the complacent. Hooker, in typically Reformed fashion, would have them bring the law to bear upon their own cases, whereupon a guilty verdict would be rendered.

> To whom shall I looke (saith God) even to a man that hath a contrite heart, and trembles at my Word: this is the roote, and this is the fruit; the heart must bee contrite and broken by the hammer of God's Law, before it can shake at the hearing of the Word. (Ibid., 223)

This increased use of the Law of God, as a tool to bring the soul to contrition, may have been a factor in the subsequent labelling of Hooker as a "legal preacher" during the Antinomian controversy.

Echoing 1 John 3:4 "sin is the transgression of the law," and anticipating the answer of the Westminster Shorter Catechism (Q.14), "Sin is any want of conformity unto or transgression of the law of God," Hooker defined sin as "a breach of the Law of God" (Hooker 1632, 100). He then made this pastoral application as he sought to show the place of the law in the "laboring after contrition."

> Therefore it is good for a man is this case to examine every Commandement of God, and breach thereof: You know not your sinnes, therefore get you home to the Law, and looke into the glasse thereof, and then bundle up all your sinnes thus. (Ibid.)

Thus the Law becomes for Hooker, not only the means by which the knowledge of sin is "brought home," but also a crucial starting point for the difficult and even agonizing work of contrition. To the place of meditation and introspection in this "difficult work," attention is now to be drawn.

Hooker's calls for contrition were given a sense of urgency by the utter necessity of preparation.

> If there bee no preparation for Christ, there can be no true evidence of grace, nor of God's love in Christ; if there bee no preparation for a building, there can bee no building set up. (Ibid., 177-178)

The place of contrition in this preparatory process was regarded as essential.

> It is the onely old way to heaven, for God never revealed any other but this way in the old Law: the onely way for the leaper to be cleansed, was to come out into the congregation, and to cry, I am uncleane, I am uncleane. (Ibid., 55)

Yet more than just a general awareness of one's plight is necessary. The minister, by his ministry of the Word, has a duty to bring into light particular sins.

> A speciall application of particular sinnes, is a chiefe meanes to bring people to a sight of their sinnes and a true sorrow for them. (Ibid., 166)

Such statements as this are about as near to casuistical teaching as Hooker ever comes (Bush 1980, 276-280). Curiously he does so, not in the late stages of his morphology, but here at the initial stage.

The *Soules Preparation* is characterized by an emphasis on meditation and introspection. To lay the foundation for his calls for contrition, Hooker, the student of human psychology, explains why the awfulness of sin is not easily perceived.

> First, because wee judge not of sinne according to the Word and verdict of it, but either in regard of the profit that is there in, or the pleasure that wee expect there from. . . . Secondly, another reason why wee see not the vileness of sinne, is, because wee judge the nature of sin according to God's patience towards us, as thus, a man commits a sinne and is not plagued for it and therefore he thinks God will not execute judgements upon him at all. (Hooker 1632, 19-20)

Hooker is ever the systematizer of his morphology. Not only is the conversion process carefully chronicled in the major stages of the morphology, but each step is also "opened up" to reveal its constituent parts. Contrition, as the essential work of preparation is so unfolded.

> First, he stops the soule from going on any longer in sin. Secondly, he wearieth the soule with the burthen of sinnes. Thirdly, by hatred the soule is brought to goe away from those carnall lusts and corruptions, with a secret dislike of those sins which he hath been wearied withall. In all this the soule is a patient (and undergoes the work of humbling and breaking) rather than any way active and operative. (Ibid., 232)

In the last sentence of this quotation, Hooker is careful to remind the listener of the source of the operative power in the work of preparation.

Richard Sibbes' "The Soul's Conflict" had not yet gone to press when Hooker's work on contrition appeared. Yet the sentiments of the "heavenly doctor" Sibbes (d. 1635) were well known. As to introspection, Sibbes maintained:

> A sincere heart will offer itself to trial. And therefore let us sift our actions, and our passions, and see what is flesh in them, and what is spirit, and so separate the precious from the vile. . . . This course will either make us weary of passion, or else passion will make us weary of this strict course. We shall find it the safest way to give our hearts no rest till we have wrought on them to purpose and gotten mastery over them. (Sibbes 1864, I, 165)

Hooker stressed this sort of "sifting" of the soul, and particularly employed it in the preparatory process. As a part of the larger agonizing striving, meditation is to be thorough, not cursory.

> As it is with a man which goeth into the house and puls the latch, when he was without, he might see the outside of the house, but hee could not see the

roomes within, unlesse hee draws the latch, and
comes in, and goe about the house: meditation puls
the latch of the truth, and sees this is my sinne,
this is the cause, here is the misery, this is the
plague: and thus meditation searcheth into every
corner of the truth. (Hooker 1632, 80)

The importance of this meditation to contrition is pressed.

Meditation is like fire, the heart is like a
vessel, the heart is made for God, and it may be
made a vessel of grace here, and of glory
hereafter: Meditation is that which melts the
soule, and drosse must be taken away from the
soule, and sinne must be loosened from the heart.
Now when you have your heart in
some measure melted, keep it there, doe not
let it grow loose again and carelesse again.
(Ibid., 107)

Using the language of faculty psychology, Hooker was careful to trace the "windings" of the soul.

Never leave meditation till you finde your heart so
affected with the evill, as your mind and judgement
conceived of the evill before; namely, let the
heart feele that evill it conceived, let the soule
feele that gall to be in sinne, which the minde
apprended to be in. (Ibid., 151)

Hooker here appears to align himself with the received psychological system of the day which was repeated by Puritan preachers throughout the century (Miller 1939, 246-256). The systematization inherent therein was well suited to the Hooker's emphasis on meditation and introspection as means to chronicle the windings of the soul.

So the understanding is like the dore or entrance
into the house, and sinne is of a fiery and
scorching nature, if there be no passage, if the

mind know not, the will will not be affected with sin, it will never schorch his conscience; though a man carry enough sinne in his bosom, to sinke his soule forever, yet we suffer it not to worke upon us, and we attend not to it, because the brazen wall keepes it off. (Hooker 1632, 31)

The different faculties are clearly noted by Hooker.

As the understanding is setled in the head, and keepes his sentinell there, so the will is seated in the heart, and when it comes to taking or refusing, this is the office of the will. (Ibid., 122)

Perry Miller presented Thomas Hooker as the most dramatic of the faculty psychologists among the New England preachers (Miller 1939, 248,253). According to Miller, Hooker was in the mainstream of that system of thought which would not be challenged until after Hooker's death. In 1658 Gershom Bulkeley authored a thesis in which it was maintained that the will may propel actions against the reason (Miller 1939, 249). Yet Hooker himself, moved by his voluntarism, had before 1632 already begun to modify his own understanding of the role of the faculties.

Understanding and reason are but the underlings of the will, they are but servants and subjects to it, they onely advise the will what is good, as a servant may suggest to his Master what is good, and yet his Master may take what hee list, and refuse what hee please in this kinde. (Hooker 1632, 116; cf. Hooker 1637a, 296)

Thus it appears that Hooker did depart, at least partially albeit not too consistently, from the given constructs of faculty psychology. Hooker thereby provided a foretaste of the views of Jonathan Edwards a century later, though Hooker's departure went in a different direction than did that of Edwards.

For Hooker, the examination of the interior

life, leading to contrition, involved a laborious striving. As the soul strives for contrition, itself a gift of God, there is relentless pain.

> As it is with a man that hath the stone in the reines, or some stitch in his side, or where ever his paine or trouble is, there he complaines most; and when the Physician comes to feele on his body, hee saith, Is it here? No saith he: Is it here? and when he cometh to the right place, he saith, There it is, cut there, and launce there; so it is with the man stung with the vile nature of sinne, when he comes to complaine of sinne, hee doth not altogether complaine of his horrour, nor of death, but he saith, Oh! that chambering and wantonness, that pride and stubbornenesse. (Hooker 1632, 140).

The "physician of the soul" is fond of medical metaphors.

> A man that hath a bone long out of joynt, and it now festered, it wil make him cry man and oh, before it be brought into his right place againe; so it is with a man whose heart is full of filthinesses, it will cost him much paines and difficulty, and heart smart, before the Lord will bring the soule to a right set againe. (Ibid., 10)

Hooker was careful to maintain that sin must be properly viewed before the soule can truly be broken. His voluntarism moved him to call for an earnest "endeavor to get mercy at the hands of the Lord." Though the soul agonizes all its days, the Lord remains sovereign in his distribution of grace.

> You must not thinke to have the foule stains of sinne washed away with a few teares; no, no, you must rub your hearts over and over again; it is not a little examination, not a little sorrow will serve the turne; the Lord will pull downe those proud hearts of yours, and (it may be) let you goe

a begging for mercy all your dayes, and well if you
may have it at your last gaspe when all is done.
(Ibid.)

The sinner must pass a "death sentence" upon
himself (Ibid., 33), though he must be aware of the
dangers of self delusion. "It is possible for the most
stubborn sinners upon earth to get a broken heart"
(Ibid., 4), yet the specter of being "hoodwinked" ever
casts its gloomy shadow.

Thou that thinkest it such an easie matter, aske
thy owne heart this question. Canst thou be
content to lay open all thy cursed sinful courses,
and all the wrong that thou hast done? Consider
what a hard matter it is to bring thy heart to it;
to confess all thy close adulteries; and when thou
hast done all this, thou mayest be as farre from
salvation as Judas was, who went and hanged
himself. (Ibid., 49)

With this stark statement Hooker seeks to awaken
or prod the complacent. This, though, might naturally
cause utter despair in the soul, subject as it is to
"many shakings." But the Lord provides a "secret hope"
in the soul which drives away despair, as the Lord
"meltes the heart of a poor sinner but consumes him
not." Therefore the psychologist is careful to not only
prod the complacent but also to comfort the doubter.

If the Lord did not leave his hope in the heart,
a man's endeavors in the use of the meanes, would
bee altogether killed; if there bee no hope of
good, then there is no care of using the meanes.
(Ibid., 196)

The Soules Preparation is marked by explicit
voluntarism. The sinner is exhorted, "bring your heart
under the power of the Lord Jesus" (Ibid., 73), and to
be careful to look to Christ and his merit alone.

For it is not sorrow for sin, nor humiliation, nor

> faith itself, that can justifie us in itselfe, but
> onely as they make way for us to a Christ, and
> through him we must receive comfort. (Ibid., 110)

Echoing Calvin in his emphasis upon "looking to Christ," Hooker is careful to make the motions of preparation only the instrumental causes of justification and not the formal grounds thereof. To look to Christ is for Hooker the goal of contrition and humiliation.

Before leaving this examination of this extremely important work in the Hooker corpus, it must here be asked whether or not these preparatory motions represent saving graces. Hooker ponders these questions himself and gives explicit answers. If true contrition is being worked, then undoubtedly the soul "will have faith powered into it." But the heart is "not yet conceived to be in Christ, but onely to be fitted and prepared for Christ." Yet the ground for comfort is prepared for though such a one is truly lost, being "not yet settled on Christ," he is aware of that lost estate and "shall have faith and Christ . . .and be saved everlastingly" (Ibid., 154). While one is in the midst of the preparatory work, he is not reckoned to have any grace by which to be "able to do anything for himself" (Ibid., 155).

This raises the old question of the difference between contrition and sanctifying sorrow. This was first put forth by Hooker in his preface to Rogers' Doctrine of Faith and later in his answers to Paget's Twenty Questions. Echoing the convictions expressed in those works, Hooker notes:

> You must know that there is a double sorrow, First
> there is a sorrow in preparation; Secondly, there
> is a sorrow in sanctification. . . . Because the
> soule is a patient, and the Lord by the Almighty
> hand of his Spirit, breakes in upon the soule, so
> that this sorrow in preparation is rather a sorrow
> wrought upon me, then any worke coming from any
> spiritual ability in my selfe. (Hooker 1632, 155-
> 156)

Given that the sorrow of preparation is "wrought from above," Hooker as an orthodox Calvinist can go on to affirm that both levels of "sorrow" are saving graces though "they differ marvailously." Using the Pauline ordo salutis of Romans 8:30, Hooker insists that because glorification implies prior sanctification, in the same manner justification implies a prior work of preparation. Thus, every saving work, contrary to the opinion of many, is not a sanctifying work (Ibid., 156). It is an idle question to inquire of the eternal state of one who dies while in the midst of this preparatory process. This follows since contrition is the work of God's Spirit wrought upon the elect all of whom God "shall have them" before they die (Ibid., 155). Preparation viewed through such Calvinistic eyes, though it be agonizing, is also a great ground of comfort viewed as it is as God's drawing of his elect. Hooker the pastoral theologian was careful to so use this initial stage of his developing morphology.

Though Hooker could speak of a "holy sort of violence" by which God draws a sinner from his sin, unlike some of his Puritan colleagues, he did not demand that conversion always come in a violent seizure. His own conversion was evidently a prolonged experience and he acknowledged diversity in the Lord's dealings. Some are "pricked with a pinne," others "with a speare" (Ibid., 166). Especially among "covenant children" God works gently and they hardly perceive the work, "though wise Christians may approve that which is done" (Ibid., 170). Just as Hooker's convictions regarding the salvific nature of preparation provided him with good grounds to comfort the "poor doubters," so did his view of the diversity of God's gracious dealings allow him to exercise his charitable judgment and eventually to promote a less stringent narrative requirement for church membership in New England (Bush 1980, 77, 331n).

For Hooker, contrition was at the center of his preparationist theology. In this early formulation of his doctrine of preparationism, he showed himself a skillful psychologist of the soul. From The Soules Preparation, attention must now be focused upon the second stage of Hooker's morphology as found in The

Soules Humiliation (1637).

THE MAJOR MORPHOLOGICAL WORKS: THE SOULES HUMILIATION

Like the works examined above, The Soules Humiliation, though not published until after Hooker had left England, contains sermonic material that antedates his silencing and departure in 1630. Along with The Soules Preparation For Christ, to which this work is a sequel, the pair constitute the two most important early formulations of Hooker's preparationism. Indeed, because Hooker viewed contrition as the essence of preparationism, the work of humiliation is merely something of the final stage, the natural outgrowth of contrition. While contrition involves a self-knowledge, humiliation proceeds to a self-rejection.

As always, Hooker is careful to define his terms early in this extended sermon.

> But what is this Humiliation of heart? It is thus much. When the Soule upon search made, despaires of all helpe from it selfe: hee doth not despaire of Gods mercy, but of all help from himselfe and submits himselfe wholy to God, the soule strikes sale and falls under the power of Jesus Christ, and is content to be at his disposing. (Hooker 1637b,8)

This understanding of humiliation is further unfolded in three stages. First, the wounded sinner seeks comfort inwardly and from others, but fails to go to Christ for help. Then follows a recognition of the total inability of such means to bring comfort to the soul. This finally leads to a falling at the throne of grace in submission to Christ. Self sufficiency is totally abandoned and a contentedness with the sovereignty of God marks the soul (Ibid.).

The parable of the "prodigal son" from Luke 15:14ff provides the Biblical text, something of a ready made plot line to Hooker's sermonic purposes (Bush 1980, 165). The labors of the soul to find comfort,

looking in every direction and trying every means, is traced in this chronicle of a spiritual sojourn leading to the completion of the preparatory process. Throughout the work, Hooker's words express an intense anxiety and dissonance, until the pilgrim finally comes to the point of relief on this arduous trek.
 Like the previous work in the morphology which found revision in The Application of Redemption IX-X, this work would no doubt had been revised in an enlarged form had not Hooker's death prevented so much. As it stands, being a sequel to The Soules Preparation, the Soules Humiliation is a work of 224 pages in which Hooker describes the means by which contrition is completed and comes to fruition in humiliation, thus completing the preparatory process.
 Hooker uses approximately the first quarter of the work to exhort his listeners to use the means, but to look to Christ in them. The means lead to Christ, yet sadly for many, the means themselves become a source of false security. In essence, instead of finding comfort in Christ, the deluded sinner uses the means themselves as one of the many other things in which comfort is sought. The various turnings of the prodigal provide a picturesque description of this sort of groping after false sources of comfort. The means themselves can become idols, preventing access to the only source of comfort found in Christ.

> Thus Humiliation pares away all a mans privileges and all his hearing and praying, &c. not that a man must use these no more, but hee must not rest upon them
> for strength to help and succor himselfe withall.
> . . . . I confess the best of Gods Saints must use these meanes, they must heare and pray, and fast, but they must not rest upon these. (Hooker 1637b, 7,9)

 Hooker the psychologist notes that many a sinner, having been brought low in contrition, and seeing the gravity of his own sin, "dares not be so proud as to thinke that he shall have any favor at Gods hands" (Ibid., 11). Thus the sinner shrinks away from the only source of help and goes to all other means he views as possible sources of comfort.

    Again in *The Soules Humiliation*, Hooker places great importance on the need to be "pierced" by the Law of God. But even then, with the sinner brought low in contrition, conscience continues to condemn and the way of relief is beclouded.

> As the guilt of sinne cannot be removed by all his duties, so his conscience cannot be quieted by all that he doth; if his heart be thoroughly pierced by the Sword of the Law, still conscience calls upon him, and quarrells with him, and takes exceptions against him in the best of his duties, so farre they are from yeelding any satisfaction to God, or from bringing any peace to his conscience; if hee rest upon the bare performance of them. I speake of a broken hearted sinner: for the conscience is now Eagle eyed, it was full of filme and scales before, but now it is open and Eagle eyed, and can spy all his weaknesses, and picke matter of disquiet, even in the best of all his duties that are done. (Ibid., 24)

Hooker goes on to maintain that it is only God's gracious work in humiliation that "will make thee see that thou and the world can doe nothing, that Christ may take away the guilt of sin, and quiet thy conscience" (Ibid., 27).

    Hooker thus returns to the anthropological themes that he covered so thoroughly in *The Unbeleevers Preparing For Christ*.

> However you pranke up yourselves, and thinke your selves somebody, yet there is no spirituall good in you; unlesse God worke upon your hearts; whatsoever you have thought, or done, is all in vaine. . . . There is no carrion in a ditch smels more loathsomely in the nostrils of the Almightie: There are some workes of a dead body; it rots, and stinkes, and consumes: so, all the works of a

naturall man are dead workes and all the prayers of the wicked are an abomination to the Lord. (Ibid., 33-34)

One can hardly imagine how by any careful reading of Hooker he can be charged with attributing to man a significant amount of ability and freedom. Yet this Kendall, and to a lesser degree Pettit, both do (Kendall 1979, 131; Pettit 1966, 22, passim). Pettit repeatedly portrays preparationism as including a part that man plays. He seems unclear as to whether man "plays a part" in an active and operative way, or if God's working upon the soul in contrition and humiliation constitutes a sine qua non in the process of conversion. Pettit also seems to have rearranged Hooker's "ordo" by remarking, "Lydia looked to the promise and therefore God opened her eyes and melted the heart" (Pettit 1966, 95). As it is being shown here, humiliation involves the looking to the promise. But this occurs only after the heart is "melted." Pettit has seemingly inverted the two stages of Hooker's preparationism.

Hooker's work takes something of a turn as he anticipates an objection. Here he seeks not to be overly harsh. Indeed, he seeks to encourage the struggling doubter.

> Some will say, you do nothing but reprove us for duties and labor to pluck us from them: then why should we pray and heare, and what good shall we have by all that we do, if we cannot be saved by these means; then, what use is of them? (Hooker 1637b, 58)

Hooker is quick to bring assurance that he does not depreciate the properly appointed means, the sacraments and other duties. On the contrary, "there is great use in them and much good to be had by them" (Ibid.).

> We must use the means that God gives us as guides, to leade us by the hand to the Lord Jesus Christ; and as lights to shew us where life is to be had. .

> . . They are means to convey grace, mercy and comfort from Christ to our soules. Though they are not meat, yet they are dishes that bring the meat. They are the meanes whereby salvation hath been revealed and conveyed to us. There is a fountaine of grace in Christ, but the Word, and Prayer, and Sacraments, and Fasting, they are the conduits to convey this water of life, and to communicate this grace to us. You doe not use to drinke the conduit, but the water that the conduit brings. (Ibid., 59-60)

So performance and use of the means is necessary, but in them Christ must be found. The necessary performance remains non-meritorious as none must think that "your duties can pardon one sinne, yet they must be used and bless God for them" Ibid., 61).

One "triall" to discover whether God is working humiliation is to ponder if the soule sees itself as helpless even while attending to the means. For Hooker it is a ground of confidence when one sees this helplessness and looks beyond the properly appointed means to Christ for refreshment of the heart. This he calls a "heavenly skill" (Ibid., 69). It is "heavenly" in that this work of preparation is from above, being nothing less than the work of God himself.

> The Soule is like the Ship; and the precious ordinances of God are faire Sailes and good Masts; and it is good hearing, and good reading, and good fasting; but except the Spirit blow with these; thou canst get no good by them. (Ibid., 75)

Here is a further evidence that for Hooker, preparatory contrition and humiliation is always wrought upon the soul and not by the soul.

When the prodigal was brought to his lowest depths, then the way of return could begin. All other means had failed, he must then look only to grace and mercy. This would serve to as "a boat to carry us and land us at Heaven" (Ibid.). There is no merit in returning, for the Lord drives even in this. The sinner comes, as true humiliation is wrought, to be content at his Father's disposing. Orthodox Calvinism shines as Hooker notes that the sinner now sees God as completely sovereign. He may do what He will and none can resist Him (Ibid., 83-84). The soul is now disposed to realize that it can only pray for mercy. Only when the prerogatives of the sovereignty of God are explicated does Hooker's voluntarism appear.

> If a drunkard, or an adulterer will submit to the Word, there is remedie for them; but there is no remedie for him, that will not yeeld to the Spirit of God. The Lord be merciful to the soules of them. (Ibid., 93-94)

In typical Hookerian fashion, the complacent church member is prodded.

> Thou that livest in the bosome of the Church, where Angels come downe from heaven, and rejoyce in this free grace of God in Christ, and hast thou the offer of mercy, and doest thou despise it , then thy drunkennesse is no bare drunkennesse, but there is a treasure of vengeance in it. (Ibid., 57)

Sargent Bush is an interpreter who has properly read Hooker as to his unwavering Calvinistic soteriology, even amid his "do something," voluntaristic exhortations.

> The tension between this assumption of the need for activity and Hooker's clear anti-Arminian position that one cannot earn grace or force God's hand created the intellectual and stylistic demands that made his sermons on the preparative stages some of the most dynamic in Hooker's entire canon. (Bush 1980, 162)

The latter portion of The Soules Humiliation stresses that only with true humiliation is preparation for grace completed. A chief sentiment that colors the work is that of "contentment." Humiliation has as an integral component the recognition of God's utter sovereignty.

> Now I come to this last passage in this worke of humiliation, and this is the dead lift of all. The Prodigall doth not stand it out with his Father and say, I am come now againe if I may have halfe the rule in the family, I am content to live with you. No, though hee would not stay there before, yet now he cannot be kept out, he is content to be anything. (Hooker 1637b, 98)

The soul that is truly humbled will likewise be content to be disposed of by the Almighty however it might please Him.
The extent of this contentment is such that the humbled but hell-bound soul also must be content.

> What if God will not heare my prayers? and what if God will not pacifie my conscience? nor shew any mercy to mee, I have my owne, and doth the Lord doe me any wrong, vile hell-bound that I am, I have my sinne and my shame, wrath is my portion, and hell is my place, I may goe thither when I will, it is mercy that God deales thus with me. (Ibid., 106)

The truly humbled will acknowledge his own "wound" and be content to bear it himself if God so wills. Yet one must question the sincerity of this "contentedness" as Hooker portrays it in such extreme terms. This follows since, by Hooker's own words, only the truly humbled are so disposed either to enjoy glory or to be assigned to everlasting destruction. But elsewhere, he insisted that because this work of true humiliation is God's work, where it is truly found faith will be inevitably and eventually "powered in" (Hooker 1632, 154-156). God shall have such a one who is truly brought low. Nevertheless, and curiously, Hooker maintains that the heart properly brought low "is content to beare the estate of damnation" (Hooker 1637b, 112).

Yet happily, this contentedness also involves a willingness that mercy should take one from one's sins.

Hooker specifically makes note of the common sins of drunkenness and profaning the Sabbath. His exhortation is one that if sounded later in New England, would raise the suspicions of the Hutchinsonian party: "Deceive not your selves: mercy will never save you except mercy may rule over you too" (Ibid., 200). Such calls for a moral amendment of life were later construed by some as efforts "to build justification upon one's sanctification" (Hall 1968, 43-59).

Hooker is ever ready to call upon his listeners to be active. Even in the context of contentment, where the heart is disposed to be content regardless of God's decree concerning it, Hooker has an exhortation.

> The soule that is thus contented to be at God's disposing, it is ever improving all meanes, and helps that may bring him nearer to God, but if mercy shall deny if, the soule is satisfied and rests well apaid, this every soule that is truly humbled may have, and hath in some measure. (Ibid., 114)

Because Hooker is so careful to stress that salvation is of the Lord alone, the sinner is exhorted to work for grace.

> The Lord hath taken the staffe out of his (man's) hands and salvation must bee no more put in his owne power.... So that faith is a gift, and a poore sinner is as able to create a world, as to receive mercy of himselfe. (Ibid., 108, 121)

This being the case, though one is to "labor to get a humbled heart," he must wait for God's mercy.

> You know the Dog must stay till his Master comes in, and when his is come hee must stay till he sit downe, and then till he cut his meate, and hee must not have the meate from his trencher neither, when he hath stayed all this while, he hath nothing but the crums. So it is with the poore sinner; you must not thinke that God will bee at your becke;

> No, you must be content with the crums of mercy, and pity, and lye under the table til the Lord let the crums fall. (Ibid., 127)

As as been shown in the biographical section above, Hooker was in New England accused of preaching a "covenant of works." In The Soules Humiliation he shows his sentiments to be far from any such thing. After noting the contrasting conditions between the two covenants, he says,

> Now what wee have done amisse, Christ has satisfied for it, and what wee cannot doe, Christ hath done it; he hath fulfilled all righteousness. And hence it is, that these two are so professedly opposite the one to the other; the Law, and Faith. The first Adam and the second Adam. . . . The Covenant of Works and the Covenant of Grace, cannot stand together in the point of Life and Grace. (Ibid., 128-129)

Warning is issued against the danger of an overly introspective and objectionable heart. Perhaps the Joan Drake incident is being remembered.

> They that have beene long over-whelmed with these cursed carnall cavellings, they will rather labour to oppose a direction, then to hold it, and to walke in the comfort of it, onely because of the weaknesse of their understandings, and their carnal reasonings are so violent against them. Upon this hinge it is, (as I take it) all the objections of a company of poore broken hearted sinners doe hange, and by this meanes they keep out that comfort which they might have; and in the strength whereof they might walke all their dayes. (Hooker 1637b, 174)

For these doubters, the remedy is to look to Christ. Nevertheless, the interior life must ever be probed because man is apt to be content at God's disposing "in an outward conformities," but not in order to honor God but rather for "some base ends" (Ibid.,

164). There is a real difficulty in examining the depths of humiliation.

> Take a mightie castle, though it be battered down, yet there remaines many heapes of rubbish, and happily some of the pillars stand many winters after; So it is with this frame of spirit, in an high abomination, in these Towers of loftiness. Though this Dagon of mans selfe be fallen downe, yet still the stumpes remaine and will doe many years. And it will cost much horror of heart, and much trouble before this haughtinesse of heart will be every wall pull'd down, and made agreeable to the good will of God. (Ibid., 170-171)

Hooker made it his practice to grant a charitable judgment in regard to others. In this sense Hooker provided a foreshadowing of another Connecticut River "giant," Solomon Stoddard. But Hooker was careful to call upon others not to become self-assured of their own safety too quickly. The need carefully to probe the interior life remained. Yet, in pastoral fashion, there was a difference to be seen between proper humiliation and discouragement. Unlike discouragement, humiliation leaves the soul content and yet active in its "attending upon God in any service, without hankering after his own ends, and without quarrelling, and this drawing backe from the Lord" (Ibid., 186-187). Again, contentment in humiliation is seen not be be equated with complacency. The complacent must ever be prodded to activity.

As *The Soules Humiliation* comes to an end, so does the crucial and agonizing preparatory process near its point of release from its arduous pilgrimage. The voluntaristic tones are heard once again as Hooker explicates his "last use." The sinner is to strive to receive a humble heart and to labor to get it above all.

> You must not thinke that God will bring you to heaven before you be aware of it, and that a humble heart will droppe into your mouthes. The saintes of God have alwayes had it before they received Christ, and thou must have it too, if ever thou

wilt have him, there-fore make it a chiefe part of thy daily taske to get it. (Ibid., 206)

The sinner is to be assured that he can not pull down his own heart (Ibid., 208). But Hooker's last words are encouraging ones as he employs his psychology to encourage the poor doubters. It is indeed possible to have this requisite heart because the Lord himself in his mercy may grant it. Here is the comfort and confidence that belongs to those of a contrite and humbled heart.

> Get but humble hearts and you have all. Men, brethren, and fathers, if there bee any soule here, that is content in truth and sinceritie to be humbled, and to be at God's disposing in all duties to be done, doe not you make too much hast to goe to heaven, the Lord Jesus Christ will come downe from heaven and dwell in your hearts, hee will sit, and lye, and walke with you; his grace shall refresh you, and his wisdome shall direct you, and his glory shall advance you. (Ibid., 220)

Here at the conclusion of the work, Hooker resorts to direct address and draws in his hearers as participants in the drama. "Mee thinkes your hearts begin to stirre" (Ibid., 219). This "gate" to life is the humiliation of the heart. Hooker earnestly desires it for those in attendance to his ministry. His exhortation "go and be humbled" (Ibid., 167) is no more a departure from orthodox Calvinism than is the call to "believe the Gospel." The analyzer of the interior life has good confidence that many indeed will get this humble heart. His concluding words are benediction-like. They express the central tenet of the latter half of the work.

> Therefore be wise, and be humbled under the mightie hand of the Lord. It is a mighty hand, and the Lord will be honored, either in your humiliation and conversion, or else in your damnation forever. Let all the evill that is threatened, and all the

good that is offered prevaile with your hearts, and though meanes cannot, yet the Lord prevaile with you: the Lord empty you, that Christ may fill you, the Lord humble you, that you may enjoy happinesse, and peace forever. (Ibid., 223)

Before moving on to the third formal stage of Hooker's morphology, this is an appropriate place to introduce his thoughts regarding these initial stages in the conversion process as gleaned from a supplementary work from the period. Foure Learned and Godly Treatises was not published until 1638, but the work contains sermonic material that clearly antedates 1630. Much of the work is of the nature of an "occasional sermon" as Hooker decries the contemporary English scene. For this reason, much of the work lies outside the scope of this dissertation which is particularly concerned with Hooker's morphology of conversion. Yet there are salient points in regard to Hooker's morphology that can be drawn from the work.

In the sermon entitled "The Deceitfulnesse of Sinne," is found Hooker's characteristic attribution to the Law of God of a great place in the process of conversion. Commenting on the 119th Psalm Hooker remarks:

> Among 176 verses there in not above one or two but mentioneth the Law of God, either Law, or precepts, or Commandments, or Word, or statutes, testimonies, or the like . . . as if the Prophet David had bestowed himself wholly, and had beene eaten up with the Law of God. (Hooker 1638a, 178-179)

This not only demonstrates Hooker's conviction of the necessary place of the Law in the preparatory process but explains David's great desire to have sin removed.

To the complacent ones who feel that they have dealt adequately with their sin, Hooker writes,

> If you will have sinne dwell in your soules, God will never dwell with you, nor you ever with him, if you will harbor and hold you sinnes, you must

hold your shame too, you will not part with your
sinnes, you must part with heaven, for there is no
coming there for you with your sinnes. (Ibid., 252)

But characteristically, there is this word of
encouragement late in the volume. Though the mockers
seek only when they are in great distress and then not
whole heartily, this assurance remains:

> Seeke the Lord with all thy heart, thus seek him
> constantly, thus seeke him with your whole heart,
> and hee will be found of you in mercie and
> compassion. (Hooker 1638a, 293)

An understanding of this early work is crucial
to a proper view of Hooker's preparationism. The work
of humiliation is seen as completing the work of
contrition. In contrition the sinner is brought to know
himself. In humiliation he is brought to reject
himself. As has been shown, the psychologist of
conversion has used the "prodigal son" parable as his
paradigm. The sinner first seeks comfort from a variety
of directions but fails to go to Christ. He then senses
the hopelessness of all such avenues and finally falls
at the throne of grace in submission to Christ. Self-
sufficiency is abandoned as contentedness with the
sovereignty of God marks the soul.

THE MAJOR MORPHOLOGICAL WORKS: TRANSITIONAL VOLUMES

In sequence, the next major work in Hooker's
morphology is *The Soules Effectual Calling To Christ*
(1637). But logically prior to that important work are
three volumes which linger over the stage of
"humiliation," and yet also point to the ensuing stage.
The Soules Ingrafting Into Christ (1637) is a
short transitional work evidently designed to be bound
with *The Soules Effectual Calling To Christ* whose first
page is numbered as 33. The thirty-page *Soules
Ingrafting* also appears singly. Whether by reason of
its brevity, its scarcity, or its transitional nature,

the work has not received adequate scholarly attention. The work loses some of its power as it became "buried" amid two subsequent enlargements: first as the second sermon in the 266 page The Soules Implantation: A Treatise (1637), and then again in the 320 page The Soules Implantation Into The Naturall Olive (1640).
As a work of pastoral encouragement, this energetic sermon on Malachi 3:1 contains some of Hooker's most concise statements as to the nature of preparation as he understands it. It is also a work in which this "do something" preacher actually speaks of a certain passivity in the conversion process. Hooker assumes that the prior works of contrition and humiliation are now understood. The transitional nature of the present volume is quite clear.

> Two things must be wrought in the soule, before it be made partaker of saving grace: 1. A preparation, 2. An implantation. (Hooker 1637d, 1)

Because the sinner is "not naturally capable to receive grace," the Lord sends this work of contrition and humiliation and "pierces our soules with it, and so upon this we desire a change" (Hooker 1637d, 1-2). But to be plucked away from sin is to be like Israel wandering aimlessly in the wilderness. A positive "planting" is needed.

> The soule is like a graft, first it is cut off, then pared, then ingrafted. So contrition cuts us off, and Humiliation pares us. The next point is, the ingrafting into the Lord Jesus Christ, the heart being prepared, it is implanted into the true vine, the Lord Christ. (Ibid., 2)

Looking prospectively at this point, Hooker characteristically defines his terms, almost in catechistic tones.

> Our implantation into Christ is the worke of the Spirit, whereby the humbled sinner stands possessed of Christ, and is made partaker of the spiritual

good things in Him. (Ibid., 3)

Hooker recognizes his own monergistic doctrine here and articulates it further.

> I use the word possession, because it is rather wrought upon the soule, than comes out of any principle in the soule . . . a man is more passive than active, the worke lyes on God's part. The childe holds the father, because the father holds him. So we hold God, because he holds us. (Ibid.)

This unusual passage is of extreme importance for an understanding of Thomas Hooker. He appears to be everywhere the activist preacher, a clear advocate of voluntarism. And so he is. But Kendall, while charging Hooker with voluntarism, also suggests that Hooker claims for himself a "doctrine of preparation that is mostly passive" (Kendall 1979, 133,138). The passage quoted above might appear to provide grounds for Kendall's view of Hooker's own estimate of his preparation. But such a view is a misreading of Hooker. As one grapples with the entire Hooker canon, it becomes transparent that passivity is one thing that Hooker clearly did not teach. Even here he uses the relative phrase "more passive than active." Indeed, Calvinistic soteriology, in its most pristine form, does not put forth a passivity in the salvation process (Heppe 1978, 521). Maintaining that God makes of an unwilling heart, a willing one, Hooker stands squarely in the Augustinian tradition. Because God has chosen to have his people, He embraces them and they are moved to embrace him in return.

In Ramistic fashion, Hooker dichotomizes the concept of "receiving." Because Christ comes to the humbled soul as King, with the harbinger of preparation having down its work, the soul lies at his disposal.

> The sinner receives the worke of grace and mercy, being empty: The Lord may power in what he will . . . and this is called passive receiving, namely whereby God fits the soule to receive mercy, and

prepares it, that it may come and the soule being emptied, entertaines the worke of mercy. (Hooker 1637d, 29)

This is reminiscent of Calvin's doctrine of faith.

We compare faith to a kind of vessel; for unless we come empty and with the mouth of our soul open to seek Christ's grace, we are not capable of receiving Christ. (Institutes III,xi,7)

Hooker likewise put forth this "empty vessel" concept and like Calvin said that the soul must seek and go out to "fetch" Christ.

The soule being emptied, and having received vertue from God, returnes an answer to this call; and this we call active calling. (Hooker 1737d, 29)

So by virtue of power received, an answer is returned to God. From the Malachi text, "And the Lord who yee seeke shall suddenly comé into his temple," Hooker insists that the Lord Jesus cannot possibly be hindered from his entry into "the heart prepared and humbled" (Ibid., 7-14). Looking to the subsequent stages of his morphology, Hooker notes that as King, Christ will bring "provision enough of vocation, adoption, justification, and sanctification" (Ibid., 6-7).

The thirty-page sermon reached its final form in the 1640 publication The Soules Implantation Into The Naturall Olive. That work was an expansion "carefully corrected and much enlarged, with a Table of Contents prefixed" (Hooker 1640c, title page), of the 1637 The Soules Implantation. The sermon's final length reached some eighty-five pages. It is the central sermon of five in the 1640 work, this itself reflecting its important transitional character.

The initial two sermons in the work, "The Broken Heart," and "Preparing The Heart To Receive Christ," both look back over preparationist themes. The latter sermon especially stresses the need for a powerful

ministry as one of the means by which a heart is brought
low.

> When a faithfull Minister out of undauntedness of
> spirit doth in a speciall and particular manner
> apply the Word unto the soules of them, over whom
> he is set: this is a powerful ministry. . . . This
> must be a speciall meanes soundly to prepare mens
> hearts for the entertaining of the Lord Jesus
> Christ. (Hooker 1640c, 69,72)

Leaving aside the expanded version of the "Souls Ingrafting" for now, the final two sermons look forward past the preparational stage to effectual calling and sanctification. The fourth sermon, "Spiritual Love and Joy," is a 113 page sermon concerned with the actual embrace of Christ and the consequential growing love for him by the child of God. It is essentially the same sermon that appears in the next major morphological work, The Soules Effectual Calling To Christ (1637). It is therefore more appropriate that this portion of the volume be examined in the next section below.

The final sermon in the 1640 volume, "Spiritual Joy," is a new one, it not having been a part of the 1637 Soules Implantation. It is a thirty-five page work primarily concerned with sanctification, particularly in the midst of troubled times. Its text is Habakkuk 3:17,18 which Hooker calls "the poore mans comfort in a deare yeare" (Ibid., 295).

Significant to the present examination of Hooker's morphology are two passages from "Spiritual Joy." Hooker reminds his listeners of his frequent warning not to expect God "to be at your becke."

> Because Beggars must not be chusers, nor may the
> holy One of Israel be limited, therefore resolve to
> wait the Lord's leasure until he have mercy on you.
> (Ibid., 307)

Hooker is here principally concerned with the struggling child of God, but the emphasis on waiting upon God is elsewhere directed to the one undergoing the contrition-

humiliation process.
In a second significant passage, Hooker summarizes his whole view of the nature of conversion, particularly noting the place of the Law in the process. The prerogatives of God's sovereignty lay in the forefront.

> In the act of conversion unto God, there is much fear and sorrow, both by the law condemning, and especially by the Gospel aggravating sin to the height of heynousnesse. The Christian is wearie, heavie lade, poore in Spirit, mournfull, ready to despaire. But here Christ comprehends him, and gives him faith to lay hold on his merit, whereby hee is blessed and comfortable, Math.5:3,4 and godly sorrow worketh repentance unto salvation. (Ibid., 309-310)

Yet in the main, this sermon remains primarily a work dealing with sanctification. It therefore belongs to a relatively small group within the Hooker canon.
The middle sermon in The Soules Implantation Into The Naturall Olive remains the central work, not only in its placement but also due to the transitional position it holds in the development of Hooker's morphology. Above it was maintained that the sermon, in its original thirty page form, is extremely significant to Hooker studies. In its final form the sermon reaches to 185 pages. The added importance of the final form lies chiefly in Hooker's concern to encourage certain doubters in regard to their "possession" of the Christ. Matters related to the Puritan concept of assurance are handled directly.
Hooker the psychologist entertains an objection. Can it be possible that that one be possessed of Christ and yet not apprehend this? He answers, "yes it is not onely possible, but it is too ordinary" (Hooker 1640c, 133). Hooker then goes on to explicate four reasons "in us" that this great work might take place unawares.

> First, Christ may come into thy Soule, and thou dost not know him. As one man comes to another mans

house, and happily one that he hath loved and
desired too, yet his geste is such, and the
distance of time so long since he saw him, that he
may be there and his friend never the wiser. . . .
Secondly, as the soule of a poore sinner knows not
Christ though he meet him in his way, and out of
the weakness of his judgement, and by reason of his
ignorance, he knowes not his presence....The third
is, because we judge Christs presence by our own
sense, and by some extraordinary sweetness the
soule imagines should be with him if Christ were
there. This is the nature of the poore creature.
The fourth also is on our part . . . when our eyes
bee hindered that wee cannot see Chris though he
were before us: when the sting of conscience
remaines, and the fiercenesse of some temptation
presseth in upon us, or some worldly inconvenience
sits hard upon us and the strength of our
imagination is wholly bestowed upon those, how to
prevent them. (Hooker 1637c, 134,136,139,143)

Armed with such convictions, the very same
pastor who could call upon sinners to "labor to get a
contrite heart," would seek to reassure the "poor
doubter when any evidence" appeared to Hooker's mind
that God had wrought his work of grace. By the time
these words were published, Hooker was already settled
in Hartford. The "charitable judgment" was entrenched
policy there, though back in Newtown, Thomas Shepard,
Hooker's son-in-law, was vigorously applying "the
relation" requirement (Selement and Wooley 1981,
passim; Morgan 1963, 107; Caldwell 1983, 99-100). One
has hardly to comment that such encouragements as Hooker
gives above would never have fallen from the lips of
John Cotton, as he was ever looking for the violent
seizure of the soul.

In the original thirty-page version of The
Soules Ingrafting, Hooker marked the transitional
character of the work.

Now we have cut out our worke, and for the further
handling, we have chosen this text, which is, to

discover this worke of vocation. (Hooker 1637d, 30)

This statement, along with the printer's pagination, demonstrates Hooker's intention that the sermon, in its virginal form, was to be bound with The Soules Effectual Calling To Christ (1637). The transitional works analyzed in this section were formulated with the assumption that the prior works of contrition and humiliation had been understood. While lingering over preparationist themes Hooker has hinted at the necessity of a "positive planting" in Christ. This master chronicler of the windings of the interior life, having explicated the crucial stages of preparation, now presses on to matters of calling and faith.

THE MAJOR MORPHOLOGICAL WORKS:
THE SOULES EFFECTUAL CALLING

The 668 page The Soules Effectual Calling To Christ, containing sermonic material dating from the Chelmsford period of Hooker's career a decade before, was published in 1637. With the addition of a "Table," it was reissued in 1638 under the title The Soules Vocation or Effectual Calling to Christ. Happily, pagination remained the same, whether or not the work was bound with the short transitional Soules Ingrafting. Following the stages of contrition and humiliation, this large work clearly explicates the third major stage in the morphology of conversion as Hooker understood it.
Here, more fully than in any other work, one finds Hooker's doctrine of faith, and his understanding of the will, presented in a systematic fashion. Hooker's definition of faith, as found in his preface to John Rogers' 1627 treatise on the subject, dates from the same Chelmsford period.

Faith being nothing else but the going out of the soul to God through Christ to fetch a principle of life which in Adam we lost and now need. (in

Williams et al. 1975, 144)

In Hooker's extended treatment of the subject in the work now under discussion, he follows in the train of thought of William Ames. Ames had maintained,

> Faith is the resting of the heart on God, the author of life and eternal salvation, so that we may be saved from all evil through him and may follow all good. . . Faith is our life as it joins us to God. But it is also an act of life because it is a virtue and our
> duty towards God. (Ames 1968, 80,242)

The Soules Effectual Calling finally traces the windings of the soul to the embrace of Christ whereby the renewed sinner begins to partake of the actual benefits of Christ's sacrifice. A sense of drama builds as the work unfolds and one presses on towards that climatic point of finding rest. The importance of this work is well stated by Sargent Bush. Of The Soules Effectual Calling he wrote:

> . . . (it) may be the fullest analysis of the process from the sinner's perspective and for his benefit published by any man in the Reformed tradition, including Calvin himself. (Bush 1980, 206)

In typical fashion, Hooker is careful to define his terminology. "Vocation" is said to be,

> The putting in of the soule, when the soule is brought out of the worlde of sinne, to lye upon and to close with the Lord Jesus Christ, and this hath two particular passages in it, partly the call on Gods part, partly the answer on ours. (Hooker 1637a, 33)

So again, using a principle of Ramistic dichotomies, Hooker launches into a detailed investigation of the interior life (Habegger 1969, 342-354).

Hooker, throughout his works, is careful to prod to activism by pointing to the appointed means of grace. God works through the means but his sovereignty is always guarded. As sinners attend to the ministry of the Word, the Law brings terror and the Gospel brings man home.

> By the work of his Spirit hee doth bring all the riches of his grace into the soule truly humbled, so that the heart cannot but receive the same, and give answer thereto. (Hooker 1637a, 34)

Hooker's first doctrine is that there is all sufficiency in God's mercy to fill up all the "chinkes" of the soule. Only in mercy will rest be found for this arduous sojourn. The sinner who is brought low by God's Spirit can find no comfort but in fleeing to the proffered mercy of God (Ibid., 37).

Using the covenant schema, Hooker maintains that as a condition of the covenant of grace is to believe, the fulfillment of this is "worked" into the elect by God.

> God doth not leave thee to thyselfe. . . . This is the tenor of mercy: God requires of a man that he should beleeve; now mercy doth helpe to perform the duty commanded . . . for the Lord he requires that the soule should rest upon him, and he make him also to doe it. (Ibid., 40-41)

This leads to a second doctrine in which Hooker maintains that even while the means are faithfully attended unto, the teaching of the heart effectually is the proper task and work of God. God is the "chiefe Master," others are but "underling ushers to convey the minde of God to us" (Ibid., 49). This assurance of God's "proper task," should serve as a comfort to the "feeble, silly, and weake." For since it is God's work, the doubter should "go to him." Even in the attendance of the means, whether the minister reproves or exhorts, one is to look not to the means but is to hear God reproving and exhorting. Such was Hooker's high view of the ministry (Ibid., 50, 51).

A decade after these sermons were first put forth, Hooker would find himself in New England amid the raging Antinomian Controversy. Anne Hutchinson would finally seal her own doom with her claims of revelation from God. Hooker's orthodox views in this regard had been established early on. His third doctrine in the work here under discussion maintained that in using the means, the Word and Spirit must go together. Hooker was no visionary nor familist. In the previous century Calvin had spoken in no uncertain terms as to the nature of effectual calling.

> Even the very nature and dispensation of the call clearly demonstrates this fact (that it depends on grace alone), for it consists not only in the preaching of the Word but also in the illumination of the Spirit. (<u>Institutes</u> III, xxiv, 2)

Hooker's own commitment to the Scriptures is clear.

> Because we not be cozened by our owne fancies, the Lord to prevent all inconveniences and conceits of the Eatonists and familists, that thinke they have the power of the Spirit in themselves, whereas Gods Spirit goes alwaies with the Word. (Hooker 1637a, 65)

This commitment to the Word as the basis of heart religion has a sobering effect which Hooker uses as a prod to the complacent.

> Be watchfull and carefull, lest we lose the comfort that we have: lightly come, lightly goe, got with little paine, lost with lesse care; Therefore the Lord will make us seeke unto the meanes. (Ibid., 66)

Clearly Hooker fears making the reception of grace appear too easy.

One of the characteristics of <u>The Soules Effectual Calling</u> is the promotion of several "trials,"

found throughout the work. The one who professes to have faith must examine whether he has a "spiritual heart or no." He must examine his thirst for the Gospel because if he will not have the Gospel he will "misse of the Spirit, then Christ will have none of thee." This typical Hookerian call for introspection would have the soul contemplate the source of faith itself, and whether it has as its object to "match with Christ onely" (Ibid., 66, 423-433).
Such trials may in turn produce assurance of salvation. To this frequent Puritan theme Hooker turns directly in his fourth "doctrine," which insists that the Spirit of the Lord gives "special notice of God's acceptance to the soule truly humbled" (Ibid., 72). Hooker here gets ahead of himself in that he has not yet explicated the actual process of "closing with Christ." Nevertheless, after the Spirit necessarily brings one through contrition and humiliation, He "strikes through the bargain and makes the understanding close with that grace and mercy." This "testification" is discovered as the Spirit evidences to the contrite one that the soule has a genuine interest in mercy and "that it was appointed for it." Consequently that interest is "ratified," and it is made "sure to the soule (Ibid., 72, 76-77, 81).

> (This) witnesse makes the soule yeeld unto what the Spirit hath witnessed: As the witnesses in open court in a matter of law, they make the case cleare and evident, the Jury they take it. (Ibid., 85)

R.T. Kendall's work, which has been frequently cited in this study, was largely concerned with the Puritan doctrine of assurance. He laments that Hooker seeks assurance in a "reflex act" (Kendall 1979, 137). This is indeed Hooker's method.

> There is a reflecting act, when a man lookes over his understanding, and labours to discern the worke thereof, not only apprehending what was laid before him, but when he doth apprehend what he doth apprehend, when he knowes that he doth know it,

> marke that place, for we will carry Scripture with us, 1 Joh. 2.3. 'Hereby we know that we know him' saith the text, 'if we keepe his commandments.' A man may know a thing, and yet not know that he doth know. (Hooker 1637a, 87)

Clearly for Hooker, assurance of salvation is possible and it is to be longed for and sought after, though it is not of the essence of faith. Because such assurance is a great prize to get, Hooker lingers long over the means thereunto. As shown above, not only must God's effectual call come through the Word, but likewise the assurance of God's acceptance comes also through this "appointed means." Because this assurance is from the Spirit, it "must needs be certaine . . . infallible, and undeniable, in those who have it" (Ibid., 109).

Hooker the morphologist seems never to miss the opportunity to chronicle the way to grace. Were it not for his very frequent and earthy similes, one might quickly tire of his many lists of "meanes," and "trialls." Hooker the activist, in delineating the means to receive the witness of the Spirit, sounds the old theme that "you must labour to be such a one, to whom the Spirit belongs. Labour to be a humbled sinner." One must not hearken to the cavils of reason or the clamoring of a corrupt heart. In this Hooker is presupposing the Spirit's work of contrition and humiliation. Furthermore, one must "labour to bee informed and to understand aright the language of the Spirit . . . those gracious promises which God hath made to poore humbled sinners" (Ibid., 102, 103, 105, 106).

But the pastor-psychologist presents his listeners with this double "pronged" exhortation lest any feel the way too easy or some poor doubter fail to embrace the gracious promise. The one who embraces the promise will receive, but the one who receives must depart from his sin.

> Therefore art thou content to sue out a bill of divorce to all thy sins, how ever heretofore thou

wert married to them, yet now art thou resolved to bed with them no more; art thou contented God should make known whatever is amisse in thy soule, and subdue every distemper, that is the meaning of the promise, and if it be thus with thee, the promise belongs to thee. (Hooker 1637a, 106)

With Hooker's fifth "doctrine," the journey nears its end though more than 500 pages remain in the work. Hooker is concerned to trace the motions of the various "affections" as the sinner is brought to "close with the Lord Jesus Christ." His fifth doctrine opens up this lengthy discussion.

The Holy Spirit of the Father doth stir the heart of the humbled and inlightened sinner to hope for the goodness of the Lord: the Lord calleth all the affections: come joy, come desire, come love; but the first voyce is hope. (Ibid., 110)

For Hooker, once the soul is brought low and enlightened, thus being fitted to receive mercy, the "faculty" of hope is best suited to then be employed for it is its "office" to "looke and expect for a good to come" (Ibid., 112).

When the Lord saith, mercy is coming towards thee, mercy is provided for thee; now this affection is set out to meet mercy a farre off, namely hope; this is the stretching out of the soule. (Ibid., 113)

With a curious twist, Hooker handles the old objection that if grace be free, can't a man "live as he list?" Here it is the faculty of hope that provides the negative answer as the Lord stirs up the desire for and the knowledge that sins may be pardoned (Ibid., 117).

But always, even when the sinner seems to be near to "closing" with Christ, patience and contentedness are imperatives.

Wait . . . and bless God that you may waite: if you

> may lye at God's feet, and put your mouth in the dust, and at the end of your dayes have one crumb of mercy, it is enough. (Hooker 1637a, 148)

If impatience should rear its ugly head in this "hoping,"

> Check you heart and say, it is not for me to know, it is for me to be humble, and to be abased, and to wait for mercy but it is not for me to know the time. (Ibid., 149; Cf. Bush 1980, 208-210)

This "hope," in Hooker's "morphology within a morphology," gives way to "desire." Hooker's sixth "doctrine" affirms that the Lord instills a longing for the riches of his mercy in grace. Once again the importance of the Scriptures is plain.

> You must not thinke to bring desire with you to the promise, but receive desire from the promise: it is a vaine thing to thinke that if the oares be in the boat, the boat must needs goe; indeed the oare will move the boat, but the hand of the Ferri-man must first move the oare: The soule is like the oare, and unlesse the hand of the Spirit moves our desire, it cannot move towards the Lord. (Hooker 1637a, 150)

Here Hooker appears to be thinking prospectively to the actual exercise of faith and the teaching of Scripture that this arises from the hearing of the Word (Romans 10:17). Clearly at this point, no less than in the first movings of the Spirit in contrition, the prerogatives of the sovereignty of God are being guarded.

The physician to the soul anticipates another objection from some poor doubter. "How shall I know if my desires be sincere?" Here is the often repeated fear of being "hoodwinked." Hooker resorts to the "reflex act," as he insists, "if thou desirest earnestly, thou will worke accordingly." But even in this working and using of the means, one is warned not to rest in ones

own labors. Thus Hooker's own answer is quite a restrained one. But there is more. With a hint of the Edwardsean view of the affections, Hooker exhorts the doubter to look for a desiring of "Christ for himselfe." This involves a relishing after God in view of His own beauty and goodness. Its intensity is likened to "a maid that desires a man in wedlocke, she doth not desire the portion, but the person of the man" (Ibid., 157, 158).
A third "triall" is to examine one's own readiness to receive grace with thanksgiving (Ibid., 159). This in turn sets the stage for an extended reproof of all hypocrites who do not have these true and sincere desires after grace and salvation wrought into them.
That these sincere desires are absolutely necessary presents no indifferent matter. For these affections of hope and desire are "the very wheels of faith upon which faith is carried" (Ibid., 197). In the preparatory stages, the sinner is brought low. Without these "affections," the soul remains, as a vehicle without wheels, lying in the dust.
As Hooker nears the end his discussion of "desire" in this "mini-morphology" of the affections, he sounds another rapturous call to action.

> Labour to spread forth the excellence of all the beauty and surpassing glories that is in the promises of God. (Hooker 1637a, 197-198)

These promises are to be made one's constant focus of one's admiration and desire.
Hooker maintains, just as he did concerning the earlier stages of preparation, that though they are not sanctifying graces, they are nevertheless "saving graces." If the "hand of the Lord be wanting," not one step towards heaven will be taken. But on the other hand, where these affections are truly added to contrition and humiliation, the sinner is close indeed to "matching" his heart to Christ. As a experimental predestinarian theologian himself, Hooker was happy to note his good company.

> Many judicious divines of late yeares having by experience observed in their owne spirits, and judicially scanned and delivered it, that there is a saving desire, by which God brings us and breeds faith in the soule. It is the speech of the judicious Perkins. (Ibid., 203)

Hooker moves on to reveal that the affections of love and joy follow next as the sinner moves ever closer to "closing with Christ." In his seventh "doctrine" Hooker maintains that love and joy are kindled by the Spirit who "conveyeth some rellish of the love of God into the soule" (Ibid., 217). This love and joy are kindled that the sinner might entertain and rejoice in the riches of mercy and grace. But one must not rush to assume this possession of these affections. Indeed to unveil the sincerity of love and joy "is a point of great weight and hard to discover." Because hypocrisy is so prevalent, self-trial is requisite. A earthy picture is offered.

> Meat that a man takes downe inwardly, and digests, breeds good bloud, and good complexion; but that which a man takes and digests not, but vomits out again presently breeds neither good bloud, nor good complexion. (Ibid., 241)

Hooker's verdict is that carnal hypocrites have only a taste of God's promises.

By contrast, the soul possessing these proper affections longs for a "nearer union . . . with a kind of earnest impatience and restlessnesse till it attaine a greater measure thereof" (Ibid., 254). Such a soul longs for the happiness of Christ, longs for Christ to be contented, and will be pleased to entertain Christ not only as Savior but also as King (Ibid., 244, 251, 242). These latter words especially would not sit well with the Hutchinsonians who would include Hooker among the "legal preachers."

Hooker's final doctrine concerns the will and gives way to an almost 400 page treatise on the subject.

> The will of a poore sinner humbled and inlightened, comes to bee effectually perswaded by the Spirit of the Father to rest upon the free grace of God in Christ, that it may bee interested therein, and have supply of all Spiritual wants from thence. (Ibid., 284)

At this stage, one is very near the actual embrace of Christ and his benefits. For Hooker faith involves not only an active "going out to fetch a principle of life," but also a "resting." This conjunction of voluntarism and rest is aptly illustrated.

> Roule thy way upon the Lord, as it is with a barrell that is tumbled up and down; and the earth beares the waight of the barrell, but somebody moves it; so the soul casts the waight of all its disgrace, dishonor, temptations, and all upon Christ. (Hooker 1637a, 302)

Hooker brings a sense of relief to any who are following his chronicle of positive exhortations, interrupted often as it is by doubts to be analyzed. The tension is eased when Hooker plainly comes to the point of closure with Christ. It comes quietly, as hostility has ceased and all objections are put down. Hooker explicates this in an answer to a final objection as one wonders if all is of faith, "doth not man do anything?" Hooker responds with sterling Calvinistic orthodoxy.

> This worke of beleeving is a worke of the Spirit upon the soule, rather than any worke wrought by the soule, or issuing from any principle which the soule hath in itselfe; as it is with an eccho, when God saith, thy sinnes are pardoned, thy person accepted; faith sounds again, my sinnes pardoned? my person accepted? good Lord let it be so: then it perswades the heart and that marvellously, to rest itselfe there for all good; but it is done upon the soule rather than by the soule. (Ibid., 327)

So the contrite and humbled sinner is rescued from despair. Throughout the tension-filled sojourn Hooker has given hints that this being brought low is itself a source of encouragement if such was possible. The psychologist is careful to distinguish between proper contrition and discouragement. Sin must indeed be looked upon and seen as it is. Sorrow must be present. But all this constitutes a "lower forme."

> Doe not looke into the blacke booke of conscience and expect there to finde supply; neither looke to the booke of privileges and performances, and thinke to finde power out of thy owne sufficiency: Look not on thy own sinnes to pore upon them whereby thou shalt be discouraged. (Ibid., 43; cf. Pettit 1974, 518-534)

Introspection is necessary, but it is a tool that must carry the soul further to cultivate the affections of hope, desire, love, and joy. These provide the wheels which carry the soul to embrace Christ by faith. Thus Hooker has presented a careful discussion of the role of these affections in the acquiring of the assurance of grace and faith.

The journey has been a long and arduous one. But finally Hooker, after the objections and ever threatening self delusions, after the tension of it all, and after the laboriously patient pace, has followed the sinner "over the top." The reader of Hooker's tome on the will, shares in the weariness of the "poor doubter," and both are glad to be brought home.

Hooker, as if standing atop a high mountain, looks back over the onerous pathway of the ascent.

> You see how far the Lord hath brought us, how the soule hath been prepared, and cut off from sin and himselfe, if fitted by contrition and humiliation and that the soule comes to see that there is no hope in creatures, nor any succor in heaven, but the Lord Jesus Christ, and so at last the sinner comes and lyes at the footstoole of the Lord Jesus

Christ, and knows that he must be either another
man or a damned man: now when he sees that prayer
and all other means will not profit and the power
of the meanes yet prevail not, and the power of his
corruptions is not yet mastered, then he looks up
to Christ, and is contented that he should doe what
he will with him. (Hooker 1637a, 667-668)

At this crucial point the Lord gives special notice that
He intends good to such a soul and that there is mercy
for this broken heart.

At last the will saith Amen to the promise, and
saith O that mercie I will have, and thus the soule
is come home to God by vocation. (Ibid.)

THE MAJOR MORPHOLOGICAL WORKS:
THE SOULES EXALTATION (1638)

The long and halting preparatory sojourn being past, Hooker in this 311 page work which contains three sections, addresses the matters of union and communion with Christ, especially emphasizing the objective ground of justification. With the great watershed issue now decided, vocation having brought closure with Christ, graces now become not only "saving" but also "sanctifying." The great strains and stresses are eased and the promised rest is now available. Hooker seems clearly to be beyond his main subject of concern and his work takes on a different character.

The present volume, especially in its final and longest sermon ("The Soules Justification"), contains standard Reformed theology, but Hooker's diminished enthusiasm may be reflected in that he no longer lingers over his doctrines, reasons, and uses, embellishing them at every turn with fine metaphors (Bush 1980, 252-254). Though the exhortations, the words of comfort, and the instructions as to application remain, the work has more of the character of a theology treatise, as relative to the previous works in the morphology.

While lacking the former metaphorical richness,

Hooker's explication of doctrine takes on a "crisper" quality characterized by brevity of expression. These sermons, most notably the final one, are more polemical tone and are laced with frequently used expressions such as "as most divines teach," and "as divines use to day." For example, before launching into the esoteric question of whether the soul is first united to Christ's deity or humanity, Hooker exposes his own hesitancy to even take up the matter.

> I am not greatly willing to meddle with this point in the popular congregation, because many wise and orthodox Divines, and godly too, which are of contrary opinion; they confesse both, but they differ about the order. (Hooker 1638d, 39-40)

Notwithstanding this hesitancy, and contrary to his normal practice, Hooker goes on to lay out the various views of "judicious" divines and to also render his own convictions.

Hooker's treatment of union, communion, and justification, is laid out in four sermons which bear these titles.

"The Soules Union with Christ," pp. 1-53, 1 Cor. 6:17 "The Soules Benefit From Union With Christ," pp. 55-130, 1 Cor. 1:30 (two sermons).
"The Soules Justification," pp. 131-311, 2 Cor. 5:21 (the title page to this sermon incorrectly reads ("2 Cor. 5:22").

Interested as he was in a systematic unfolding of the morphology of conversion, Hooker is careful to link the present work with the one which holds a logically previous place, <u>The Soules Effectual Calling To Christ</u>. As the previous work concerned itself with putting the "soule into Christ" as a graft, it now remains to be demonstrated how the soul grows and what is the nature of the "ingrafting into the stock." This growing together is accomplished by two means.

The first is the union which the soule hath with

Christ. The second is a conveyance of sap, or sweetnesse, or a communion with Christ, and all the treasures of grace and happinesse that is in him: then to make up the growing together of the graft and the stock, first the graft is put into the stock. Secondly, there must bee a communicating of the moisture that is in the stock to the graft so they grow together. (Hooker 1638d, 2-3)

Hooker's first doctrine is that the believer is joined or "glued," to Christ, being "firmly and neerly combined and knit to the Lord Jesus Christ." The preacher takes a measure of sermonic license when he says that "the word in the original is glued." Hooker is clearly grasping for an adequate picture. The analogies fail him in the face of the depth of the mystery at hand.

What ever by way of comparison can be alleged, concern-ing the neere combination of one thing with another, they are all tyed to this knitting of the soule to Christ: looke what a friend is to a friend; looke what a father is to a childe; what a husband to a wife; looke what a graft is to a tree; and that is neerer than a husband to a wife: nay, goe yet farther, Gal. 2.20. what the soule is to the body; the soule is not only knit to the body, as one member to another, as the hand is knit to the arme, and the arme to the sholder; but the soule doth communicate it selfe universally through the least part of the body: so the Apsotle saith, Christ is the very sole of a beleever, I live, yet not I, but the Lord Jesus liveth in me. (Ibid., 3-4)

Exhortations are everywhere implied as Hooker unfolds the meaning of this union. The soul "gathers it selfe up" and employs all the faculties of hope, desire, love, and joy, upon Christ. The soul is knit to Christ as two pieces of dough are kneaded together. Love increases as it does in the heart of a husband who is

altogether satisfied with his wife. He is ravished by
her breasts and her love alone, having not "his back
doores, and his goings out." This union is a covenant
bond in which the heart is to be kept "to the exercise
of the promise." This is a union, spiritual in nature
and yet involving the "whole nature of a Saviour and the
whole nature of the beleever" (Ibid., 5-7).
 The believer is to be made aware thereby of his
high privilege, though he be despised by the world.
Hooker reveals the precarious conditions for English
Puritans at the time the sermon was preached, by giving
an entire "use" to the high sin of persecuting God's
people (Ibid., 10-14).
 Perhaps it is because Hooker's present subject
concerns an abiding condition, and not something to
press towards, that this initial sermon flounders a bit
in its mid-section. Hooker retreats to the question of
how the union takes place. This of course pushes his
subject matter back towards the giant <u>Soules Effectual
Calling To Christ</u>, upon which union inevitably follows.
So our author once again goes over his old themes of the
Law's work of preparation, the Spirit's necessity
conjunctive work with the Word, the soul being wrought
upon and "carried" to the point where it is made to
"close with the promise," the soul itself not having the
ability to so fit itself (Ibid., 27, 29, 33).
 Since the faithful have been joined unto Christ
in such a union, examination is to be made that no
uncertainty exists that the sin of a believer is
"marvellous heinous in God's account." A final "use" in
this initial sermon is somewhat unique in Hooker and
touches upon the importance he gives to the covenanted
community of faith. Because man is a social creature,
he must "have some to keepe company with him." The
faithful are exhorted to "close with such as Christ
himselfe doth close withall." Wisdom is called for in
the choosing of one's companions.

> Yes, Oh then get you to the Saints of God, and get
> them to your houses, and lay hold upon gracious
> Christians, and say, I will live and converse with
> you, for the Spirit of Christ is with you. (Ibid.,

52, 53)

The second section of the work contains two sermons on 1 Corinthians 1:30, "But of him are yee in Christ Jesus, who is made unto us wisdome, righteousnesse, sanctification, and redemption." Following logically after the first section, Hooker here purposes to make plain the "benefits" that issue from union with Christ, namely, the "conveyance of all spirituall grace, from Christ, to all those that beleeve in him" (Hooker 1638d, 63).

The believer is to rest assured that there is all sufficiency in Christ, and more, he actually communicates to the believer "that which is fit."

> So he doth preserve what hee doth bestow and communicate, and give to the beleeving soule; hee doth not give grace to the beleeving soule, and there leave him and let him manage his own estate, but when he hath wrought grace in the soule, he preserves it, and nourisheth his owne works. (Ibid., 73)

By such statements, the road ahead does indeed seem to be an easier one than the toilsome preparatory one travelled heretofore.

In pastoral fashion Hooker portrays this day to day "conveyance" as a great ground of comfort against all manner of temptation, persecution, opposition, and one's own drooping spirits. To the foolish, Christ becomes wisdom; to the base, Christ becomes sanctification and redemption; to the weak, Christ become honor. "Thou canst doe nothing, it skils not, God the Father hath appointed it unto thee, Christ hath brought it; therefore be cheared herein" (Ibid., 87).

Yet typically, Hooker takes his "uses" in two directions. The double prong also involves "lamentation and complaint" for unbelievers.

> When thou shalt see a companie of poore creatures goe up to Christ, and receive mercie, and great redemption, and thou shalt goe without, this will

> bee gall and worm wood to thy soule, and strike thy
> soule into everlasting despaire. (Ibid., 83)

So Hooker issues an evangelical call colored by his Calvinism.

> Therefore, the Lord open thine eyes, that thou
> maist come in, and receive mercy at his Majesties
> hand. (Ibid., 84)

For the Christian, Christ alone is sufficient as a daily supply. The believer, as did the elders of the Apocalypse, is to lay at the feet of Christ, and glory only in him. But as the soul draws from Christ its efficiency for daily duties, the physician to the soul recognizes the tendency to pride.

> The heart is thine, and the worke is thine, and all
> is thine; when therefore thy heart findes any
> succor from God, any assistance in the performance
> of duty, if it begins to lift up it selfe and say,
> aye this is somewhat, then checke thy soule with
> that of the Apostle, what hast thou, which thou
> hast not received? What, bragge of borrowed fruit?
> who did this? let him receive all the praise.
> (Ibid., 95)

Hooker can not long linger over human duties nor his exhortation to the same, without a statement of the effective mover behind the fulfillment of such duties. His is, from start to finish, even given his constant calls to activism, a theology of grace.

The second sermon in the middle section of the present work concerns itself with the basic Reformed understanding of justification. It overlaps with the final and longest sermon of the volume, concerned as the latter work is with a formal discussion of justification itself. The "conveyance of grace" that Hooker is here concerned to describe is accomplished both by means of "imputation," and "impartation." The judicial aspect of the Reformed understanding of justification is highlighted, thus leading the preacher into the polemical arena, wherein the Roman concept of infused grace as the formal ground of justification refuted. The polemical nature of the rest of the volume becomes one of its distinguishing features in the Hooker canon. Hooker's polemical intent is obvious in that as "The Soules Benefit" nears its completion, his first "use" is a "confutation of the Church of Rome." In a radical departure from his normal practice, Hooker cites and reads from the proceedings at Trent regarding the implantation of righteousness in justification. Hooker's retort is that only the Reformed doctrine argues that "I have and can doe nothing" (Ibid., 122).

The final section of the volume, "The Soules Justification," is an extended treatise on 2 Corinthians 5:21. Its polemical nature exceeds that of any in the Hooker canon with the exception of his final work on polity, A Survey Of The Summe of Church-Discipline (1648). Psychological and morphological matters make only occasional appearances in "The Soules Justification," as Hooker is more concerned to explicate the objective grounds of justification. The fare is standard Reformed orthodoxy, as indicated by Hooker's formal definition of justification.

> Justification is an act of God the Father upon the beleever, whereby the debt and sinnes of the beleever are charged upon the Lord Jesus Christ, and by the merits and satisfaction of Christ imputed to the beleever; hee is accounted just, and so is acquitted before God as righteous. (Ibid., 132)

Citations will not be made here of Hooker's views in regard to counter imputations, his concurrence with Anselm's understanding of the atonement, or his several attacks upon Bellarmine and the Jesuits (Ibid., 139-140, 216, et passim). Rather, the present focus, given the more narrow scope of this study, will remain upon matters psychological and morphological.

Given the Father's verdict rendered in the high court of heaven, Hooker's doctrine of justification has as one of its uses, a great "ground of admirable comfort to beare up the poore sinner against all the accusations . . . of the enemy against us" (Ibid., 143). Since the acquittal has been rendered from the highest possible court, no care should be given, and surely no despair should arise, in the face of troubles, opposition, or persecution. Happily, Hooker regathers some of his picturesque homiletical skills.

> Let the gates of hell bee set open, and Belzebub and all the Devils come roaring out against him, and let the wicked come that beare him ill will, and let all his sinnes come and his own conscience too, yet hee need not feare any thing the ground is hence, because it is God who justifies. (Ibid., 145)

Because God can be the only accuser to be feared, when he is satisfied, no other "suit" can matter.

But because the fact remains that many others do bring "suit," the saint is open to the threat of discouragement or even to begin to despair of his union with Christ. Hooker is quite aware of these daily snares. He prescribes a preventative.

> Looke not what sense and feeling, and feare and suspicion say, for they speak killing words, and will tell you that your condition is naught and damnable: what all this vilenesse, and basenesse, and stubbornnesse, and yet goe to heaven? that cannot be: Good brethren hearken not to these, for they are not the Judges of the court, the sentence must come from God, and remember that God will speak peace and comfort unto his people; hee will comfort your distressed consciences: and therefore let not Satan, nor your owne distempered hearts be hearkened unto, for though they speake never so much terror to your consciences, yet God will justify you. (Hooker 1638d, 150-151)

In two places Hooker urges his listeners to see contentment in God. This reflects back to the final stages of contrition where the soul was content to be at

God's disposal whatever he might decree concerning it. There, as here, Hooker maintains that such contentment is a sign of saving grace being wrought into the soul.

> If thou art content to goe to God, and depend upon mercy, and let it doe what it will with thee, then mercy shall certainly save thee; if thou wilt come to beleeving, thou art sure to be acquitted. (Ibid., 152; cf. 149)

But Hooker fears that many poor humbled ones fail to embrace grace because they only look within, and their conscience provides "a bad jurie" and so their hearts go drooping and are discouraged. These Hooker, if he can can hope to discern between them and the stiff-necked, seeks only to encourage as their very contrition is postulated as a sign of saving grace.

For others, the gracious act of God in redemption serves only as a ground of terror. Their complacency serves to "sinke their soules to Hell." But in this mostly optimistic work, Hooker carefully notes that he speaks "not to those that have some doubtings and troubles arising in their hearts, but to such as never yet beleeved in Christ" (Ibid., 154).

Real tension remains as the physician of the soul tries variously to administer the proper prescriptions. The twin dangers of over-introspection, and that of complacent self-confidence ever remain. One must judge himself properly and not "gloss over" his own sins. He must see that he is worthy to be condemned, but then he must look elsewhere, that is, to Christ the vicarious sacrifice.

> I say not that a man should say, that the Lord will condemne him, but that he is worthy to be condemned for them (his sins), and he deserves condemnation.

Even for the one who has "closed" with Christ the danger of self-righteousness remains.

> Though God hath accepted of a poore believer, yet hee must see his sinne, and lay his mouth in the

> dust, and never pranke up his heart more, but walk humbly before the Lord; and yet hee is accepted and pardoned, yet hee shall judge himselfe worthy to bee condemned. (Ibid., 184-184)

The extent of Hooker's anticipation of objections and various impediments to godly living is remarkable. The one who has recently fallen anew into sinful behavior, being grieved thereby, ought not to assume quickly that he had never been joined to Christ. The Lord sometimes allows such a wallowing as a form of chastisement.

> Every sinne is like a great bandog that is muzzeled, if hee bee once let loose, he will teare all in peeces: so the Lord sometimes muzzels a man corruptions and keeps them under, and if the Lord doe but now and then let them loose, then they pull a man downe; and hence comes all those pale lookes, and discouragements of soule, these are they that will thus worry a man: Thus every beleever must acknowledge that is were just with the Lord to let loose his sinne, howsoever not to condemne him. (Ibid., 186-187)

By no means is sin to be taken lightly. If fact Hooker uses the Anselmian view of the atonement, with the awful wrath of the Father poured out upon the Son, as the measure of the depth of human sin. With the cross in view, the sinner is to "looke upon sinne in the Lord Jesus Christ, and there see it in its colours, and see what vexation it brought on our Saviour" (Ibid., 261-262).

The present volume, though its material dated from an earlier period, appeared just after the Antinomian controversy had wrecked havoc in New England. In answering an inquiry concerning the moral "danger" of preaching sovereign grace, Hooker clearly demonstrated on which side of the Antinomian controversy he would come to be aligned.

Thus, as I may say with holy reverence, they make

Christ a stall for all their sinne: therefore let me show all such loose libertines of this last age of the world, what fond conceits they have: I mean the Anabaptist, but specially the Familists, who think it unprofitable for a beleever to trouble himselfe for his sinnes. . . . This is the cursed opinion of the Familists. (Hooker 1638d, 181)

While there is immeasurable comfort in the soul's justification by grace alone, the Familists, "sucke as much poison from it" (Ibid.).

Late in the work, as Hooker presents his final "uses," words of encouragement and exhortation to action predominate. That by sovereign grace Christ became a substitutionary atonement for his people is put forth as a great comfort to all believers. But the "hard hearted and unbeleeving wretches" are told to "bee packing" (Ibid., 166-167). This deliverance from wrath, hell, and punishment is an "incomparable chearing of the soule, to all the faithful of God." But Hooker says that he seems to hear some begin to "cavill" that though this be great blessedness for those with title to the same, "did Christ suffer the death of the crosse for me, my sinnes so many, and my condition so bad?" The psychologist answers any who doubt because they deem themselves too bad.

> This is your own fault, for this mercy is for thee, for every faithful beleeving soule, bee his estate never so low, be thy faith never so weake: Hast thou faith but as a grain of mustard seed, that thou canst scarcely know whether thou hast faith or no, yet if it bee true faith, there is grace and mercy enough for thee in the Lord Jesus. (Ibid., 293-294)

Hooker here places himself in the mainstream of Puritan thought, holding that even weak faith, if it be true faith as wrought by God, is saving. The assurance of salvation need not depend on the strength of faith, for even a "seed" of grace could save (Cf. Perkins 1626, I, 637-639). For Hooker this view of weak faith was almost necessarily assumed, given the great encouragement he gave when the anterior phases of contrition and humiliation could be discerned. Addressing the "poor doubter," Hooker exudes confidence.

> Do not think that God will pass by poore little ones, no he will not lose one of you, but he will in his appointed time helpe and deliver you: therefore be not troubled nor dismaied, but resolve on this and say, I shall bee delivered, and therefore let my soule be ever cheared. (Hooker 1638d, 297-298)

After handling several other objections, mainly of the sort in which the sinner claims unworthiness, Hooker concludes his treatise on the soul's union with Christ with a characteristic "do something" exhortation. An "answer" is to be returned unto the Lord. He is to be loved "in all things by all means, and at all times." The very sacrifice of Christ requires so much. The complacent are in that "scanty desire, and a few lazy wishes" will not suffice.

> Muse of him, speake for him, worke for him, and doe all for him, in all miseries and troubles, sorrowes and vexations, temptations without and terrours within; love Jesus Christ therein . . . thinke nothing too good for Christ, but love him in all things, and by all means, the Lord grant wee may. (Ibid., 307, 310, 311)

In this way the somewhat uneven volume comes to an end. The polemical nature of parts of the work, while revealing Hooker's determined zeal for theology, nevertheless give the work a different flavor then those before examined. With the anxiety of the preparatory pilgrimage eased, so was some of the metaphorical richness lost. Yet in the end, the voluntarism of Hooker remains obvious, whether the need be for humiliation, comfort, or a life characterized by a greater love for Christ. As always, the doubters are to be comforted in the all sufficiency of Christ. Yet the ominous tone is periodically sounded to the complacent, at no time more dramatic then when Hooker employs the tool of direct address. "Now tell mee Judas, is it good to be covetous now?" (Ibid., 263).

THE MAJOR MORPHOLOGICAL WORKS: SANCTIFICATION

Tracing as we are Hooker's morphology in its pre-New England formulations, the final stage represented by publication is the work of sanctification. One finds relatively scant treatment given to this theme. This is surprising, given its relevance to such a large portion of the saint's life. Surely, Hooker the pastor must have spent in his weekly preaching duties much time over matters of holiness of life. Because sanctification involved the marks by which one might by reflection gain assurance, the suggestion of Sargent Bush that Hooker probably did not slight sanctification in his *ordo salutis* as much as his published remnants may suggest can hardly be doubted (Bush 1980, 270).

The extremely rare 170 page The Soules Possession of Christ (1638) provides Hooker's main treatment of the subject. The posthumously published The Saints Dignitie and Dutie (1651) dates from Hooker's time in New England and is something of a revision of The Soules Possession. Accordingly, it will be examined below as Hooker's morphology in its final form is treated. Though on occasion in other sermons, practical matters are of course brought up, apart from The Soules Possession, only The Christians Two Chiefe Lessons (1640) qualifies as a major Hookerian work on sanctification. This evaluation is in contrast to that of Sargent Bush who in his bibliography describes the latter work, especially in its first sermon on "Self Deniall," as being closely related in subject matter to The Soules Preparation (1632) (in Williams *et al*. 1975, 408). In the eyes of the present writer, The Christians Two Chiefe Lessons constitutes a work primarily concerned with the process of sanctification.

For Hooker, the essence of sanctification is an

amendment of life that results from the impartation of righteousness. That this is the next logical stage in his morphology was foreshadowed in Hooker's careful distinctions between the imputation of righteousness and the impartation of the same, as previously delineated in The Soules Exaltation (Hooker 1638d, 139-140). As a work of grace, and because of God's persistence in that he will finally have his elect, Hooker views sanctification as inevitable. The morphology will be completed because God is the prime mover. Yet sanctification is hardly "automatic," as Hooker remains the activist, calling on his hearers to labor for holiness as they look to Christ. Thus human responsibility remains. Sanctification involves a new obedience.

> It is a work of the Spirit, whereby a man that is already justified doth by vertue of grace received bring forth fruits worthy of amendment of life. (It is a worke of the Spirit.) Ezek.36.27. I will put my Spirit within you, and cause you to walk in my statutes. (of him that is already justified) that is acquitted of his sins, and made righteous in the sight of God. (Hooker 1640a)

No Antinomian charge could be leveled against Hooker given his constant calls for an improved life. He guards against complacency, yet is careful to maintain the gracious character of the ongoing work of God (Bush 1980, 271). This double emphasis is obvious as Hooker in one of his "uses," notes that because Christ is the leader of his Church, the faithful "see what Christ saith, and follow him." He is the "Author and finisher of our faith" (Heb.12.2) and therefore the faithful look to him and are guided. The faithful one, in weakness, goes to him and says "I am thy servant, teach me to keepe thy Commandments." But on the contrary, that Christ is indeed Commander of the Lord's hosts, "it is a word of Terrour to the wicked" (Hooker 1640a, 18-19).

Practicality comes to the forefront as Hooker answers the question of the seemingly complacent one, and the objection of a poor doubter. The complacent one asks how he should know the will of God? Hooker wonders if this one really wants to know.

> See the pillar of fire, that is the word of God goe before you. Would you know whether you may buy, or sell, or bowle on the Sabbath day? Aske, would the Lord Jesus bowle, or buy or sell, on the Sabbath day? Would hee drop into Ale houses? And if thou knowest these things and wilt not reforme them, thou walkest not in the wayes of Christ. (Ibid., 28)

The poor doubter, who claims he is "weake and feeble," is encouraged to get busy, to "do something." The words are comforting, being laced as they are with assurance.

> Then plucke up those feeble hands, bee not sluggish but presse on as farre as thou canst, and looke up to Christ. the child that knowes not the way to market, when he is weary, he cries, father, father, leade mee, and then his father takes him and carryes him in his armes. Oh you little ones, you younglings in Christ; goe as fast as you can; follow your father; what Christ did performe, doe you; doe not go away
> and say I cannot pray; hast thou not the spirit of Christ, and canst thou doe nothing with it? endeavor what you can; and when you cannot, seeke to heaven and cry, my father help mee; call on your Father, and he wil carry you on Eagles wings, and though you have not then ability, you will have it after-wards. (Ibid.)

In accordance with the title of the first sermon ("Selfe-deniall") in The Christians Two Chief Lessons, and following the model of Perkins (Perkins 1626, I, 110-116), Hooker asserts that sanctification not only involves a looking to Christ for guidance, but also involves mortification as a necessary component. The believer must have no other Lord but Christ. Denying all makes one a disciple of Christ. The Christian must

"lay downe selfe . . . lay down all at Christ's feet .
. . never love them more (nor) let thy affections be
hankering after them" (Hooker 1640a, 46-47). The saint
is to recognize his redeemed condition, and talk to
himself as it were, reminding himself "ye are not your
own," (1 Cor. 6:19) and is therefore to refuse to be
subject to self as "its Master" (Ibid., 37). To be
subject to self is blatant idolatry for "a mans selfe
naturally is a God to his soule" (Ibid., 38).

In mortification, the saint puts off his
"menstruous clothes," and his "bosome abominations"
(Hooker 1638e, 24). Hooker here aptly combines
Isaiah's metaphors with that of St. Paul in Hooker's
text, "Put ye on the Lord Jesus Christ, and make no
provision for the flesh to fulfill the lusts of it"
(Romans 13:14). This "fitting" of the garment of
Christ's righteousness is a lifelong process, and the
saint strives to perfect the wearing thereof (Ibid.,
15).

Hooker is indeed the sane churchman. He proves
himself no sectarian as he rebukes those who reject the
ministry of the Church of England (Hooker 1640a, 204),
though he bemoans mere formalism (Ibid., 223-232). The
means of grace as found in the sacraments, prayer, and
the preaching of the word, are to be attended unto as
the proper vehicle of sanctification. But in all, the
saint is to look unto Christ as he is found in Holy
Scripture.

> Maintaine in thy soule the authority of the truth:
> thou seest the evill of selfe, and selfe-seeking,
> and the good of selfe-denyall, then let the
> commande-ment of God be above thee, let that be the
> supreame over thy soule, and be moved in the power
> of this. There will be a God for ever in thy
> soule, and there-fore set up the truth, and let
> that be the spring of thy actions, and this will
> crush all privy pride and secret corruptions.
> (Ibid., 63)

Sanctification plays a part in an important
question for the Puritan mind, that of assurance of

salvation. Hooker insists that assurance is indeed possible and should be sought. This follows on the plain teaching of Scripture (Psalm 14:1; John 5:13; and 2 Peter 1:10) as well as upon the promised testimony of the Spirit (Romans 8:16) (Ibid., 204). This provides a use of exhortation.

> To provoke men to use all meanes that they may be assured touching the welfare of their estates. . . If they be so earnest for earthly blessings which they must forgoe, how hot and eager should they be in pursuit of getting of an assurance of those spiritual good things which shall never be taken from us! (Ibid., 205)

But the "physician of the soul" knows that self delusion lurks at every turning of the soul. The soul may be satisfied with mere "civil" or "formal" righteousness. It may move but a "temporary professor," only having a taste of the grace that overflows from the corporate community of faith (Ibid., 214-244). All the while this poor deluded hell-bound creature may be "hoodwinked" by his own heart which is "not onely blind but also deceitful," and by the "continuall endeavor of Sathan, whereby hee laboureth nothing more then to be a lying spirit in the mouth of a mans owne heart" (Ibid., 207).

So though the way may be a bit easier than that hard preparatory journey, trials and testings are part and parcel of the way of sanctification, though now constituting "sanctifying graces."

> The text (Matthew 16:24) doth not say, let him take up his crosse and leave me, no, but take up his crosse and follow me; as who should say, persecution will stand with perseverance in obedience, Christ and a crosse accord. (Hooker 1640a, 94)

Afflictions present no ground for excuse not to follow in the way of the cross, the way of holiness. Hooker's high view of the perpetuity of the Law of God, and therefore its place in the sanctification process is obvious. Indeed the Law of God for Hooker has a primary place in his morphology due to its various "offices" of showing sin, restraining sin, revealing the need for a Savior, and giving guidelines for holy living.

> The Law bindes at all times, to all times, it is an old rule in Divinity; there is no time wherein sinne is to be granted, our condition may alter, but duty is that which God ever cals for; poverty may take away riches, but no condition should take away duty. (Hooker 1640a, 96)

No persecution or poverty, nor any time of trouble, can excuse a man from duty. Least of all does Hooker, who takes transgression very seriously, allow for such a lame excuse as "my neighbor did hinder me" (Ibid., 99).

True faith does persevere. It is determined, the way being "painefull, laborious, joyned with a most earnest using of the meanes." The way of true sanctification is marked by persistence, time being a legitimate test. Such patience will expose the fickle temporary professors of faith (Ibid., 241). The "markes" of true faith are discernible. True faith purifies the heart and sends up "strong cryes" to the throne of grace for a "filling of the heart with saving grace." This constitutes a modification of the "reflex act" as a means to assurance. Hooker shares with the more pristine Reformed faith the need to be "looking to Christ" as the objective grounds of salvation and the assurance thereof (Ibid., 251). This "looking to Christ" is a frequent refrain of Hooker's, especially in his urgings that the appointed means be attended unto.

Poor doubters can find comfort that "true faith wrestleth with doubting; and is assaulted with feare within and terrours without" (Ibid., 252). But in looking to Christ true faith finds contentment in all estates.

William Haller described the Puritan world view as involving much more than a collection of prohibitions. Rather it was a program of an active life (Haller 1938, 123). In no other Puritan does this description become more luminous than in Thomas Hooker. Sanctification was a work of God's grace. Yet the renewed will, now more than ever, was exhorted to activity. The saint is bound to be active and energetic in his pursuit of holiness. He is to be ever striving to be "fitted," that is, to be clothed with Christ (Hooker 1638e, 24, 35, 60).

One other work should be mentioned in regard to the place of sanctification in Hooker's morphology. When the transitional "implantation" volumes reached their final form as <u>The Soules Implantation Into The Naturall Olive</u> (1640), a new sermon "Spirituall Joy," appeared. This addition to the 1637 kindred volume primarily concerns itself with matters of sanctification, especially the "improvement" that is to be made even in troubled times. Its text is Habakkuk 3:17,18.

> Although the Fig-tree shall not blossome, neither shall fruit be in the vines: the labour of the Olive shall faile, and the fields shall yeeld no meat, the flocke shall be cut off from the fold, there shall be no heard in the stalls: Yet I will rejoyce in the Lord, I will joy in the God of my salvation.

Hooker calls this text "the poore mans comfort in a deare yeare" (Hooker 1640c, 295). Though beset by all troubles, if Christ and with him salvation are "come into the house," the saint is as comfortable "as Zachaeus and the Jaylor." Though losses and "crosses," are near to the heart and may threaten life itself, "God is nearer."

Hooker's Christocentric emphasis appears again, for "salvation" is nearly synonymous with Christ.

> That one word (salvation) is an epitome of all blessings, it comprehends the causes, meaning, effects, and perpetuitie of our blessedness, and absolute overthroe of the enemies; and speciallly the immediate authour of salvation, which is Christ. (Ibid., 301)

This being the case, the activist preacher in his "uses" calls "all true hearted Christians to stirre up themselves to rejoyce in God and the sure mercies of David." In so doing they are also exhorted that each one be sure of his personal apprehension of Christ that he might be able to exclaim, "he is the God of my salvation" (Ibid., 302, 305).

But predictably, the double prong comes. For the Christian, melancholy is culpable and therefore finds reproof from the psychologist-preacher,

> It is utterly a fault in Christian, if they be melancholy and dejected, because of crosse years, bad harvest, losse in that or any other kinde, casualties, calamities, or other evils, that come by the hand of God or man . . . as if you had no hope in God. (Hooker 1640c, 304)

Prescriptions differ according to the malady. For the faithful and active Christian who is nevertheless encountering great difficulties, Hooker urges patience with continued activity.

> It were unreasonable to sow in September and look to reap in October, No, stay till the month of harvest, and then see what blessing God will give (Ibid., 311).

But the slothful saint is exhorted more vigorously.

> My brethren be awakened from security: you finde your evidences for heaven somewhat muddy, and that you need renew your covenant with God, and Oh that you could get the old feelings and the comforts that you sometimes had! To do that, renew your repentance: sow a little more though in teares; digest all well, because you do all in hope, and with a promise that those who sow in teares shall reap in joy. (Ibid., 320)

The important part played by the affections is obvious

as is also the necessary underlying covenant commitment to Christ. To look to him in faith, and to continue to press on, these for Hooker in large measure constitute the gracious work of sanctification, as Christ is being "put on."

VOLUMES SUPPLEMENTARY TO THE MAJOR MORHOLOGICAL WORKS

The present section is intended as a brief overview of Hooker's "lesser works," especially those that have not found treatment above in relation to any of the stages of the morphology. Some works will be noticed merely by summary statements, while others will be drawn upon where they provide aid to a proper understanding of Hooker's morphology,
Two early Hooker sermons, "The Church's Deliverances" and "The Carnal Hypocrite" have much in common and were both probably preached in 1629. They were published in 1638 as the first two of the Foure Learned And Godly Treatises. The final two sermons of this 1638 volume were examined above due to their close connection with the second stage of Hooker's morphology, The Soules Humiliation. Unlike those final two sermons, the two presently to be examined have been reproduced in Williams et al. 1975, 60-123.
Because "The Church's Deliverances" was probably preached on Guy Fawkes Day (November 5) of 1626, it clearly has the tone of an occasional sermon. Though its theme is the gracious providence of God, tension is apparent throughout as allusions are made to the sorry state of Protestantism on much of the continent, especially in view of the ongoing Thirty Years War. With England itself, God appears to be losing patience. Thus the sermon portrays a real urgency as Hooker seeks to evoke fear of God's wrath. This is evident in his choice of scriptural text, Judges 10:13: "Wherefore I will deliver you no more." Yet his complementary practice of nurturing assurance and confidence is present as well.

If God be the deliverer of his people, then it is a

great ground of confidence to bear up the hearts of poor souls in affliction. If God will deliver, who can destroy? If God will keep, who can hurt? (in Williams 1975, 70)

This is the kind of confidence that Hooker especially put forth in his discussion of justification in <u>The Soules Exaltation</u>. The preacher wants this confidence to issue in action. Since the Lord has so wondrously delivered, Hooker asks introspectively, "What will you then do for God again?" Voluntarism is in the forefront of this urgent plea, "Make God on your side and all will be well." As the war raged, as plots from the Evil One were discovered "just in time," the saint was to know that deliverance was not in men, nor in policy, power, or shipping, but only in the Lord (Ibid., 71, 72).

On the other hand, those who boast in wickedness are only readying themselves for the slaughter. Watchfulness is enjoined that the saint not grow senseless and numb in an ungodly course as many cry "peace, peace" (Ibid., 85, 87). So it is that Hooker's double prong never allows even the saint to become too comfortable, especially in such a sermon as this with its national concern. This follows as Hooker reminds his people that corporate destruction will affect even the godly (Ibid., 76).

"The Carnal Hypocrite" likewise reflects concern for the national welfare. But here Hooker more directly addresses the difficulty of pursuing holiness in a society filled with temptation. He urges an open and unashamed profession of godliness. To illustrate the nature of hypocrisy, Hooker invokes Machiavelli who could speak of virtue easily because he took no pain nor "disquiet" in the practice thereof. By contrast, godliness involves the possession of truth inwardly and the expression of holiness outwardly.

(It) implieth that gracious frame of spirit whereby the heart is disposed and the soule of a Christian is fitted to express some gracious work outwardly. For what the oil is to the wheeels of a clock, it makes them run glibber, so godliness to the soul; when the soul is oiled and anointed therewith, it is fitted to perform any good duty. (Ibid., 92, 93)

The mere "form of godliness," of Hooker's text (2 Timothy 3:5) is an outward show like that of a "stage-player." But the word of terror comes from this preacher so concerned with heart religion.

But when God plucks him off the stage of the world and his body drops into the grave, and his soul goes to hell, then it appears that he had not the power of godliness; he was only a stage-player, a stage professor. (Ibid., 93)

In Hooker's *The Soules Possession*, his major work on sanctification, the inevitability but not automatic nature of sanctification was taught. But perhaps here, even better then in that volume, does Hooker make his point.

Look as it is with a clock: if the wheels run right, the clock cannot but strike. So it is with the trees of the field: if there be sap in the root, it will discover itself in the branches by the fruit and greenness of them; though it be hidden in the winter, yet it will appear in the spring and in the summer.
So it is in the souls of God's servants. The frame of a man's heart, that is like the wheels of a clock. If a man have an humble heart, he will have a holy life; it will make the hand work, the eye see, the foot walk, and the actions be proportionable unto the disposition of the heart. (Ibid., 94)

This activism and the inevitability of sanctification flow from Hooker's concept of the radical nature of regeneration as "the power of grace . . . imprinted upon any soul, it will break through and make way for itself" (Ibid., 95). Because godliness does indeed have a "form," Antinomian tendencies are absent from the preaching of this high Calvinist.

For Hooker, one who hates the outward form of godliness hates the very power of godliness. On the contrary, the path to assurance is partly by reflection. It comes quite naturally as true godliness is actually practiced. By heeding the preacher's call to action, one provides for himself the evidence of God's gracious work.

> If you desire any evidence to your souls or testimony to your hearts that God hath wrought grace in you, then show it in your lives. Express the virtues of him that hath called you from death to life. (Ibid., 99)

Admittedly the church consists of a mixed multitude. But Hooker shows himself to be no separatist. "We confess this fault; let it lie where it is; we cannot reform it. We can only mourn for it, and that God will accept" (Ibid., 111; cf. 1640a, 204). Time will do its duty of exposing the hypocrites in the church. Vigilance to one's own life is necessary.

> The lawyer goes up to London in term time, but he hath a vacation time too. So sinners have their vacation time; the drunkard, usurer, adulterer have their vacation times. But so soon as the term-time comes, so soon as the occasion is afforded and the opportunity offered, they fall to their old trade. (in Williams 1975, 106; cf. Hooker 1640a, 241)

While addressing the well known troubles in the English church and commonwealth in his Danger of Desertion (1641), Hooker also expressed his strong desire for the spiritual health of his hearers. To such the present comments must be limited. The sermon has as one of its purposes to deflate the egotistical confidence of Hooker's hearers. In this sense it is quite typical. The intensity of the sermon gives it an apocalyptic tone.

> Plead with God: And though his hand be up, and his

sword drawne; yet suffer him not to destroy; but to sheath it in the blood of our enemies. (Hooker 1641, 15)

But Hooker fears that this will not happen because there is a lack of heart religion in England. "No man stirs up himselfe to lay hold upon God (Isaiah 64.7) . . . thus we play mock-holy-day with God."

> God is going, his glory is departing, England hath seene her best daye, and now God is packing up his Gospell, because no body will buy his wares, nor come to his price. Oh lay hands on God! and let him not goe our of your coasts, he is going, stop him, and let not thy God depart, lay siege against him with humble and hearty closing with him. (Ibid.)

The individual must prepare room for God for he is a King. He must be given consent: "let him have his will." Hooker stands aghast at complacency. "Our God is going, and doe you sit still on your beds?" (Ibid., 3, 7, 13).

This jeremiad is one Hooker work that does not exude confidence. All here is an urgent call for action because God can "unchurch a people." He can still be God without England. If the people are weary of God, Hooker says "get thee down to hell." Hooker lets it be know that he does desire spiritual health in his hearers. If their desires are holy, he assures them that they will be fulfilled by God's favor through the ordinances. But if any tire of attending to the means, he ought to know what a terror it is when "a merciful God doth show himselfe unmercifull" (Ibid., 7, 11, 19).

"The Faithful Covenanter," which was preached in the Dedham pulpit of John Rogers in 1629, is of the same genre as the two sermons described above. Personal faithfulness in the troubled times is everywhere urged in this work which has received previous treatment in this dissertation as the earliest Chelmsford period works were examined.

Three additional Hooker sermons were published in 1638 under the simple title, <u>Three Godly Sermons</u>.

The Work was reissued during the same year, in exactly the same form apart from a new title page which gave the work the barest of titles, Three Sermons.[1] In 1645 an expanded edition, with different pagination was issued as The Saints Guide In Three Treatises.

In an initial sermon entitled "The Wrath of God Against Sinners," certain light is cast on Hooker's preparationism as it related to the important question of just what man, before he is in a state of grace, can do. Though one comes from reading even Hooker's earliest works such as The Soules Preparation (1632) with a necessarily deflated view of man's spiritual abilities, still Hooker's critics both then and now, have charged him with, or praised him for, attributing to man a theretofore unheard of amount of ability. But Hooker was a high Calvinist who also was a common sense observer of the human condition. He offered this answer to the question, "Is it in our power to make the word effectual?"

> No, but it is in your power to doe what you are able to doe; your leggs may as well carry you to the Word, as to an Alehouse; your ears may heare the Word as well as Songs; you may reade good books as well as Play bookes. Do what you are able and cry to God, and see what he will doe . . . the Lord may give what he will and deny what he will, but destruction is from thy selfe, thou hast free will to sinne. (Hooker 1638h, 28-29).

It is significant that in regard to this last statement, Hooker never speaks conversely regarding the will. Who can dispute that the ungodly may decide simply to attend morning prayers, and be taken thereunto by the same legs that carried him the evening before to the local tavern? Any that read Hooker's corpus at-large know that he insists upon the sovereign working of

---

[1] The 1638 volume is rare, the copy at the Speer Library in Princeton possibly being the only extant copy in this country.

the Spirit of God, in conjunction with the Word, if spiritual profit is to be gained. By attending to the means, one sets himself in the "environment" in which the gracious strivings of God's Spirit are to be found. Because the sermon was considered the primary means whereby the Spirit does his effectual work, Hooker constantly calls his hearers to an attendance to the same. The sinner is to go to the meeting house seeking to have his heart subdued by sovereign grace. Yet even in the proper attendance to the means, the carnal heart resists the work of conviction and cannot endure to have its sins removed (Hooker 1638h, 30, 39).

But in such resistance, the one who will strive with God's "striving Spirit," is utterly culpable. Thus the warning, "take heed of taking up of Armes against the Spirit of God" (Ibid., 75). In the spirit of Ramistic dichotomies, and in predictable fashion, Hooker also warns against the one who too quickly assumes his safety. One might reason in syllogistic fashion, that "since Christ came to save sinners, and I recognize myself to be in that dreadful company, indeed deliverance is an easy thing." Expressing sentiments painful to the familists, and anticipating the 1637 New England crisis, Hooker revolts against "cheap grace." "The truth is that Christ came to save sinners, and not to save them merely, but to sanctify them" (Ibid., 85).

The third and most famous of the sermons in this volume, "The Plantation of the Righteous," has as its Biblical text Psalm 1:3. Much of the sermon is concerned with an extended exhortation to proper use of time. Insufficient excuses aside, the reality is that the saints of God in the process of sanctification waste much time.

> So that the proofe is plaine, that the Saints of God must have their opportunities for the performance of duties. (Hooker 1638h, 117)

There is a seasonableness to be considered in the performance of duty. But Hooker notes that this might be an excuse for the complacent to neglect such duties. Taking note of St. Matthew 6:34, the sluggish are to consider that today may indeed be a good day (Ibid., 120), and hereafter "circumstances and occasions" may not concur for the performance of a particular duty (Ibid., 118, 121-122).

Since duties are to be taken up so to be helpful to one another (Ibid., 124), an introspective "use" is offered.

> See and bee humbled for what hath been amisse in us; let each man lay his hand on his mouth and bewaile and look backe add view our former course, to consider the opportunities and seasons we have had. (Ibid., 134)

So in characteristic fashion, the Christian life involves a checking and a re-checking of the profession against the realities. Even in this a Ramistic influence is mirrored in the constant comparison of perceptions and realities. The danger of self-delusion always lurks. Though no life is as blessed as that of the saint, nevertheless his is a halting and arduous one.

> The life and conversation of a Christian is a marvelous, tedious, and laborious life that will marveilously (sic) put a man to it, if ever he come to be sincere, and to walk uprightly with the Lord in a holy conversation of life. (Hooker 1638h, 136)

In summary, Three Godly Sermons (1638) is largely a work concerned with the sanctification process though there are certain "lapses" into Hooker's consuming area of concern, preparationism. In these, culpable activities are ominously rebuked while orthodox Calvinistic anthropological convictions are carefully safeguarded.

Hooker's views regarding the roles and authorities of the faculties have not been well understood by students of his works. He indeed recognized a hierarchical structure among the faculties, as understood in his day. The Patterne Of Perfection (1640) contained a clear statement of Hooker's understanding of the ordo within that hierarchy. The preeminence of the will in the human psychological makeup is obvious.

> Now the faculty of the Will, is like the hand, that puts away or takes any thing. The will is like an unruly horse, that casts his rider; I will do what I will do though reason crosse it. (Hooker 1640b, 61)

Much of this work is an examination of pre-lapsarian Adam as a "pattern of perfection." The work, which often resorts to a catechetical format, concerns the nature of man, the imago dei, and matters of the soul, holiness, righteousness, free will, and the covenants. The pre-lapsarian man is described as to the true freedom of his will and the imago dei which resided in his understanding, will, affections, and body.

While in "innocency" the faculties operated in a much different fashion as compared to sinful man with his will acting as an "unruly horse." Although Hooker's picture is one of harmony and consonance, his faculty structures remain obvious. He does not approach the monistic psychology that Edwards sought even for fallen man. Hooker describes the faculties as they operated in Adam before the fall.

> (There was) sweet agreement, and submission which they did yeeld unto holy will, and right reason. The Understanding directed what should bee done, the Will imbraced that, and the Affections yeelded serviceably to the command of Reason and Holinesse. (Hooker 1640b, 149-150, 151)

The Patterne of Perfection contains a standard discussion of the "covenant of works" made with Adam. But Hooker uses this as a prod to action. If the "ideal man" was bound to obedience, certainly so are we. The encouragement to "poore doubters" that Hooker gives is the the closest thing he offers that might cause concern to the more doctrinaire of his observers.

> We learne what care to use in walking in obedience; that is that which gives God contentment. Do as thou canst, and God will accept of what thou dost, if it be sincere. Wee must not think to performe exactly what Adam did, but to endeavor what we can. (Hooker 1640b, 228)

    This voluntaristic statement might indeed seem to reduce godliness to a cooperative effort between man and God who only requires some semblance of human determination to be all that one can be. But given his entire corpus, the word "endeavor" is an important operative word here. The Christian life is not one without strivings and toil. It is a laborious life calling for constant introspection designed to discover sincerity or the lack thereof (Hooker 1638h, 136).
    The "self-denial" theme, prominent in The Christians Two Chiefe Lessons, appears also here.

> A man must part with all his sinnes and corruptions, for a mans sinnes will never doe him any good but hurt, and therefore he ought to forsake them. (Hooker 1640b, 264)

    Bonhoeffer's "cheap grace" terminology was employed above to describe Hooker's fears. The transportation of this phrase back across the centuries seems fitting given Hooker's use of a "going to market" theme. One must go purposefully to buy.

> Because the meanes of grace and salvation is a thing of as great excellencie and price as can bee; therefore in reason wee should lay downe a price for them. For the better the commodity is, all wise men will lay down answerably. (Ibid., 297)

    It is the succor and Lordship of Christ that is to be sought above all else. The voluntaristic sentiments here are obvious. But Hooker urges no life of ease as a result of a crisis commitment of faith, but rather a life of obedience under the Lordship of Christ.

> This is our misery, we stand puddling our selves for a little honor, and for a little riches; go (I say) and buy the Lordship, and then all will be made sure to thee. (Ibid., 303; Hooker 1638h, 85)

The latter portion of The Patterne of Perfection consists of three "miscellanies" primarily related to the realm of sanctification. Only certain psychological insights and Hooker's handling of cases of conscience will here receive treatment. In "The Prayer of Faith" (James 1:6), Hooker explains, with acute insight into the soul's windings, what it means to "waver."

> A distressed, distrustfull staggering heart need nothing to vexe and trouble it; because it wil be racked and tormented in it selfe in restlesse disquiet: for such a man is like unto the sea waves, whirling now this way, tossing againe that way. Feares and hopes are the hangmen of the heart: Hope sayes, It may bee, and Feare says, I suspect it wil not bee; thus a man becomes like a wave. (Hooker 1640b, 320-321)

The preacher seeks to prod such wavering ones by a "use" of "terrour." But conversely, God's people should see how highly they should "price" faith (Ibid., 336-337, 338).

The doubting theme appears again in "A Preparative To The Lord's Supper," as Hooker attempts to explain how one may know if he has a title to the Lord's Supper. Certain requirements are set forth.

> He must have these graces, Faith, Repentance, Knowledge and Love; for without these no man can receive good from the Sacrament. (Ibid., 369)

But this does not mean that doubters are thereby automatically excluded. Rather, the one who can admit his own doubts is to seek to have them removed. The place of the minister in handling cases of conscience as a physician to the soul is given a high place by Hooker.

> Openly, nakedly, plainly, and to the full hee is to lay open his estate unto some faithful, judicious, and holy-hearted Minister; and if upon sincere relation of his estate, the Minister, out of the Word, shall answer all the objections that he can make against himselfe. . . . Then he is bound to submit to the Word, and to address himselfe unto the partaking of the sacrament. (Ibid., 370)

The tenor of this sermon as a whole is that full assurance is not necessary for access to the "table of the Lord." Poor doubters may come, and Hooker, true to his common "judgment of charity," encourages them to do so. In this he does not seek to deprecate the sacrament but only to utilize the spiritual nourishment therein available to those even of weak faith.

Some may insist that they must not attend to the sacrament by reason of sin. In view of the warnings of St. Paul in this regard, Hooker allows abstinence as proper. But the activist and probing preacher reminds such that it is by reason of sin that he does not come. None should find comfort in their not coming.

The final "miscellanie" contains seventeen "markes" or tests by which one may evaluate the soundness of his own faith. These marks provide a handy "checklist," but given their brevity and standard nature, this "miscellanie" is one of Hooker's more unremarkable pieces. Yet "marke xv" provides the characteristic Hookerian emphasis on examining the interior life. The urgency of self-examination is thereupon insisted.

> If thou makest conscience of secret sinnes which none eye sees; as a hard heart . . . if thou lookest not so much to the matter of good duties, as to the manner, if they bee done in truth and sincerity.
> Use often to try and search thy heart and all thy actions. Take an often account of thy life, concern-ing thy progress in the course of godlinesse: for want of this examination, many live and die hypocrites, and know it not, but suppose

their case is good. 1 Chron. 29:17; Rev. 2:19; 2 Tim. 3:7; Ps. 119:59; 1 Tim. 4:15; Gal 1:14; Heb. 5:2. (Hooker 1640b, 391-391)

The heart needs to be examined over and again to discover whether it really desires Christ "for his holinesse sake." The soul which does will find contentment even amid shame, disgrace, or persecution.

The year 1638 was truly a bounteous one as to the appearance in print of Hookerian sermonic material. Another volume from that year is a singly bound sermon published under the title of The Sinners Salvation. This is a relatively rare little work consisting of a seventy-three page sermon on the answer to the cry of the Philippian jailor from Acts 16:31. The initial fifteen pages of the volume provide an extended evangelistic call on the part of the voluntarist preacher. Hooker insists that the question of the jailor, "What must I do to be saved," is the most important one a man may ask, yet it is indeed a "hard question to ask."

> The Lord was driven to terrifie him with feare and terror, and astonishment, before hee would aske this question, what hee might doe to be saved. (Hooker 1638c, 5)

After Hooker outlines the ingredient parts of the proper answer to this hard question which include the act of believing, the proper object of faith (Christ), the blessed effect (salvation), and the communication or spreading of this effect (the believers household) he entertains an objection. This is an answer that seems easy. Why should Hooker insist that both the question and the answer are "hard" ones (Ibid., 12)? This sets the stage for Hooker to "open up" what faith is.

> There are many things to be done before a man can beleeve, give mee leave to insist upon them. (Ibid., 15)

Of course without waiting for permission, the author begins to explicate the main themes of the sermon, four antecedents to faith. These requisite antecedents provide a convenient summary of Hooker's preparationist views. Hooker first insists that there must be a knowledge of one's transgression of the Law, "the Law must kill him" (Ibid., 17). In the second place, the sinner,

> . . . must be emptied, and evacuated of himselfe, he must be wrought upon so as to be sensible of his own nothingnesse . . . that he is not able to set one step forward towards his own deliverance. (Ibid., 18-19)

With unblemished Calvinism as formulated in the federalist mold, Hooker goes on to note that man is as unable to keep the condition of the "covenant of grace" as he is unable to keep the condition of the "covenant of works" (Ibid., 20). A third required antecedent of faith is that there must be a "dogmaticall knowledge of all the Gospell of Christ." Grand truths such as the incarnation and God the Father's propitiation must be grasped for "true faith cannot dwell in an ignorant heart" (Ibid., 22,24). A fourth antecedent involves Hooker's insistence upon the Spirit-Word connection. The sinner must be taught from above even "more than all the preachers of the world can teach him" (Ibid., 25).

To this preparationist preacher, these antecedents are absolutely necessary given human "deadness" and inability to submit or come to the Lord. The human soul, carried along by its own "windings" and "shifts," will "content itself with vaine conceits and false delusions of Sathan, than with Christ itself" (Ibid., 26, 27, 31-32).

Considering the entire Hooker corpus, it is in this little work that Hooker most directly attempts to relate his voluntaristic view of faith to his Reformed theology. These four antecedents "hem in" the soul. But Hooker insists that this is necessary because a man must be "allured" because "faith is not a compulsive act, but

a free act of the heart" (Ibid., 32, 33). This supplies Hooker's understanding of the "freedom of the will," one which he has imbibed from the standard Augustinian and Reformed views.
As might be expected, and contrary to the views of John Cotton, Hooker denies that conversion involves a violent seizure. For Hooker the "reformation of the soul" is begun in the preparatory process. With sentiments that would disturb Cotton, Hooker notes,

> This vilifying of the creature is in part begun before faith comes in, because that Christ will not come into a soule that is not worthy of him. (Hooker 1638c, 45)

Preparation, which involves the removal of the stubbornness of heart is insisted upon because Christ will not "enter by violence" into a heart that is "not fit" for him (Ibid., 48).
Hooker's "uses" clearly demonstrate his voluntaristic stance. The sinner must "labour to see that faith is a hard thing to attain." Once faith comes, the "hardest is done and the worst is over." True faith is a "rare" thing which carnal men hate. One must not suppose that it will suddenly come by "one sermon" or "one minister." An introspective prod is thrust forward.

> . . . hadst thou faith without rending and tearing of thy bowels, without being emptied of thy selfe, with-out being touched by the Law? (Ibid., 69)

In summary, the much neglected The Sinners Salvation briefly but lucidly expresses Hooker's preparationist theology with its utterly requisite antecedents to faith. The material itself, dating from Hooker's English career, early sets him on a "collision course" with the one who became something of a New England rival, none other than John Cotton.
The present writer has purposed to analyze the entire Hooker corpus that a better understanding of Hooker's morphology of conversion might be gained.

Given this stated goal, only The Survey of the Summe of Church Discipline (1648) and The Covenant of Grace Opened (1649), being more polemical in nature, lie outside the scope of this study. Here it remains only briefly to survey the remainder of the writings from that feverish publication year of 1638.

Spiritual Thirst (1638) is a singly bound seventy-seven page sermon on John 7:37, "If any man thirst, let him come unto me, and drinke." This rare little work stresses the all-sufficiency of Christ alone to "satisfie spiritual thirst." Hooker insists that this "thirst" is a component part of preparation, wrought in man during the "fitting" process (Williams et al. 1975, 406).

The Stay of The Faithful (1638) was bound with "The Properties of an Honest Heart," the latter being a fifty-three page handbook for the practice of introspection. In the one hundred page first sermon of the volume, Hooker stresses the all encompassing providence of God. Internal evidence clearly marks the sermon as dating from the turbulent 1620's in England. The sentiments of the work would later be reflected in the Westminster Confession of Faith (V,vii) where those divines affirmed:

> As the providence of God doth in general, reach to all creatures; so after a most special manner, it taketh care of his church, and disposeth all things to the good thereof.

Hooker's briefer statement is that "the reason for all God's providence in the world is the church" (Hooker 1638f, 39).

Unlike the Danger of Desertion, this work is of a calmer character, being less apocalyptic in tone. The Christian is to rest in the providence of God as he is humbled by the knowledge of its all encompassing scope. The very "mystery" of providence is to humble the Christian (Ibid., 41). Because England is indeed seeing such troubled times, the activist preacher urges his hearers to "seeke the Lord," and to "frame your hearts to such a milde and meek spirit, that you may adorne the

Gospel of Christ" (Ibid., 89, 95). This section has analyzed Hooker's "lesser works" as they relate to his morphology of conversion. Whether in the jeremiad-like "The Carnal Hypocrite" and "The Church's Deliverance," the evangelistic The Sinners Salvation, or in the introspective Three Sermons, Hooker's concern is for "heart religion." His fellow Englishmen seem to care little that "God is going" from their land. They seem only to be playing religious games. Our author insists that Christ came both to save and to sanctify sinners (Hooker 1638h, 85). Regeneration if it be real, will flower in sanctification. The Christian life is one of strivings and toil and along its entire path lurks the danger of self-delusion. By reflection the sinner is to check and recheck the reality of his spiritual condition against his profession.

CHAPTER FOUR:
HOOKER'S PREPARATIONIST THEOLOGY AS FORMULATED
IN HIS WRITINGS FROM THE ANTINOMIAN PERIOD AND BEYOND

The Antinomian crisis of 1637, with the "prophetess" defaming the greater part of New England's clergymen, threatened to topple the very authority structures of the Bay Colony. The context and outcome of the controversy have been briefly overviewed in the biographical section above. Details can be easily traced elsewhere, especially in works by Battis (1962), Hall (1968), and Larzar Ziff (1962). Perry Miller, in his "Preparation For Salvation" (1943), has shown that preparationist theology as championed by Hooker, was at the center of the Antinomian storm. Indeed it was the "hidden issue" in the crisis which saw the two theological "giants" of the day, Cotton and Hooker, in direct opposition to one another.

This portion of the study is designed to examine the significant works of Hooker that owe their origin to the period of the controversy itself, and also to examine Hooker's morphology in its final form as presented in the Application of Redemption (1656). A judgment will be made as to any "tailoring" of Hooker's views as a result of the Antinomian controversy. Four major works will here receive treatment: The Saints Dignitie And Dutie (1651); The Application of Redemption (Books I-VIII, 1656); The Application of Redemption (Books IX-X, 1656); and A Comment On Christ's Last Prayer (1656).

Thomas Hooker served with Peter Bulkeley as a co-moderator for the synod of ministers that convened on August 30, 1637, in Boston. He therefore was all too painfully aware of the intricate issues of the controversy, made even more difficult by John Cotton's disturbing habit of providing elusive answers to his inquisitors (Battis 1962, 163-164). In pre-synod private councils, the majority of ministers expressed their convictions that conversion was not normally a "violent seizure" as Cotton maintained, but often came in stages leading to the embrace of Christ and his benefits by faith.

Also of particular interest to these Augustinian voluntarists was Cotton's view of the relationship and order that existed between faith, union with Christ, and justification. Cotton somewhat downplayed the instrumental role of faith, and maintained that union with Christ preceded faith's embrace of Christ (Battis 1962, 163). For a brief time during the three week proceedings of the synod, Cotton even maintained that "God may bee said to justifie me before the habit, or act of Faith, and the habit is the effect of my Justification" (Ibid.). To the relief of the other ministers, Cotton returned eventually to a more moderate position as to the relationship of faith and justification.

Other areas of concern included the question of to what degree, if at all, can sanctification be an evidence of justification, the differences between the covenant of works and the covenant of grace, and the usefulness of self examination and grieving over sin.

THE SAINTS DIGNITIE AND DUTIE (1651)

To this point no examination has been made of The Saints Dignitie and Dutie. This has been owing not only to its late and posthumous date of publication, but also to this writer's view that the sermonic material contained therein is later than that heretofore examined.

Frank Shuffelton, in his 1972 dissertation, "The Light of the Western Churches: The Career of Thomas Hooker," appears to have been the first to suggest a connection between The Saints Dignite and Duty and the Antinomian controversy. Shuffelton suggested that this work was written, along with A Comment Upon Christ's

Last Prayer (1656), several years after the crisis and that both works were designed to stamp out any lingering Antinomian sentiments. For Shuffelton, The Saints Dignitie and Dutie represents a unified series of sermons whose ultimate purpose was to refute any Antinomian contention that works of sanctification were irrelevant in the redemption process (Shuffelton 1977, 258).

Taking this lead, Sargent Bush has now provided an extensive analysis in which he convincingly argues that the work belongs, both in its origin of thought and in its actual formulation, to the immediate temporal and intellectual context of the controversy (although actual publication came years later) (Bush 1980, 78-95).

John Winthrop's A Short Story of the Rise, Reign, and Ruine of the Antinomians (1644) was prefaced by Thomas Weld who glowingly spoke of the many "antidotes" put forth by faithful ministers against the Antinomian heresy.[1] It appears, especially based on the internal evidence as articulated by Bush, that the seven sermons of The Saints Dignitie and Dutie represent the type of "antidote" specified by Thomas Weld. These sermons appear to have been preached in Boston, possibly in August of 1637 or shortly thereafter. As will be demonstrated below, each of the major issues in the Antinomian controversy receives some degree of treatment in the 1651 volume.

Finally, by way of introduction to the work, notice should be taken of its preface, signed simply by a "T.S." Though he died two years before the publication of the volume, most readers have concluded that the author of the preface is none other than Thomas Shepard (Walker 1891, 193; Bush 1980, 79). Bush wonders if Shepard, possessing the manuscript of his father-in-law, may have edited out any overly explicit references to the Antinomian controversy (Bush 1980, 79-80). Such may have been done for trans-Atlantic considerations in the 1640's, without negating the basic nature of the

---

[1] Weld was a co-prosecutor of Anne Hutchinson at her trial (cf. Hall 1968, 212; McGiffert 1972, 65).

book which consistently runs counter to Antinomian sentiments. The author of the preface "To The Reader," makes it clear that the subject matter concerns the place of works in the life of the saint, the relationship between faith and justification, the need for an active faith and the value of self-inspection.[1] Adopting the conclusions of Bush as to the social context of this work, it clearly is Hooker's fullest and most careful treatment of the central issues in the gravest crisis that afflicted the first generation Puritans of New England.

The title page itself, including as it does the Scriptural text, Hebrews 10:38, "Now the just shall live by faith, but if any man draw back, my soul shall have no pleasure in him," may have been carefully chosen with Antinomianism in mind (Bush 1980, 82).

The first sermon, which has Titus 2:14 for its text, clearly contains the emphasis that redemption was wrought by Christ not only to justify a people, but also that they might be a holy people, "zealous of good works." To embrace Christ as Savior is also to recognize his Lordship.

> To beleeve in Christ then, is nothing else but for a man to goe out of himself, and to receive the Lord Christ in all his Offices, to be to us in particular,
> a King to govern us, a Prophet to teach us, and a Priest to make intercession for us. (Hooker 1651, 3)

This counters the Antinomian sentiment that godliness may be irrelevant to the question of whether or not one possessed saving grace.

In an earthy simile, Hooker stresses the need

---

[1] The "double prong" so characteristic of Hooker, is captured by "T.S" who notes that "those that will not sweetly be drawn by the cords of love shall bee violently surprised with the chains of wrath (in Hooker 1651, "To The Reader").

for the Christian to be continually purged. The sanctification process is likened to the "scum" that a good housewife takes from the top of a boiling pot. Whenever it arises, she takes these impurities off and throws them away (Hooker 1651, 4-5). Not only does life involve purgings, which might be regarded as passive, but these also have an active "propertie." This conviction is far from the Antinomian way of thinking.

> Where ever there is faith, it is working. Faith is not an idle grace; it is not a fancie or an opinion that Christ hath died for us, and there is the end, but it is a working grace, where ever there is faith, there is work, and what work is it? it is a work of love. (Hooker 1651, 5)

This comment by Hooker on Galatians 5:6 "Faith works by love," reminds one once again just how detestable was passivity to Hooker. Hooker's voluntarism is of the Augustinian strain, not the scholastic intellectualist variety.[1]

As to the ransom price, the sinner can do nothing, but "in the point of deliverie of ourselves from under iniquitie, we must do a great deal" (Hooker 1651, 37-38). Only by the Spirit of Christ and the grace of Christ are any delivered. Yet, Hooker insists, we must "labor" and Christ will help us. One wonders whether Hooker may suspect the Antinomian position to be a cloak for sluggishness.

> Christians are miserably guiltie of being under the power of iniquitie, much more then they might, because they are lazie and idle, and they do not labour to deliver themselves from under the

---

[1] For this important distinction and as to how Augustinian voluntarism could combat both idle scholastic intellectualizing on the one hand, and Arminian moralizing on the other, see Fiering 1972, 515-558.

remainder of iniquitie. (Hooker 1651, 39)

But conversely, no hint of Arminianizing is allowed to stand either, as Hooker balks at any suggestion that anything can be added to the redemption of Christ, especially by those to whom "slaverie to sin is of the bodie and soul both" (Hooker 1651, 40).

John Cotton had driven a large, almost absolute wedge between "grace and works" (Hall 1968, 97-98). Hooker's text is carefully chosen to combine the two concepts. While ever holding both justification and sanctification to be gracious, Hooker nevertheless pleads, "labour to have in your souls this grace of faith" (Hooker 1651, 21). Years before, Hooker had rejected the doctrine of the "Anabaptists" and "specially the Familists, who think it unprofitable for a beleever to trouble himself for his sinnes" (Hooker 1638d, 181).

"The Blessed Inhabitant," the second sermon in the volume, is a rather direct attack upon several tenets of Antinomianism. Especially in focus is the Antinomianian view that self-trial is of little value. Hooker repeatedly advocates self-trial (Hooker 1651, 55, 57, 58, et passim). A good and sober examination is urged upon his listeners.

> Here you have a cleer looking-glasse, wherein you may be able to judge of the faces, of the face and temper of your souls. I beseech you consider it well, and the Lord set it home upon your hearts; either you have Christ in you, or you have him not in you; If Christ be in you, then you have this imperfect death of sin, and the life of righteousnesse; but if you have not this, then Christ is not in you. Be exhorted therefore I beseech you to try yourselves by this touchstone. (Hooker 1651, 57-58)

By reason of union with Christ, there is a death to sin and a life of righteousness. For Hooker, this is very clear from his text, Romans 8:10, and he insists that though expositors carry the text this way and that, the doctrine remains, "In whosoever Christ is, there is a death of sin and a life of righteousnesse" (Hooker 1651, 53-54). Thus, a basis for assurance, based on reflex, is established.

> The death of sin and the life of righteousness, they are the Evidences of Christs being in us, the evidences of the goodness of our estates; therefore the more these are, the more our comfort be, and we shall make more sure our calling and election. (Hooker 1651, 76)

In similar fashion, Hooker had concluded the first sermon by noting that assurance can be gained by the experiential knowledge that one loves Christ above all else (Ibid., 43).

This constant self-trial in itself would be odious enough for Hutchinsonians, but Hooker's emphasis on the Law clearly branded him as a "legal preacher." For Hooker, the Law of God was to be the measure in the process of introspection. He everywhere grants that sin is only "imperfectly" dead (Hooker 1651, 50, 56-58), yet the life of righteousness is characterized by "an agreement of the heart to the whole Law of God" (Hooker 1651, 63).

So it is that in the third sermon is found Hooker's fullest answer to the charge that he preached a "covenant of works." "Grace Magnified, or the Privileges of Those that are Under Grace," is based on Romans 6:14. The over-arching theme of this sermon is that grace puts one in communion with Christ who then enables as to the performance of Christian duty.

The "Law" in Hooker's text, "You are not under the Law but under grace," is understood by Hooker not to denote the Decalogue, but rather the "covenant of works," that is, that made "with us before the fall with Adam in paradise." This "Law" orders, and demands obedience, but gives no power to obey (Hooker 1651, 107, 108). All mankind stands condemned thereby, but grace, delivereth us from under the curse, and fetcheth us out of condemnation. . . and give us dispositions inward, answerable to the outward commands of the Law of God. (Hooker 1651, 112)

But that grace enables is no reason to be idle. Hooker, stressing that God's grace provides "no incouragement to lazie Christians," calls upon his hearers to use the means and therein find God's promised help (Hooker 1651, 83). His last use of the doctrine is a pastoral application that there is indeed "consolation to all God's children." The constant refrain of the sermon is that what God has bidden his people to do, "hee by his promise hath undertaken to make thee able to perform" (Hooker 1651, 90).

In "Wisdomes Attendants: Or the Voice of Christ To Be Obeyed" (Proverbs 8:32), Christ is seen as wisdom personified and therefore the proper source of spiritual wisdom. This being the case, the question of authority, seemingly so threatened in 1637, comes into focus. The means are to be faithfully attended to and in them Christ is to be sought. Over the multifarious voices being sounded Christ is to be heard.

Howsoever we sometimes heare the counsell of others, and hearken to the voyce of the Minister and of private friends, yet we ever use them, but as means to bring us to Christ, and to reveal his counsell unto us. (Hooker 1651, 128)

The 1637 crisis may be reflected in this fourth sermon by the extent to which Hooker extols not faith alone, but faith and obedience. Throughout, the role of the minister in pointing to Christ and in exhorting to obedience has a certain prominence. The minister calls "hear and obey," but if the minister cannot successfully "perswade you to yeeld up your selves to the practice of this duty. then let the Lord himself prevail upon you; and woe to that soul that will not be perswaded by the Lord himself" (Hooker 1651, 145). This high view of ministerial authority is nowhere set forth more clearly than in this passage:

> The word of God in the Scripture ever hath the voice of Christ in it: Whatsoever the word speaks, the Lord himself speaks. . . . Whatsoever any faithfull Minister shall speak out of the Word, that is also the voice of Christ. (Hooker 1651, 135)

But of course these types of sentiments were held also by Anne Hutchinson and provided the ground for her allegiance to both John Cotton and John Wheelwright.

The sermon contains a remarkable passage, lacking any personal reference, but seemingly directed to both the kind of "private authority," and the kind of "absolute allegiance" to the minister, that was found in Hutchinson.

> Justly to be reproved are those that captivate their opinions to the judgement of men. There are a poor kind of deluded creatures in the world, that have made themselves so far servants unto men, that they have pinned their conceits and judgements to the opinions and commands of those upon whom they depend, and from whom they expect either profit or preferment; They look what their great masters say, whatsoever they speak, that they account as Gospel . . . and their judgements must entertain nothing to the contrary. (Hooker 1651, 140)

Even in the process of self-trial, so frequently urged by Hooker, the "many voices" must be discerned. The Lord Himself must be allowed to be Judge. Here Hooker employs a pastoral psychology in which he seeks to comfort "poore doubters." Neither the voice of Satan nor that of one's own sinful weakness is to be allowed to prevail. The minister is to be heard when he speaks "out of the Scripture," and self-trial is to be "by the Word of God." This is the great need of doubting and confused Christians.

My brethren, the ground of all our feebleness, and

distrust, and distemper lieth especially in this, that we neglect our grounds, and doe not fix upon those truths which God hath revealed and made known unto us either publikely or privately. (Ibid., 144)

But by the cunning subtlety of the enemy, too many were hearkening to "Heretiques," including "Familists and Anabaptists" (Ibid., 131). In the end, even Cotton came to rebuke the opinions of Hutchinson which he said "infect farr and near, and will eate out the very Bowells of Relgion" (in Hall 1968, 380-381, 383).

Hooker's fifth sermon in the volume, "The Activite of Faith," returns to approach more closely the crucial question of the crisis. John Cotton admitted, in his little book <u>Sixteen Questions</u>, that discerned sanctification could provide an evidence of salvation, but assurance must await the witness of the Spirit of God. Though Cotton was willing to consider sanctification a concurrent sign of justification, he dampened the sentiment by warning that if one builds "his justifying faith upon such evidences, he shall . . . go aside to a Covenant of Works" (in Emerson 1965, 117).

Hooker's sermon puts forth activity as a test of true faith. He addresses directly the proper place of works in the life of a believer, implicitly defining the nature of faith, and explicitly revealing its effects. Because of his view of the radical nature of regeneration, that faith "brings Christ into the soul," Hooker insists upon a formulation that where there is no fruit, there is no faith (Hooker 1651, 165). The true son of Abraham "is a walker, is a worker," and "by the footsteps of faith you may see where faith hath been" (Hooker 1651, 164-165).

By means of these "footsteps," and against the warnings of Cotton, Hooker employs the reflex. He does so, he explains, at the urging of the Apostle.

I can say no more, but with the Apostle, 2 Cor. 13:5. Examine your selves, whether yee bee in the faith. Why doth not the Apostle say, Examine whether faith bee in you, but whether yee bee in the faith? His meaning is, that as a man is said, to be in drinke, to be in love, or to bee in passion, that is, under the command of drinke or love, or passion; so the whole man must be under the command of faith . . . if he pray, faith must indite (sic) his prayer, if he obey, faith must work; if he live, it is faith that must quicken him . . . and wheresoever faith is, it will do wonders in the soul of that man where it is, it cannot be idle, it will have footsteps. (Hooker 1651, 164)

Because Hooker is careful to speak of "the grace of faith bestowed," his demand that a faithful man be a fruitful man is seen to follow from the gracious character of the work. The works are not "instrumental," but rather constitute a sine qua non in the believer's life because faith holds a certain "spell" over the saint (Hooker 1651, 163). There is a "Use of Comfort" in the observance of these "footsteps" in that those who indeed walk with Abraham will one day also rest with him (Hooker 1651, 185).

Cotton's more abstract theological views, whether he realized the danger or not, provided a natural seedbed for extreme Antinomian opinions. Since assurance of conversion and was granted only by the witness of the Holy Spirit, the threat of subjectivism loomed large. Hutchinson's personal "revelations" confirmed the worst fears of the orthodox party and would have brought Cotton's own downfall had he not moderated his views, at least in the articulation thereof. As Norman Pettit has summarized it, John Cotton "realized in time than an extreme emphasis on the freeness of grace posed hazards that could not under all conditions be controlled" (Pettit 1974, 527; Cf. Murray 1978, 55-57). Preparationist theology was carrying the day. Its voluntarism, especially as expounded from the pulpits, served as a means to insist both upon human responsibility, and the sovereign irresistible grace of God.

The Antinomian crisis had threatened the basic authority structures of New England. Hooker's final two sermons in The <u>Saints Dignitie and Dutie</u> addressed the matter of proper attitudes toward authority. More minute theological considerations aside, that the "heretics" posed a threat to society may have been the largest issue in many New England minds. The Antinomians may well be in view when Hooker announces that God will lay his correcting hand upon "carelessness." The careless fail to see that not only is God a God of order, but he has demanded certain duties of his people.

> Many are loth to have some points to be true, as that a man should exactly observe the Sabbath; it is just with God to give such up to a profane spirit, to deny the Sabbath; Others are loth to have this true, that they must pray duly every morning and evening in their family; it is just for God to give such up to a stupified course, that they can be contented to go and be like beasts. (Ibid., 204)

In "Wilful Hardness of the Means of Grace Abused," the final sermon in the volume, Hooker appears to be addressing a congregation very near to the Antinomian storm. Possibly it is even the Boston congregation of Wilson and Cotton (Bush 1980, 92). Throughout the sermon a spirit of rebellion against both the magistrates and ministers is perceived and rebuked.

> Take notice of this evill that is in our hearts. I say, all of us, for howsoever wicked men doe professedly oppose the truth of God, and his word in the faithful ministry thereof, yet the Saints of God themselves, so farre as they are flesh, have resistances in them; but with this difference,
> a godly man, when he perceiveth his heart stubborn and rebellious against God in his Word, yet he notwithstanding joyneth and sideth with the Word, and laboureth to oppose that corruption of the flesh. (Hooker 1651, 238)

Even under the "best means" the wicked may grow more

rebellious and vex both the minister and the magistrate "if he be more zealous to reform abuses amongst men then ordinary" (Hooker 1651, 221, 228). Undaunted by the Antinomian crisis and any charges leveled at him of being a "legal preacher," Hooker's voluntarism remained uninhibited. The paradoxes in his activism remain. Sovereign grace, human inability, and Hooker's "do something" exhortations, appear side by side.

> Labour to work upon thy own soul a kind of reasonable contentedness, to part with that beloved corruption that lieth in thy bosome. I doe not say thou canst doe it, but I say labour to bring thy heart to a reasonable kind of contentednesse this way. . . . Work thou when God works, and move thou when God moveth. (Hooker 1651, 240, 245)

The Saints Dignitie and Dutie is too consistently taken up with the issues of the crisis of 1637 to not have been formulated with Antinomian troubles in mind. For Hooker and his colleagues, their brand of voluntarism carried no presupposition of human ability with it. Rather it arose from a recognition that God requires certain duties and these are fulfilled in the faithful by the enabling and gracious power of the Holy Spirit alone. The third sermon, "Grace Magnified," was especially concerned to exhort to the use of the means, while stressing that God graces his children with ability. Throughout the work, a perceived careless attitude is rebuked as the saint is to soberly try himself by the Word of God, as in a "cleer looking glass."

For Cotton assurance could only be found in union with Christ. In turn, the works of sanctification are "the effect and consequences of our assurance of faith," and never the basis of the same. For this understanding Cotton credited "Calvin and others, our best Protestants" (in Hall 1968, 133). Cotton insisted that to rely upon the discernment of one's own sanctification is "to go on in a Covenant of Works" (Hall 1968, 53). Yet even Cotton affirmed the value of

sanctification as a "secondary witness" (Murray 1978, 58; Hall 1968, 177-178). Much more emphatically Hooker maintained that by self-inspection, the walk of faith in the "footsteps" of Abraham could be discerned. Danger of self-delusion remained, yet reflection upon these "footsteps" could provide pastoral help toward certain "poore doubters" as a judgment of charity was rendered.
That God was a God of order demanding both faith and obedience provided the structures needed for an orderly society, as his prophets and deacons, ministers and magistrates, announced and carried out his will. But the crisis had struck a severe blow against this orderliness.

> The heart of New England had been rent, not as John Norton thought, in the relatively minor Quaker annoyances of the late 1650's, but in the much more fundamental and decisive eruption which had taken place two decades earlier. (Maclear 1968, 50-51)

Hooker could easily remain undaunted in 1637, for in every point he and his colleagues were triumphant. It remains now to examine Hooker's final works, which systematically present the definitive form of his morphology of conversion. In this examination, evidences of any "tailoring" of the morphology, by reason of the 1637 crisis, will be sought.

THE APPLICATION OF REDEMPTION (1656)

Given the popularity of his published works and the acceptance of his preparationist theology as an ingredient of the New England way, as Hooker approached the twilight of his pastoral career, it was natural that he should set himself to offer an "authorized" explication of his morphology. During the years of his Newtown and Hartford ministries, Hooker had once again gone over its constituent parts with his congregants. This no doubt served as a honing process to his own formulations begun first at Emmanuel College, rehearsed again during the Chelmsford ministry, and then finally in New England (Hooker 1656b, "To The Reader"). Goodwin and Nye, editors of *The Application of Redemption*, note that by reason of preparation by "unskilful hands," and given Hooker's removal to such "remoter parts of the World," previously published works "deformed" and "misrepresented" the author in places. But this 1656 work, published nine years after the author's death, was to be different.

> Here, in these Treatises, thou hast his Heart from his own Hand, his own Thoughts drawn by his own Pencil. This is all truly and purely his own, not as preached only, but as written in order to the Press. (Ibid.)

The ten books in *The Application of Redemption* volumes are followed by "Book Seventeen," *A Comment Upon Christs Last Prayer*. It is doubtful whether the intervening six volumes ever existed even in some nascent form, let alone in full manuscript. Nevertheless, Peter Cole, the ambitious printer of these final Hookerian works, presented an advertisement in each of them which indicated "there are six more books of Mr. Hookers, now printing in two volums." Perhaps he had hoped that editors such as Goodwin and Nye could construct two additional "authorized" works from previously prepared material. It is clear that when Hooker in the 1640's set about to formalize his understanding of the conversion process, preparing it for publication, he would carefully articulate those initial stages of the morphology which most interested him.

Even then, the two volumes bearing the title *The Application of Redemption* are concerned only with the initial "contrition" stage. This is the subject of "Book Ten" while the first nine books were designed to provide theological background to the morphology.

It seems fair to assume that Hooker wished these volumes, being more carefully prepared as they were, to supersede his earlier works which covered the same themes. Frank Shuffelton insists that certain modifications can also be seen between these final works and their earlier counterparts, The Soules Preparation (1632), The Soules Humiliation (1637), and The Soules Vocation (1637). Noting a change of emphasis, but offering no contrasting citations, Shuffelton writes:

> In the earlier preachings on conversion he (Hooker) struck a balance between natural man's passivity in the work of salvation and his concurrent need for voluntaristic action, but he was more forceful when urging men to react under the influence of preparing grace than when reminding them of their essential helplessness before union with Christ. This rhetorical, if not doctrinal imbalance was what laid him open to the Hutchinsonians' charge of preaching a covenant of works. Now in the 1640s he was much more careful to articulate the precise relationship between supernatural and natural action in the process of salvation. (Shuffelton 1977, 254)

Because Shuffelton did not linger long over his suggestion that Hooker "tailored" The Application Of Redemption volumes for a post-Antinomian New England, he offered little concrete evidence in that regard. The thesis that these "more mature" works demonstrate a greater emphasis on helplessness is one that will here be tested. The Soules Preparation (1632), with its sermonic material originating from the Emmanuel and Chelmsford periods, provides the best touchstone of comparison for these purposes. This especially follows since the Application of Redemption volumes ventured only so far as to explicate the very initial stage of the conversion process, the same stage that was revealed in the 1632 volume. Because Hooker in The Application of Redemption rehearsed the same preparationist themes, often using the same imagery, as in the earlier works, special focus will given here only to that material germane to Shuffelton's thesis.

It does appear to be significant that in Hooker's final revision of his life's work, he does not plunge immediately into the preparationist themes of contrition or humiliation. Rather, a 430 page volume of

THE ANTINOMIAN CRISIS AND BEYOND 215

theological background is offered ("Books I-VIII"). The initial two books concern themselves with emphasizing the primacy of Christ's work in redemption. Early therefore in the volume, Hooker's orthodoxy as to the main points in Calvinistic theology is clearly reaffirmed.

> First, there must be a Redemption wrought by the death and obedience of Christ, that Gods justice and holiness which were wronged might be satisfied. Secondly, there must be an Application unto the Souls of such for whom it was paid . . . such only unto whom God hath intended it (Hooker 1656b, 4).

That Christ has purchased all spiritual good, and that only for his elect people, sets a tone of high Calvinism for the entire volume. Redemption is described in substitutionary terminology within the schema of the Covenant of Grace. No double indemnity can be charged, for the wicked lay outside the realm of purchased redemption and will suffer for their own offenses (Hooker 1656b, 13, 13, 15, 17). None of these standard points of Calvinistic theology need serve to provide any connection of the material with the events of the Antinonmian controversy.

But having established that man can not bring the application of Christ's merits to himself, Hooker ponders a question that also appeared during the heat of the 1637 crisis. "May not the Spirit of God witness to him without and before faith?" Hooker quickly answers in the negative (Hooker 1656b, 27-28). Of course, as has been shown, John Cotton, depending upon his mood at the time of articulation, sometimes affirmed that faith itself was a sanctifying work that only followed union with Christ. Nowhere else in the Hooker corpus, including The Saints Dignitie and Dutie, which is so related to the Antinomian crisis, did Hooker answer this doctrine of Cotton's. But here these ordo questions are taken up directly.

Hooker denies that union with Christ and the testimony of the Spirit precedes faith by noting that no unbeliever has any claim to the benefits of Christ's redemption. The Spirit of God, being a Spirit of truth, would never "deceive" one by affirming that one is in a state of grace when indeed he remains in a state of sin. Any doctrine to the contrary, as that indeed sometimes put forth by Cotton, Hooker labels "little less than blasphemy" (Hooker 1656b, 28). There can be little doubt that the Antinomian controversy, with Hutchinson and Cotton themselves, are all quite in the forefront of Hooker's thoughts.

> This Opinion that sayes, that Christ may be united to soul and so he be Justified and Adopted before he have nay Faith; it is a dangerous Opinion, a desperate Delusion; that I may say no worse of it. Mark what follows, here's the plot of all prophaneness, the ground of all looseness and familism: A man may have Christ and be Justified and Adopted while he is without faith, and therefore though a man fall into any Sin, or live in any sin whatever it be, he may have recourse to this Revelation, the witness of the Spirit, and thats enough. (Hooker 1656b, 29)

Hooker manifests his preference for assurance gained by "reflex" as he demands of the one who claims a state of grace, "prove it then!" Immediate revelations, and here Anne Hutchinson surely comes to mind, are delusionary for the "Spirit of God and the Word of God ever go together" (Hooker 1656b, 30). The Spirit of God does give testimony, but only in conjunction with "some Qualification, gracious disposition, or Condition in the Soul" (Hooker 1656b, 34). By resorting once again to an assurance based on reflexive considerations, Hooker seeks to avert Antinomian carelessness. Yet he is ever careful to guard his Calvinism.

> Free Grace is the Fountain of all: It makes the Condition, it works the condition, it maintains the Condition which is wrought. (Hooker 1656b, 33)

In another place, Hooker notes that man's spiritual deadness makes it such that he is no more able to help himself out of his plight than is the Devil himself (Hooker 1656b, 61).

Contrary to Cotton's views, Hooker insists on the utter necessity of the instrumental nature of faith in the application of the merits of Christ. Here is Hooker's voluntarism unveiled in logical fashion.

> No work of Application is without respect to a Qualification; but Evidencing is a work of Application: without an act of Receiving there is no Application, for the applying of any thing to another, ever in common sense, implyes some to whom it must be applyed, and who must receive it; But without respect to a Qualification there is no act of receiving the Priviledges, therefore without respect to a qualification, there is no application of them. . . . Thus then, Without a Qualification of Faith, there is no Receiving; and without Receiving respected, there is no applying of any Priviledges; and without applying, no evidencing; therefore without respect to a Qualifica-tion there is no Evidence given by the Spirit, nor enjoyed by the Soul. (Hooker 1656b, 42)

There can be no true evidence, unless the "qualification" of faith precedes. For Hooker, standing against the Antinomians involved charging them with being "careless" about sin. A life of holiness growing from faith provided the proper ground for the Spirit to witness with the Word of one's state of grace. While remaining careless about sin, and by a "Familistical dream," some might seek assurance without the Word (Hooker 1656b, 44).

> These sensual self-deceiving men make the gate of Mercy and Salvation so wide, that so they find room not only for themselves, but to carry their sins to Heaven with them also. (Hooker 1656b, 58)

This first "book" is indeed polemical in tone. The crisis of 1637 does seem to have provided much of the impetus for Hooker's rather direct attack on

Antinomian views. There is a different "tone" found here which is not evident in the rest of the Hooker canon. Shuffelton remarks that the type of quotations provided above provide the closest thing to a personal attack in all of Hooker's writings (Shuffelton 1977, 257).

Yet this is not to say that there is any theological shift for Hooker which can be perceived in this late work. Nor does man appear to be more helpless now than he did in Hooker's earlier works. In preliminary works like The Unbeelevers Preparing (1638) and The Soules Preparation (1632) the odiousness of sinful man before the holiness of God, and man's utter helplessness as to self improvement, were set forth with intensity. Because these were Hooker's themes from the beginning of his career, they neither needed to be nor were they intensified after the heat of the Antinomian battle. On this point Hooker's theology needed no doctoring.

This is all to say that Shuffelton is correct to notice that certain notices of the Antinomian crisis are taken by Hooker in this later work. These include the notions of personal revelations apart from the Word (Hutchinson's claim), and Cotton's primacy of union with Christ as relative to faith. But in "Book I" of The Application of Redemption, the only one cited by Shuffelton for evidence for his thesis, this writer sees no change, even in emphasis, as to Hooker's anthropological views.

Though the work is concerned with more basic theological considerations, Hooker hints at his favorite preparationist and voluntarist themes.

> The Gospel doth not require a Man should Beleeve of his own power, but that he should be willing and content to be made able to Beleeve and Partake of that Grace he is called unto. (Hooker 1656b, 61)

This being the case, this polemical work is not without its voluntaristic urgings.

And now, al you that sit by, and here of al this:

> me thinks your hearts should sink within you, You that never knew what is was to be Humbled, and to be Called, and to Beleeve in Christ: Behould, al is gone before you: beleevers have al; Awaken therefore, and arise to follow hard after the Lord that you also may be Humbled, and that you also may be Called, and Comforted and for ever Saved by Jesus Christ. (Hooker 1656b, 57)

So while including a blast at Cotton's view of faith, and while stressing a highly Calvinistic view of the atonement using the language of particular redemption, Hooker nevertheless stands firm in his voluntaristic urgings. His was the prevailing position in the resolution of the 1637 crisis. There was no need for him to alter his views and little reason for any change in emphasis.

In "Book II" of The Application of Redemption, Hooker continues carefully to lay the foundation for his most precise presentation of his preparationist theology. Prominent among the themes taken up is that of man's utter inability to work his own salvation. Yet in typical fashion this is juxtaposed with the insistence on "the active involvement of the individual at all stages of the redemptive process" (Bush 1980, 157). The tension is obvious between Hooker's view of the plight of mankind, and his voluntaristic urgings. But his activism is properly understood, not in juxtaposition to passivity which Hooker abhors, but rather to inability which he everywhere maintains. This important distinction is to be preferred over the characterization of Shuffelton who continues to speak of Hooker's understanding of natural man as "passive" in the work of salvation (Shuffelton 1977, 254, 255).

Hooker urges a "holy admiration at the riches of Gods mercy and freeness of the Covenant of Grace in Christ" (Hooker 1656b, 95). Hooker's brand of preparationism contains no concession to Arminianism for "it is not in any mans power to make application of any Spiritual good which Christ hath purchased" (Hooker 1656b, 82). The early pages of "Book II" stress that redemption is particular in intention, and that it is both accomplished and applied by the grace of God.

> The Application of Mercy and Grace purchased, depends not upon mans will, for then our Savior had died at uncertainties, and it had been in the power and pleasure of man, to have made frustrate the death of our Savior and the end of our Redemption purchased thereby. (Hooker 1656b, 77)

The "familists" find mention again as Hooker explicitly denies any notion of passivity. With the favorable outcome of the 1637 crisis, Hooker is "standing tall" upon his insistence on activism.

> This meets directly with that vain conceit of the Familists, Doth the Lord do all the work? it seems then a man may sit still and do nothing, nothing is required of us, and there is nothing for us to do. It was a wise speech of one of the Ancients, He that created thee without thy self, will not save thee without thy self; know therefore we must, God by his Almighty Power, is the Principal Cause, and those means that he hath appointed are the Instrumental Causes. (Hooker 1656b, 133)

Hooker then urges an attendance to the means, emphasizing the ministry of the Word "rightly opened and applied."

This second "book" also contains passages in which Hooker chronicles the windings of the interior life. Preparationism involves a "saving work" which is not though a sanctifying work. Of course this tenet was denied by Cotton, yet it is integral to Hooker's preparationism in which God Himself is the "Principal Cause."

> Manie a Saint of God can say that the Lord hath been wrestling with him from the time of his childhood, and all along in the places where he lived, sometimes strange horrors and strokes of conscience, and strange sins that he fell into sometimes and then strange humiliation and

abasement for them. Grace is not wrought yet thats true, but its working, the Soveraigne vertue of the blood of Christ is now at work, and will never leave the Soul for which Christ died until there be a full and effectuall application of all saving good. (Hooker 1656b, 79)

The "psychologist of conversion" notes that relative to this experience of "wrastling" with the Lord, Augustine confessed that "when he prayed against his lusts, he secretly wished that God would not hear his prayer" (Hooker 1656b, 83). But because God not only provides a gift but also the hand to take it, this is reason for encouragement to the "poor doubters."

Here is matter of cordial refreshing to support the hearts of sinners, from sinking into desperate discouragement, when they see the weakness of their own abilities, not able to reach this work, the stifness of their own will, as ready and resolute to oppose it and out of both, an utter impossibilitie to attain it or any spiritual good unto themselves. (Hooker 1656b, 96, 101)

Hooker approaches near to his preparationist themes which will be more fully explicated in the third book. The struggling sojourner is not to be deterred. He is to use the means and in them be looking to Christ. His is to be a resolute determination to press into the Kingdom of God.

Now the Lord is working, be you sure to follow the blow, and give not over wrastling and striving with the Lord until he bless you with the effectual working of his Word and Spirit, and so apply unto thy soul all Spiritual Good in Jesus Christ. (Hooker 1656b, 139)

It was not until "Book III" that Hooker directly began to directly unfold his preparationist theology. Much of the "book" is a revision of the transitional volumes, The Soules Ingrafting (1637), The Soules

Implantation (1637), and The Soules Implantation In The Natural Olive Tree (1640). No change can be noted in either Hooker's definition of preparation, its utter necessity, or his understanding of the means by which preparation is worked. Echoing in verbatim fashion the opening words to The Souls Ingrafting, Hooker announces that he is about to enter into a discussion of what is a broad outline of much of his pastoral ministry.

> The parts thereof come to be considered in the next place. There are two, I. A Preparation of the Soul for Christ. II. An Implantation of the soule into Christ. (Hooker 1656b, 141; cf. 1637d, 1)

Hooker defines preparation as "a fitting of a sinner for his being in Christ" (Hooker 1656b, 142). His chosen text, "To make ready a people prepared for the Lord" (Luke 1:17), provides a natural springboard from which to explicate his doctrine. Using one of his very common tropes, Hooker insists on the utter necessity of this work of preparation.

> Before the Soule can be engrafted into the true Vine Christ Jesus, it must be prepared and fitted there-unto by the powerful work of the Spirit of God upon it, being not fit to receive a Christ by nature, and unable to fit itself thereunto, by any liberty of Will, or any sufficiency natural it hath. (Hooker 1656b, 141; cf. 1632, 177-178)

It suffices here only to note that Hooker obviously attributes the work of preparation to the Spirit of God. Throughout this third book, his Calvinism remains undiminished. Indeed, in the following statement Hooker comes close to approaching a concept of man's passivity in salvation, though that thought is more then sufficiently denied in his corpus as a whole.

> The soul of a sinner is meerly a patient herein, it is wrought upon him, not wrought by him, by any power he hath inherent in himself. (Hooker 1656b,

150)

Repeating his convictions as expressed in *The Unbeleevers Preparing For Christ* (1638) and *The Soules Implantation Into The Natural Olive* (1640) Hooker the churchman notes that "a plain and powerful ministrie is the only ordinary means to prepare the heart soundly for Christ" (Hooker 1656b, 205; Hooker 1638g, I, 2; Hooker 1640c, 69,72). From this Hooker draws a use of introspection. The ones who have been privileged to live under a powerful ministry and have not yet been humbled and moved to close with Christ are warned.

> Oh take heed of it, for he that will not be fitted for grace, shall be made a firebrand in hell forever. Therefore all you that have lived under a powerful ministry, and are not yet prepared, go home and reason with you souls, and plead with your own hearts, and say, Lord, why am I not yet humbled and prepared? Shall I thus be alwayes under the hacking and hewing of the Word and never be framed? (Hooker 1656b, 219)

A house for God is not only to be "hewn" and "framed," but once constructed the sinner must be careful to "make room" for Christ. This is typical Hookerian language and provides the second main trope in "Book III."

> The Lord hath promised to come into our souls if we humble them and make them fitting to entertain his majesty; therefore sweep your hearts, and cleanse those rooms, cleanse every sink, and brush down every cobweb, and make room for Christ; for it thy heart be prepared and divorced from all Corruptions, then Christ will come and take possession of it. (Hooker 1656b, 201)

It is apparent that the Antinomian crisis, in which the Calvinism of such preachers as Hooker was doubted by the likes of the Hutchinsonians, in no way diminished the voluntaristic zeal of this activist preacher.

> Why then when you hear the Word plainly and powerfully preached to you, labor that the Word may be so unto you as it is in itself: It is a preparing Word, labor you that it may prepare your hearts to receive Christ. (Hooker 1656b, 220)

Direct notice was taken by Hooker of the Antinomian troubles. Again rejecting the sometimes held opinion of John Cotton that union with Christ precedes faith, Hooker shows how such a sentiment breeds carelessness.

> We are the rather to have our hearts and judgment established in this Truth, because the contrary opinion, to wit, that Christ may be united to the soul remaining in the state of corruption, is a brooding Error, that brings out a whol nest and company of delusions with it, which will pollute and pervert the Judgment, and defile our practices in our dayly conversations. (Hooker 1656b, 158)

Portraying the Antinomian sentiments in the worst possible light, Hooker characterizes their carelessness.

> That a man may keep his lusts and his Christ, his comfort and his corruption together than which nothing is more contentfull to a carnall heart. A Christ and a Lust; A Christ and a proud heart; A Christ and a World; A Christ and a peevish Nature; Oh such a Christ pleaseth us well, but such a Christ will never do us good. (Hooker 1656b, 158)

So it is that Hooker takes notice of the troubles that had worked havoc in New England. But he hardly has "tailored" his final formulations to any degree as a result of those troubles. Shuffelton may have expected Hooker to show clearer signs of high Calvinism or to moderate his overt voluntarism as a result of the controversy, but he has not been able to demonstrate that Hooker did so much. The characteristic "double pronged" use remains. Hooker offers this to the "poor doubter" who finds himself afflicted by the Devil, and seemingly struck by the wrath of the Almighty.

His friends pitty himm, and the Parents conceive their child is undone, they never thought to have seen this day: Why so? It is the best day his eyes ever saw; he is now in Gods way, the Lord now seems to lay hold of him and to intend good to him; be not afraid of the work, but be afraid he should miss and spoil in the working. (Hooker 1656b, 198)

Conversely, the careless one who thinks the way to heaven to be easy, receives this reproof.

To imagine the Lord Jesus would carry the Drunkard and his Cups, the Adulterer and his Harlots also, the riotous Gamester his cards and dice, Hawks and Hounds, and all to heaven together, is impossible and incredible. (Hooker 1656b, 164-165)

All must be therefore careful to practice the art of introspection to discern whether one is "fitted and prepared for Christ." As a building project is daily and carefully checked by the one who has employed carpenters, so must the building of the soul be analyzed that care be taken that "the building go forward" (Hooker 1656b, 221).

"Books IV, V, VII, VIII," constitute a revision of the 1638 work, The Unbeleevers Preparing For Christ. It will be remembered that the 1638 work was concerned with the pre-initial stage in Hooker's morphology, being chiefly taken up with anthropological considerations and the need for God's initiative in drawing a sinner to Christ. In their reformulation, as relative to the previous volume, little new is offered. In fact, unlike the first three books, no notice at all of Antinomian troubles seems to be found in "Books IV, V, VII, VIII."
Prominent themes include the importance of "redeeming the time," yet all the while one must be patient and content with God's timing in the conversion process. The means are to be used while one arms

himself with "patience to stay God's time and to wait his pleasure" (Hooker 1656b, 239). The laboring process is to be incessant, even if grace seems to be elusive for it remains true that "while there is life there is hope" (Hooker 1656b, 249).

The fifth book, being a short sermon of encouragement and exhortation, is similar, especially in the importance it gives to patience as a recognition of God's sovereignty. This follows, especially in view of Hooker's rather stark indictment in the previous book, "You have no worth in yourselves, you deserve no favor" (Hooker 1656b, 237). Nevertheless, the work contains a clear statement of Hooker's "judgment of charity" that so governed his ministry and ideas in regard to the relation requirement for church membership.

> Learn we hence to take a lesson of sobriety, not to be too rash and censorious touching the final estate of any in this life, since it is never too late for the Lord to call though at the Eleventh hour. (Hooker 1656b, 271)

But even here the "double prong" of Hooker's ministry is apparent. The complacent must be shown to be in danger, they must be prodded from their sluggishness.

> It is not then a breach of Charity to judge the tree by the fruits, the disease by the Symptomes, yea it was folly and little less than madness to do other; As the Word judges I may judge, and so should. (Hooker 1656b, 274)

The seventh book has Romans 8:7 for its text, "The wisdom of the flesh is enmity against God, it is not subject to the Law, neither can it be." Its themes are the same as those in <u>The Unbeleevers Preparing</u> (I, 81-125). A standard Reformed understanding of the inability of man in his natural state is put forward.

The sum of this argument in short returns to thus much, That if the Will of a man be under commission

of Divine Justice, and is delivered up to the power
of sin to be possessed by it, and acted by it;
therefore it is not, nay cannot be willing to be
severed from its sins. . . . The will of a natural
man is the worst part about him. . . . To know the
Will of God and do it, to be able to close with
God, and to do what is acceptable to him, this is
far estranged all the sons of men by nature.
(Hooker 1656b, 325, 327)

Because this is true, a radical change, wrought from above must take place. Mere profession will not do. Prayers may be practiced, tears may be shed, the tongue may express godliness, but one must ask his heart, "Heart, what sayest thou" (Hooker 1656b, 343)? Here is Hooker's insistence upon "heart religion," an insistence found everywhere in his sermonic material. Amid the striving, the toiling, and the attendance to the means of grace, the sojourner who seeks grace must "look to him in whose hand our hearts are that he may do that for us which we cannot do for ourselves" (Hooker 1656b, 347).

"Book VIII" continues these anthropological considerations, being a reworking of the second part of The Unbeleevers Preparing. In both works there is an extended treatment of John 6:44, "No man can come to Me, unless my Father which sent Me, draw him." The theme throughout is the necessity of preparation set against the text which provides the emphasis upon human inability. The material found in "Book VIII," has received treatment above as its earlier formulation was examined. Its post-Antinomian form is no different except perhaps in the finality with which Hooker wants to be understood.

Let me leave this upon Record for ever amongst you.
This effectual drawing and quickening of the heart
is the alone work of God. It is not in him that
Wills, nor in him that Runs, but in God that shews
Mercy. (Hooker 1656b, 451)

The sixth book in the volume appears not to be a

revision of any earlier work. It is concerned with the danger of the soul becoming secure and complacent in its sinful condition. As repeated in "Book VIII" (1656b, 349), Hooker suggests that it is by a "holy kind of violence" that a soul is finally severed from its sin and drawn unto Christ (Hooker 1656b, 284). But such language should not be seen as a concession to the views of John Cotton, who while denying the preparatory process, insisted that conversion usually comes by way of violent seizure. Hooker's sentiments predate the crisis of 1637, this "holy kind of violence" terminology having appeared in The Unbeleevers Preparing (Hooker 1638g, II, 3). For Hooker this "holy sort of violence" characterizes the preparatory process in which the sinner, though he be at first unwilling, is awakened from his sleep and drawn unto Christ by the hand of the Father.

The self-deluded complacent ones must know that they will not be carried to heaven "on a feather bed."

> It is easie for a Mariner to be in a Calm at Sea, he hath quiet there, but he dies there: Women in Child-birth long for Throws, if their Throws leave them, their life leaves them and all; but if they have many and strong Throws, then they hope well. So go your wayes and call for the Throws of Conversation: For a Child to be born into the world, and the Mother asleep, its against Nature, and Reason, and Sense, and Experience, and all; so before ever you be born again, before ever Christ be formed in you, it will cost you many Prayers, and Tears, and much Sorrow; but it these Throws come thick, then there is hope: Oh! Therefore call for the sight of sin, and sorrow for sin, for conviction and humiliation, as you love your lives and souls call for these. . . . Awake and call upon your God. (Hooker 1656b, 299-300)

This call to the complacent also contains within it an encouragement to the poor doubter weighed down by the knowledge of his own sin. The arduous way is the way that leads on high. The one who grieves thereupon is seeing his "best day," for he is on the way. Surveying the eight "books" of the first volume in The Application of Redemption series, Hooker's orthodoxy as to the main points of Reformed theology is quite evident. Primacy is given to the redemption wrought by Christ as Hooker affirms that all merit is found in the Savior. Man's corruption and spiritual inability to achieve any degree of purification are clearly articulated in standard fashion. That redemption has been purchased only for the elect is prominent in the first two books. Notwithstanding the charges leveled against him during the summer of 1637, Hooker remained consistent in his activist stance, calling upon his readers to labor to be "fitted" to receive Christ and all his benefits. Occasional reference to the "familists" was made, but on the whole, no change in doctrinal outlook, nor even in emphasis, can be demonstrated in The Application of Redemption (I-VIII) as relative to the earlier formulations of the same themes.

"Books IX, X" of The Application Of Redemption constitute another 1656 volume. This sequel to the previous volume reproduces the same twenty-one page preface by Goodwin and Nye. Once again the present examination will particularly be concerned with spotting any signs of "tailoring" of Hooker's sentiments by reason of the Antinomian crisis in which pastors of his sort had been labeled as "legal preachers."

The ninth book is a short untitled sermon on Isaiah 57:17 in which the Lord announces that he will "dwell with him also that is of a contrite and humble Spirit." Such a text provides a natural foundation for Hooker's preparationist theology. The sermon is a revision of one which first came to print almost twenty years earlier, "The Broken Heart" (Hooker 1637c, 1-24; Hooker 1640c, 1-28). But the 1637 version of the sermon was unrelated to the crisis of that year, the sermonic material itself dating from the Emmanuel and Chelmsford periods of Hooker's English career. A reminder may here be in order that only in such late works as The Covenant of Grace Opened (1649); The Saints Dignitie and Dutie (1651); A Comment Upon Christs Last

Prayer (1656); and The Application of Redemption volumes (1656), do any Hookerian morphological formulations from New England make an appearance.

Yet notwithstanding the upheaval caused by the crisis that had intervened between the first appearances of this sermon and its later publication, Hooker evidently felt no need to modify his formulations of his preparationist theology contained therein. "The Ninth Book" evidences no essential differences when compared to the 1640 "Broken Heart," as found in The Soules Implantation Into The Natural Olive. Both formulations use the same text, follow the same outline, and exposit preparationist theology with the same intensity.

The short work is concerned to demonstrate the utter necessity of a properly fitted heart, that is, one that has been brought to contrition and humiliation. For only to such "prepared ground" will faith come (Hooker 1656c, 5).

> An honest heart is a contrite and humble heart, so rightly prepared that faith is infused, and the soul thereby carried unto Christ, and quickened with patience to persevere in good duties. As we say of Grounds before we cast in seed; there is two things to be attended there, it must be a fit ground, and a fat ground; the ground is fit when the weeds and green sword are plowed up, and the soyl there, and made mould: And this is done in Contrition and Humiliation; then it must be a fat ground, the soyl must have heart, we say the ground is plowed well, and lies well, but it's worn out, it's out of heart: Now faith fats the soyl, furnisheth the soul with ability to fasten upon Christ, and so receive the Seed of the Word, and the brace of Sanctification, and thence it produceth the good fruit in Obedience. (Hooker 1656c, 6-7)

In typical fashion Hooker also examines the "windings" of the soul in order to expose "lets and impediments" to contrition, humiliation, and faith. A primary impediment is self-secure complacency in which one is easily persuaded and deluded that "they have no cause to alter their condition." Another is when sensing the "plague" of sin, the sinner looks for his remedy in self, outward excellencies, or some performance of duty. This is a "bar to faith, which is the going out of the soul to fetch all life and power from another." So the work of humiliation is needed, whereby "God plucks away all props" (Hooker 1656c, 6-10). One should note that Hooker maintains at this late stage of his career the very same voluntaristic definition of faith as he did in his very first published work, the 1627 preface to John Rogers' Doctrine of Faith (in Williams 1975, 144).

Examining the "uses" as the sermon comes to a conclusion, the activist stand of this preacher is apparent once again. The physician to the soul seeks to dash the hopes of the careless. Because "all grace is in his gift, and he doles it out only to the bruised and abased," a word of "terror" is sounded.

> You were never broken-hearted here for your abominations, know assuredly that you will burn for them one day; your proud hearts were never abased, and laid in the dust, the Lord will ruinate both you and them.(Hooker 1656c, 11)

Having asserted that contrition and humiliation are God's works of grace, preparatory to his "infusion" of faith, Hooker nevertheless exhorts, "labor to be humble and broken-hearted Christians." The comfort comes because this is "God's order," the contrite and humbled one, driven to the dust of death, can be assured that "then he will revive your spirits with his presence" (Hooker 1656c, 14). No less now then before the 1637 crisis, Hooker is determined to sound his activist calls, and to allow them to stand in apparent tension with his theology of grace.

"Book X" provides an extensive revision and enlargement of The Soules Preparation (1632). It is not until this tenth book that Hooker begins to provide a formal definitive restatement of any of the major stages of his morphology of conversion. The first nine books can be viewed as loosely related to The Unbeleevers Preparing For Christ (1638), concerned as they are with anthropological considerations and "foretastes" of Hooker's preparationist theology. In this tenth book, the author turns directly to the subject matter of contrition. Once again evidences of post-Antinomian "tailoring" will be sought out. Additional extracts from the work will here be provided when they demonstrate clear continuity with earlier Hookerian formulations.

Insisting on the absolute necessity of the preparatory process, and prospectively commenting on the second stage, humiliation, Hooker writes:

> Contrition loosens a man from his sin, makes him see an absolute necessity to be another man, or else he is a damned man. Humiliation loosens a man from himself, makes him see an utter insufficiency in what he hath or doth, for to procure the least spiritual relief unto his soul; now the Coast is cleer, and faith may come to us, and we by that be enabled to come to Christ. (Hooker 1656c, 15)

Following his own practice of being careful to define his terms, Hooker's formal definition of contrition is essentially identical to that found in The Soules Preparation (Hooker 1632, 2). As in the earlier work, and to the same degree, Hooker carefully guards his Calvinism. The component parts, "sight," "sorrow," "detestation," and "sequestration," are all things "rather wrought upon us by the impression and motion of the Spirit, than performed by any inward principle." Repeatedly Hooker notes that these things are "brought" to the sinner (Hooker 1656c, 16).

Making a reference from his text (Acts 2:37), which was also the text for The Soules Preparation, Hooker notes how painful a thing contrition is when it is truly being wrought.

> . . . not a slight and overly ripling of the skin but a piercing to the quick, reached unto the very heart-root, that which cut asunder the soveraignty

of the choyce of the Will and made that stand back, and go off from those loathsome corruptions which were as neer as the soul to the soul. (Hooker 1656c, 325)

These words appear in a context in which Hooker clearly posits the will as the commander of the soul. It is the cutting off of the sovereignty of the carnal will that brings such pain as contrition is being worked.

That the process is painful runs parallel to the seriousness in which Hooker views sin. For some seventy pages he lays great stress upon the seriousness of sin before a holy God and the necessity of seeing this personally. Because of the need for admitting even sinful thoughts, meditation upon sin is hailed as a special means to break the heart (Hooker 1656c, 208-280). Sincere meditation will bring "detestation" of sin. If this is not gained, the "coast" will never be cleared unto faith and unto Christ.

Thou thy self art an abomination to the Lord, if sin be not an abomination to thee. (Hooker 1656c, 702)

Yet this examiner of the interior life combines his voluntarism with his frequent refrain that one might be "hoodwinked" in his introspection. In order to see sin aright, Hooker urges a laboring to perceive the immeasurable holiness of the Lord. While one is attending to the means of grace, the Lord may well send his "Sargent or Officer," the conscience, to give a sight of sin. But as these blows are rendered, Hooker warns that many "wily shifts" of the mind will attempt to "break the blow as it were and to defeat, and put by the Authority of the Truth" (Hooker 1656c, 114-117, 118).

The psychologist perceives that one of the "shifts" of the mind which is employed to "lighten the hainousness of his evil" is to put the blame off of oneself and upon companions who either "by their inticements and perswasions, have deluded him." One claims, "It was the fault of such and such, had they not counselled it, I had never committed the sin." Hooker's verdict is that such an excuse is not only lame, but guilt is aggravated by the heeding of the counsels of man rather than to the wisdom of God (Hooker 1656c, 125-126). Later in the work a related caution is offered. "Loose company is a deadly enemy and hindrance to the conversion of a sinner" (Hooker 1656c, 240). This is especially true in that such "froathy company" is hardly the environment for serious introspection.

But these harsher judgments are balanced by Hooker's encouragement for "poor doubters." Chronicling the windings of the soul, Hooker finds reasons for a charitable judgment as he answers objection after objection from those who would condemn themselves (Hooker 1656c, 310-316). To these who are not opposing the work of contrition, but rather seem to be truly crushed by it, the physician prescribes hope.

Yet the windings of the soul are such that often excuses are offered after sin has been committed. Hooker desires that these be brought to "naked acknowledgment of their errors." Those that oppose the acknowledgment of their own sin employ many methods of reasoning.

> So many muses to escape, so many sleepy, senseless shifts to save their own stake, their credit and respect, yield nothing, though they can gainsay nothing with color of reason, they spend their wits and thoughts, and lay about them to the utmost skil of al the carnal reason they have, to latch the blow, to defeat and put by the stroak of the truth the dint and evidence of the Argument that would discover their evil. (Hooker 1656c, 646)

By the "reflective" method of gaining assurance Hooker says that evidence can be garnered as to whether the Lord "hath made any entrance upon this great work of preparation . . . to this day or no." But initial stirrings may be misperceived. Again the danger, amid the "windings" of the soul, of being "hoodwinked" remain. There is danger of falling short of the true sight of sin.

Thou has heard a confused noyse as it were that made thee a little to look about. But hath the Lord ever lifted up the latch as though he were resolved to come in? (Hooker 1656c, 101)

In recognition of the dual possibilities of self-delusion and undue doubting, the "double prong" finds frequent employment.

Thus you see the compass of this encouragement which issues from God's free grace. But lest some proud flesh should arise by this healing preservative if it should heal too fast to keep thee under this encouragement and yet to keep thee from presumption, take these cautions. (Hooker 1656c, 131)

Hooker then cautions that God will work "in his own way" and that this way must be followed. Caution should be exercised lest one "escapes from under the hand of the Lord, and fall back again to the old base course" (Hooker 1656c, 316, 317). While noting a variety in God's dealings, especially as to the Lord's timing, Hooker maintains that nevertheless "the nature and substance of the work is really and truly wrought in all that are effectually called out of the world" (Hooker 1656c, 374-375).

To the poor and downcast, Hooker assures that this sorrow and anguish is "not unto death" but rather is the "onely way and means to deliver from death" (Hooker 1656c, 439). But an objection comes from one who moans that his "terrors" are greater now than formerly. The psychologist is delighted for "therefore thy comfort is never so near as now." The crucible is being heated to an unbearable degree and in this Hooker finds reason for good hope (Hooker 1656c, 441). But on the other hand, as the windings reach a feverish pitch, all still may be lost.

Never rest until we come to the right pitch of this saving sorrow, otherwise we shall lose our labor,

> all the pains, and toil, and trouble we take, will prove indeed unprofitable, we shall lose our labor, and our souls and all. (Hooker 1656c, 447)

The "do something" voluntarism of Hooker's is no less evident in this late work than it was in the pre-Antinomian days. This indicates that the victorious preparationists saw no reason, even in the face of the charges that had been leveled against them, to modify their voluntarism. The calls to "labor" become almost a constant drone. No rest is to be taken until this "laboring" has brought a true sight of sin.

> Brethren let not Satan deceive you nor suffer yourselves so far to be deluded as to dream of another course or to devise a shorter cut to Grace and Glory, for its certain if you do, you will fall short of your hopes and comforts and all. (Hooker 1656c, 111)

The overcoming of the various "windings," "objections," and "shifts" of the soul mark this laborious process.
Before moving from these remarks regarding Hooker's "prodding," one rather unique passage from The Application of Redemption must here find notice. The "physician of the soul" makes a startling diagnosis of the ills of New England society at large.

> Walk we from one Plantation to another, from one Society to another; nay, which is yet a further misery, from one Assembly to another, all the Earth sits still, and is at rest; there is no stirring, no trading in Christianity; men cheapen not, enquire not after the purchase of the precious things of the Gospel, what shall I do to be quit of my self? what shall I do to be severed from my sins which have pestered me so long? . . . As though Christ were taking the Charter of the Gospel from the present generation, and were removing the markes, there is no stirring, Trade is dead, men come dead and sit so, and return to their habitations, there is deep silence, you shal not

hear a word. What spiritual good they get, what
they need, or what they desire; men are willing to
do nothing, and therefore they wil not inquire what
they shall do. (Hooker 1656c, 565-566)

This rare indictment against the first
generation settlers runs counter to the hagiographical
tones of their descendants. But to Hooker the activist,
sluggishness was not to be countenanced. Writing near
the end of his New England career, the above quoted
words provide a faint echo of his similar
dissatisfaction in England as expressed in The Danger of
Desertion, his 1631 farewell to his Chelmsford
congregation (Hooker 1641, 15).

Finally, consideration should be given to
certain more polemical aspects of this tenth book.
Certain remarks are put forth as to the extent of man's
ability in this process of preparation. Hooker answers
the question as to how "active" man is in the acquiring
of a true "sight of sin." His Calvinistic anthropology
seems unblemished.

There is an incapability in our minds to receive
this spiritual light by which we might be enabled
to come to the right discovery of our corruptions.
(Hooker 1656c, 43,46)

Hooker is careful to articulate that conversion
does not depend upon any preparation that we can make.
Indeed, he wants the reader to "hence forever to fear
and avoyd that haeretical doctrine of the Arminians do
deeply dangerous to the salvation of mens souls" (Hooker
1656c, 299). Though none can prepare or "fit" himself
to receive grace, nevertheless the activist preacher
revolts against idleness because,

Though all that thou canst do, can neither prepare
thee for Grace nor purchase Grace for thy self, yet
the means through Divine Institution are mighty;
God by them can work effectually, and if it seem
good to his good pleasure, he will; wait upon him
only for that good thou wantest, from whom only it

can be received. (Hooker 1656c, 306)

These are the very same sentiments that are found in The Soules Preparation (Hooker 1632, 136, 148). Our author's almost nominalistic sounding theme is that one is to put himself in the "environment" of grace, i.e., attend to the means, where grace in usually active.

If one were so predisposed, a certain "tailoring" as a result of the 1637 crisis might be perceived. But only if Hooker's orthodoxy as to Calvinistic doctrines in the earlier works is questioned might one feel that he is "firming up" his Calvinism in this later work. This writer adheres to neither supposition.

As it has been shown, especially in "Book I" of the Application of Redemption, Hooker made some direct references to the "familists" of the 1637 crisis. To Shuffelton's credit, he did not claim that Hooker modified the ideas previously preached, but rather only changed the balance of emphasis. This writer denies that even such a change of emphasis can be perceived. Professor Shuffelton's use of the respective titles of The Soules Preparation and The Application of Redemption, seems hardly sufficient to demonstrate a different emphasis in the two works (Shuffelton 1977, 253-254). As Bush has put it, Hooker, like any careful Puritan, kept well offshore from each of of the "treacherous shores" of Antinomianism and Arminianism (Bush 1980, 160).

A COMMENT UPON CHRIST'S LAST PRAYER (1656)

One final post-Antinomian work remains to be analyzed. During the months preceding his death in July of 1647, Hooker was evidently preaching and writing out in manuscript form the sermonic material which would be eventually published as A Comment Upon Christ Last Prayer (1656). This final work in Hooker's summa on the application of redemption, is identified on the verso of the fly leaf facing the title page, as Hooker's "seventeenth book, made in New-England." It therefore was designed, at least in the editorial judgment of

Goodwin and Nye, to be the "capstone" to the Application of Redemption series. The work concerns, especially in its latter portion, the final stage in the process of regeneration, that being glorification. The work appears to be a completely original one, not being a revision or reformulation of any previous material. Although the volume was produced from Hooker's own manuscript prepared with a view toward publication, the material was not ready by the time of his death.

Goodwin and Nye summarize the focus of the volume as "our mystical Union with God and Christ; a subject but rarely handled by divines." These editors go on to lament that the final product presents only a "miscellaneous treatment" of the subject as Hooker apparently foresaw his impending death and scrambled to go to print with something of this topic though it lacked the systematization found in the Application of Redemption volumes. The reader must therefore be content with this "precursory handling" of the grand subject matter. The material was originally preached for communion services where "union with Christ is sealed up to Beleevers more conspicuously than in other ordinances" (in Hooker 1656a, "To The Reader").

This final labor of Hooker's life in some ways presents a new endeavor. As relative to the Hooker canon as a whole, this is work has a more purely theological and abstract character. One immediately notices the relative absence of psychological factors and the reduced emphasis on considerations of the interior life. Shuffelton calls the work the "most speculative and radical" of Hooker's career (Shuffelton 1977, 259). If this was the final "book" of a proposed seventeen that were to detail Hooker's understanding of the morphology of conversion, the volume is indeed a disappointment. Only following a miscellaneous and somewhat haphazard treatment of themes related to union with Christ does Hooker in the latter portion of the work formally treat the stage of "glorification." Earlier pages somewhat resemble The Soules Exaltation (1638) in its treatment of inter-Trinitarian roles and the "satisfaction" view of the atonement.

In these post-Antinomian and final formulations of his morphology, Hooker lingered long over introductory matters. In The Application of Redemption (I-VIII), he had "backtracked" to anthropological considerations. Now in A Comment Upon Christ's Last Prayer, Hooker rather lays a theocentric foundation.

> Hereby the great work of our Redemption comes to be discovered, comes also to be acknowledged; when once this sending our Savior is rightly understood. Its the very Hinge upon which the Gospel turns: The very foundation, upon which the work of our Salvation hangs. (Hooker 1656a, 75)

Early on in the volume Hooker describes his text, John 17: 20-26, in this way.

> A prayer of unconceivable and incomparable worth, above al that ever was expressed or recorded in the word: Like a confection or compound of those soveraigne excellencies; beyond the highest strayn of the desires or conceiving of the souls of the Saints. That which containes the quintessance or the pith of the cordialls of the Gospel, the very marrow of al that great redemp-tion, he had wrought and purchased: the highest pitch of al that happiness, which Heaven can afford, or the very richest Diamond in the crown of Glory. (Hooker 1656a, 2)

A crucial word in Hooker's own description here is "unconceivable." As to the consideration of the saint's union with God and the ultimate glory attending thereunto, human reason and expression fall short in their analytical abilities. As Hooker was putting pen to paper, the end of his own sojourn was drawing near. The "Day Star" arising was about to burst forth for him into a glorious dawn. As he attempts to describe the anticipated bliss, his own prophetic powers do not prove equal to the task.

Hooker is at his best, though it is a somewhat new genre for him, when he slips into a mystical mode of enraptured joy. Leaving examples of this aside for the moment, the following scholastic sounding definition is demonstrable of the inadequacy of language to do justice to the grand theme at hand.

> The Glory of Christ then here attended is the meeting and concurrence of the expression of all the Divine perfections and Grace in Christ, in the highest strain of Eminency, and to the utmost activity of that power they can put forth, or the Creature can receive. (Hooker 1656a, 368)

This seems to be an amplification of Ames' more simple and calm description of glorification as "the taking away of every imperfection from soul and body and the bestowal of total perfection" (Ames 1968, 174).

In their preface, Goodwin and Nye had noted the scarcity of treatment of this subject by well known divines. Any examination of standard anthologies of the Puritans will confirm this paucity. But in one of his "cordials," Richard Sibbes had in 1629 offered his "Glimpse of Glory." There he affirmed that "God's end of calling us is unto glory" (Sibbes 1864, VII, 498). Hooker likewise notes that the Savior has an affectionate desire "to have the presence of the Faithful in Heaven with himself" (Hooker 1656a, 354).

Because this is the "end" of God's calling in the first place, the future is assured.

> We shal al be taken up with him into the Clouds, and he shall carry his Bride with Triumph into his own Country and Kingdom, into Heaven, and there we shal ever be with him. (Hooker 1656a, 356)

But this ultimate experience of union with God awaits the end of an extended process. This of course, mirrors both Hooker's own morphology and Ames' identification of glorification with the entire process of sanctification.

> The Lord redeems, not only from guilt, and punishment, and power of our sins and miseries, but

> even from the presence of them. (Hooker 1656a, 358)

In ultimate glorification the redemptive process is completed as "the Sight of his Glory is the highest step and stair of ours" (Hooker 1656a, 368). The use of "step" and "stair" here serve to connect the present formulations with the morphology as a whole.

But the most striking feature of the volume is the mystical element apparent in many places. Sargent Bush is careful to note that Hooker, as a preeminent preparationist, was classified as one of the "legal preachers." With his sequential stages of grace, Hooker would be less likely than others to reflect a mystical side. Yet Hooker dares discuss the ultimate mystical experience, communion with God (Bush 1980, 306).

> Its a matter of Admiration; we may here see and be swallowed up with everlasting wonderment, at the mysterious and incomprehensible depth of Gods dispensations in the covenant of grace and the Redemption of a sinner by Christ; where he brings the greatest good out of our greatest evil, the greatest glory out of the depth of our greatest misery; Advanceth us to the highest top of Heaven and happiness, out of the lowest most Hel of sin and wretchedness, out of the greatest estrangement from God. To bring a sinner to the neerest union and communion with God. (Hooker 1656a, 530-531)

Again the incomprehensibility of this grand theme is noted. But Hooker does allow himself a degree of speculation, though it tends towards a most orthodox Christocentricity. Noting that Christ himself will be the great source of heavenly happiness, Hooker even denies that the communion with loved ones and family members will serve as any delight.

> The sight of Gods glory gives full satisfaction. . . Its not heaven but God in Christ in heaven that makes it desirable. All desires of al the hearts of the Saints empty themselves and end here. Their

desires are to Thy Name. And the remembrance of thee. The Soul in Heaven desires the union of the Body, and the perfection and accomplishment of the number of their fellow brethren. But when the Body and Soul are raised, and the Saints completed, then, al desires are to Gods Name, and to the remembrance of Him. There is remembrance of nothing else. The things and relations of this life are like prints in the Sand, there is not the least appearance or remem-brance of them. The King remembers not his crown, the Husband the Wife, the Father the Child. . . . Only the Name of God in Christ . . . that now is their Eye and aime, that only comes into remem-brance. This is the top and highest pinnacle of perfection. (Hooker 1656a, 367)

Despite this bit of speculation, Hooker's mystical elements are kept "in check" by his typical insistence upon the necessary Spirit-Word conjunction (Hooker 1656a, 449). This distances him from any sort of Antinomian mysticism with its attendant personal revelations. Hooker has shown himself in his life's work to be a reasoned chronicler of the activity of grace, a careful student of the interior life, and a warm-hearted pastor with a special skill in raising up the down trodden "poor doubter." Here another side of the physician to the soul is seen. Hooker was a man enraptured by the thought of grace. In contemplating heavenly glory, he is filled with wonder and awe as words fail to explicate the ecstasy of ultimate union with God in Christ. This indicates that the student searching for roots of a mystical tradition in Reformed theology must go further back than Edwards.

It is enough here to affirm that Thomas Hooker's voluntaristic, preparationist stance was supple and broad enough to incorporate within it the genuinely mystical wonderment and awe that would be still another major facet of the American literary imagination in the centuries ahead. (Bush 1980, 309)

If this emergent mysticism provides the most unique feature in this final volume of Hooker's, the most vital theological consideration is his schema of "grace and glory now, but more so then." As God's grace intrudes into this realm by his Covenant of Grace, this provides the "suburbs of happinesse and of the New Jerusalem." Present grace is likened to a "porch," but future glory will be the "palace" itself (Hooker 1656a, 79).

Using the metaphor of trade and commerce, first employed many years before in The Danger of Desertion, future glory is likened to a wholesale imbibing of the excellencies of God. Commenting upon 1 Corinthians 13:12 and I John 3:2, Hooker writes:

> Al Comfort, and Peace, and Grace of al kinds, shal like a mighty stream, take up the whol man. Here by re-tale, as persons who are poor, buy, and bring in their Provisions. Then by whole-sale. Here the Light of the Sun shining in a crevis, and day hole, leaves yet a dark place. But then the Lord Christ shall arise as the Sun of Righteousness, and fil (as that the whol heaven, so this) the whol heart. (Hooker 1656a, 371-372)

Ames had described glorification as a life long process (Ames 1968, 171-174). Likewise, Hooker affirms that in the appointed means grace and glory are granted. The believers see the "Day Star arising" even now in the ministry of the Word. But only then will all shadows flee away.

> We shall see and enjoy God immediately, not by means. . . . And this is the priviledge of heaven: the unconceivable beauty and brightness of the place may dazel us (Hooker 1656a, 335).

With such anticipated bliss, all the struggles of the preparatory process and the sojourn of sanctification now seem to pale into insignificance. No doubt Hooker had given assent to Sibbes' proverb, "It is better to go bruised to heaven than sound to Hell" (Sibbes 1864, I, 47). Though A Comment Upon Christ's Last Prayer contains less pastoral psychology than the former works, Hooker cannot completely resist applying his understanding of future glory to the "windings" of the human heart.

> Have this glory of Christ in thine Eye, and keep the savor of it in thy heart. Thou canst not but have glorious peace in thy conscience, joy in thy heart, and contentment in thy course. (Hooker 1656a, 335)

If present sins seem to overwhelm and sink the soul, Hooker exhorts that the sinner not only look to Christ his surety, but to especially dwell on the glory he now possesses.

> Satan accuseth, Conscience gives its witness against thee, and the Justice of God passes Sentence. Look up to this Glory that Christ stands possessed of now in Heaven, and al these accusations will vanish immediately, nor will once appear to plead against a beleeving sinner. (Hooker 1656a, 338-339)

In conclusion, this volume adds very little to Hooker's morphology of conversion. Though glorification is called the "highest pinnacle," the "highest step and stair," in Hooker's morphology it is not the highest hill of difficulty. In glorification an inherent climax is rightly perceived. But though ultimate union with Christ involves the believer's highest bliss, a degree of energy and tension had already gone out of Hooker's preaching before he reached these themes. Towards the end of The Soules Effectual Calling (1638), the true crisis point in the morphology had been reached. Indeed, as one came to "close with Christ," the final outcome to the arduous preparatory process was assured. Hooker tries in this volume to recapture some of that "drama." But despite his glorious subject matter, much of the tension and anticipation characterized by his nervous style has disappeared.

CHAPTER FIVE:
THE VEHICLE FOR HOOKER'S MORPHOLOGY,
THE PURITAN PLAIN STYLE

As this analysis of Hooker's writings draws to a conclusion, if a balanced view is to be gained, attention must be given to that for which Hooker may be best known, his preaching. Moses Coit Tyler spoke of the aura that surrounded the man. "In the living presence of Hooker there appears to have been some singular personal force, an air both of saintliness and kingliness, that lofty and invincible moral genius which the Hebrew prophets had, and with which they captivated or smote down human resistance" (Tyler 1878, I, 194). In similar fashion, Edward Johnson's hagiographical tones praised the rhetorical ability of Thomas Hooker.

> Come, Hooker, come forth of thy native soile;
> Christ, I will run, says Hooker, thou hast set
> My feet at large, here spend thy last days toile;
> Thy rhetorick shall peoples affections whet.
> Thy Golden Tongue and Pen Christ caus'd to be
> The blazing of his golden truths profound,
> Thou sorry worme, its Christ wrought this in thee;
> What Christ hath wrought must needs be very sound.
> (Johnson 1910, 90-91)

Hooker's throne was his pulpit. "There he swayed men with a power that was more than regal. His face had authority and utterance in it; his voice was rich, of great compass and flexibility; every motion of him spoke" (Tyler 1878, I, 195). Yet these approbations of Hooker are not confined to those hagiographers of previous generations. Everett Emerson has called Hooker "probably the greatest preacher of American Puritanism"

(Emerson 1977, 96). Hooker was also a man who himself knew good preaching. Having heard Jonathan Burr, Hooker remarked, "surely this man won't be long out of heaven for he preaches as if he were already there" (Levy 1945, 9). From an analytical viewpoint, the judgment of Tyler is generally accepted. Speaking of Hooker's published sermonic material, Tyler commented, "What he wrote is literature meant for the ear, not the eye; having the rhythm and cadence of a good speech. It is constructed for swift practical effect on the minds, passions, resolutions of men" (Tyler 1878, I, 199).

It has been shown that Hooker's brand of preparationism became "part and parcel" of the New England way. It was adopted by the great majority of mid-seventeenth century New England pastors, John Cotton being the most notable exception. Nathaniel Ward characterized the rigors of the preparatory sojourn by remarking to Hooker,

> You make as good Christians before men are in Christ as ever they are after; would I were but as good a Christian now, as you make men while they are but preparing for Christ. (in Hall 1972, 165)

Despite his high scholarship, Hooker was a "people's pastor." He assured his Hartford congregation that "the meanest saint knows more of God's love and promises than the most unregenerate doctors" (Hooker 1656a, 404). Using an analogy from daily life to comfort the doubting Christian who happened to be simple and unlearned, Hooker assures them:

> And suppose one dull blocke, and a quicke wit, are both set to one trade, yet if the dullard had an expert master and learn unto him the skill of the trade, and the quicke spirit was with a master that could not teach him his trade; we see that the dull blocke is more wise in this trade than the other; so it is here, they have the Lord for their master. (Hooker 1637a, 109)

Hooker's classical training gave way to the

"plain style" cultivated by Puritans in both "old" and New England. It was especially suited to the frontier which was the Connecticut River. Obscurity and eloquence were to be deliberately avoided. It was but a waste to use "fine gilded sentences, where there is nothing but a jingling and a tinkling, nothing but a sound of words" (Hooker 1637c, 65).
Commenting on this "plain style," Ola Winslow writes,

> Colonial preachers also spoke a language the pew could understand. Their power in the pulpit owed much to this common sense discipline. . . . Plainness was imperative and for the best of reasons; the preacher had in his keeping the souls of educated and illiterate; all must understand the doctrine. (Winslow 1972, 110)

To this end, Hooker remarked, "I have accounted it the chiefest part of judicious learning, to make a hard point easy and familiar in explication" (Hooker 1648, "Preface").

The Puritans in Cambridge had been in unanimity in their detestation of the flowery eloquence of the establishment ministers. Perkins, Baynes, Ames, Cotton, and Hooker all cultivated the "plain style" to the consternation of Archbishops Whitgift and then Bancroft (Sprunger 1972, 8, 15). Plainness was to be the vehicle for Amesian practicality. The overly ornate sermon was not a matter of personal opinion or preference. It had evil consequences upon diverse congregations.

> I have sometime admired at this: why a company of Gentlemen, yeoman and poore women, that are scarcely able to know their A.B.C. yet they have a Minister to speake Latine, Greeke, Hebrew, and to use the Fathers, when it is certain, that they know nothing at all. The reason is, because all this stings not, they may sit and sleepe in their sinnes, and goe to hell hoodwinked, never awakened. (Hooker 1632, 66)

But such a determination to maintain something of a pristine Calvinism marked by "lucid brevity" did not mean for Hooker a sacrifice of dignity. Ever amid earthy and homely imagery, Hooker maintained a sober dignity in his preaching of the Word of God.

Preaching was ever to be dignified because of its very nature. Imperative to understanding Hooker's conversion preaching is to note the centrality of preaching as a means of grace (Emerson 1955, 35). For Hooker the primary converting work of the Spirit comes in the hearing of the sermon. If any oppose the preached Word of God, let him know that it is the Lord's Word he opposes (Stout 1986, 42). So high was Hooker's view of this converting ordinance, this means of grace, that he declared, "Every sermon a man heareth, he is thereby nearer either to heaven or hell, either he is made better or worse by it" (Hooker 1651, 234).

Stressing the importance of the actual, not the apparent, Hooker constantly urged introspection and meditation. It was through self-examination that assurance was possible. The difficulties of self-examination and its time consumption, ought not to be discouragements, but rather demonstrations that the heart of man is indeed full of "infinite windings and secret turnings" (Hooker 1640a, 205). This emphasis of Hooker's on introspection became a mark of New England's Puritanism. Sacvan Bercovitch has summarized Puritan psychology as one concerned with one's own soul yet while abhorring selfishness. Indeed the "basis of Puritan psychology lies in this contrast between personal responsibility and individualism" (Bercovitch 1975, 17).

The practical effects of this introspection were at times most unhappy, as immortalized in Hawthorne's guilt ridden Arthur Dimmesdale. Nevertheless, Hooker urged his listeners to look within.

> Meditation is not a flourishing of a mans wit, but hath set about at the search of the truth, beats his brain as wee use to say, hammers out a business, as the Gouldsmiths with his mettal, he

beats it, turnes it on this side and on that, fashions it both that he might frame it to his mind. . . . Meditation is the traversing of a mans thoughts, the coasting of the mind and imagination into every crevis and corner . . . . Meditation lifts up the latch and goes into each room, pries into every corner of the house, and surveyes the composition and making of it, with all the blemishes in it. Look as the Searcher at the Sea Port, or Custom-house, or Ships . . . unlocks every Chest, rummages every corner, takes a light to discover the darkest passages. . . . Meditation goes upon discovery, toucheth at every coast, observes every creek, maps out the dayly course of a mans conversation and disposition. (Hooker 1656c, 210-214)

As to the actual form of Hooker's sermons, the classic Puritan model, that of Perkins and Ames, was followed. William Perkins, in his The Arte of Prophecying, had prescribed a four step pattern.

1) A distinct reading of the text
2) An explication of the sense and understanding, by
   the Scriptures themselves
3) A collection of profitable points of doctrine 4) A delineation of the applications or uses of the doctrine in the life and manners of men. (Perkins 1612, II, 670)

Though following the received pattern, Hooker more so than other ministers of his day, often began to make application even as he explicated. Habegger has suggested that Hooker's divergence from the received methodology was a consequence of his preparationist agenda (Habegger 1969, 342-354).

Clearly the most remarkable facet of Hooker's sermonic material is his skillful use of rich imagery. He seems never to have been without an illustrative description from common life. In addition to the obvious examples in the main portion of this study, a number of other representative examples will here be noted.

Often analogies were drawn from the natural world. Here the prod is toward introspection and the seeking of assurance through reflex.

> Take but an Apple, there is never a man under heaven can tell what tast it is of, whether sweet or soure, untill he have tasted of it; he seeth the colour and quantity of it, but knoweth not the tast; so there is no man under heaven discerneth more of grace than he findeth in himselfe. (Hooker 1651, 209)

The faithful member of God's Kingdom, while here upon earth, should expect joy to be mingled with sorrow. Here the picture lesson is taken from the nautical world. The prod is toward deeper humility.

> Great revelations have great Humiliations go before them; the Eb is very low before the Tyde comes with greatest strength and height; otherwise the soul would never be able to bear such overbearing expressions of God's love, and communications of himself, but would certainly abuse them. If the Keel of the Boat were little and narrow, a large sail would overturn it, not convey it to the Haven. Great assurances and Glorious Joyes, are too large a sail for a heart that is not widened with enlarged contritions and humiliations. (Hooker 1656c, 336)

The common beggar is truly a humble soul. Hooker finds therein an analogy well suited to his voluntarism. "Though a man should beg his bread from door to door, if he can beg Christ and have him, and beg grace and have it, he is the richest man upon earth" (Hooker 1637a, 76).

On the one hand, the searching soul must avoid idleness.

Whilst the stream keeps running, it keeps clear;

but let it stand still, it breeds frogs and toads and all manner of filth. So while you keep going, you keep clear; but do not once flag in your diligence, and stand still, and oh! what a puddle of filth and sin thy heart will be. (Hooker 1637a, 13)

Yet neither must one be impatient. "We must wait God's leisure, and stay his time for the bestowing of his favors. Beggars must not be choosers" (Hooker 1656a, 98).

The intensity and thoroughness of the preparatory process is stressed in domestic terms.

Sweep your hearts, and cleanse those rooms, cleanse every sink, brush down every cobweb, and make room for Christ . . . and when thou hast swept every corner of thy house, do not leave dust behind the door, for that is a sluts tricke; do not remove sin out of thy tongue, and out of thy eye, and out of thy hand, and leave it in thy heart. (Hooker 1637c, 50)

If any are slothful or refuse to come to Christ, Hooker awards to them punishment in "good, round, English curses. He assures them of damnation right heartily. His pages gleam and blaze with the flashes of threatened hellfire. His ink has even yet a smell of theological sulfur in it" (Tyler 1878, I, 199).

In a final example of Hooker's metaphorical richness, he seeks tenderly to urge one to use the means of grace.

Let us be led by all means into a nearer union with the Lord Christ. As a wife deals with the letters of her husband that is in a far country, she finds many sweet inklings of his love, and she will read these often and daily . . . because she would be with her husband a little, and have a little parley with him in his pen, though not in his presence; so these ordinances are but the Lord's love letters, and we are the ambassadors of Christ . . . we bring marvellous good newes that Christ can save all poor broken-hearted sinners in the world. (Hooker 1637b, 73-74)

It is obvious that the "plain style" had its own brand of eloquence. The metaphors were often of the earthy sort, or at least drawn from the commonalities of life. Samuel Eliot Morison captured the tenor of Hooker's work with a Hookerian-like simile of his own: "From Hooker, eloquence flowed as easily as water from a jug" (Morison 1930, 107).

CONCLUSION

Thomas Hooker (1586-1647) was theologian-pastor of the first rank. Unfortunately, erroneous but persistent suppositions of his "democratic ideals" have detracted from his greatest contribution to ecclesiastical and intellectual history. Standing consciously in the Reformed tradition, and bridging the English and American Puritan streams, Hooker's greatest legacy is his series of conversion sermons in the "plain style." Concerned as he was with "heart religion," Hooker's preaching was designed not to dazzle, but to pierce and then to comfort. The "plain style" sermon itself was perceived as the ordinary instrument of salvation.

Modeling his entire ministry around the preparationist tenets so obvious in the conversion sermons, Hooker became a physician to the soul whose prescriptions, while including no injection of Arminianism, served rather as a healthy antidote to Antinomianism. In the seventeenth-century, ministrations to those afflicted with great distress of soul became a large part of the Puritan ministry. Few could rival the skills or renown of Hooker as an analyzer of the interior life.

Developing federalism, with its bilateral contractual conditions, provided a "seed-bed" for Puritan voluntarism. Hooker's particular blend of federalism and voluntarism was concerned to chronicle the "windings" of the soul along its halting sojourn. The road along which Christ is finally "fetched" is a low one of contrition and humiliation. Hooker's morphology became a reliable and basic scheme which, in the hands of the skillful physician, served both to prod the complacent on the one hand and to comfort the poor doubter on the other.

The emerging tradition of Ramistic philosophy

and Amesian utilitarianism provided the foundation for Hooker's "double prong." Ames' definition of theology as "the doctrine of living to God" (Ames 1968, 77), tended in the direction of casuistry. His well known insistence upon a manifest piety at Franeker is mirrored in Hooker's "do something" voluntarism. As in St. Paul's epistolary structure, and like a Ramist dichotomy, the Christian life was to be one of godly activity which finds its basis in revealed truth.

A systematic analysis of Hooker's entire corpus as it relates to his morphology has been made. Certain factors are quite obvious. Hooker feared empty professions. He called for activism and based assurance upon the presence of sanctifying graces, all of this clearly in contradistinction to Antinomianism. Yet as it has been demonstrated, little if any evidence exists that Hooker felt the need to "tailor" his teaching, or "firm up" his Calvinism during or following the crisis of 1637. In this, exception has been taken to certain themes in Shuffelton's excellent studies of Hooker's life and thought.

To say that Hooker's orthodoxy is unquestionable is not to insist that he was some sort of clone of Calvin. As to the question of one's assurance of being a recipient of saving grace, Calvin's refrain was "look to Christ" as the only mirror upon which we may contemplate our election (<u>Institutes</u> III, xxiv, 5). Hooker sought to comfort doubters by pointing them to sanctifying graces that seemed to be at work in themselves. But by reason of his knowledge of the only basis for redemption, Hooker often tempered his reflective method with a more pristine "look to Christ" exhortation (Hooker 1656b, 94).

Thomas Hooker held an important place in the evolving Reformed theology, a century after Calvin himself and a century before Jonathan Edwards. So much does Hooker deserve a place in the center of that evolving tradition that Andrew Denholm somewhat unhappily commented that Hooker was "disgustingly orthodox" (Denholm 1961, 349). More sympathetically, Emerson attributes to Hooker a "greatness" in that he was able to be at the same time a "High Calvinist" and a

CONCLUSION 257

very effective evangelical preacher (Emerson 1955, 239). Previous to the formulation of Hooker's morphology, William Perkins had been explicating at Cambridge a certain ten steps in the conversion process (Morgan 1963, 68-69). But more than anyone else on either side of the Atlantic, Hooker became the systematizer of the grand theme of the application of redemption. To restive New England minds came a comforting "order" in God's workings. They were on a new frontier. By the mysterious workings of Providence many had been tossed from England to Holland and now to these new shores. But in God's work of grace upon the elect soul, there was a discernible chronology, a morphology of conversion which could be traced. This in itself was a comfort to "poor doubting Christians." Hooker and the other preparationists sought to find in the reliability of God's covenant and the trustworthiness of human experience, an understanding of God's gracious purposes. Hooker's more comforting position, despite the charges leveled against it even by the mighty John Cotton, became the orthodox position in New England. Cotton, suddenly in the minority, would continue to be the apostle of violent conversions.

A century later, Edwards perceived that Arminian sentiments had by then arisen from excessive voluntarism. He therefore could not adopt wholeheartedly the preparationism of the Hooker-Shepard sort. Nevertheless, in his Narrative of Surprising Conversions, Edwards himself carefully chronicled the experiential side of the conversion process, thus preserving the Connecticut River tradition of evangelical preaching and experiential religion.

As an unabashed voluntarist, Hooker followed and advanced beyond William Ames in departing from the received constructs of the day as he gave primacy to the will as the "commander" of the faculties. Hooker thus stands as a representative example of the importance of the Ramistic and Amesian underpinnings of the New England Way. Having thoroughly embraced the precept of monergism in the conversion process, Hooker sounds his activist calls even if this is perceived by some to be in tension with his high Calvinism. That which has been said of Edwards is no less true for Hooker: "he realized that a voluntaristic psychology worked equally well against Arminian rationalism and Antinomian inspirationalism" (Breitenbach 1988, 184).

Driven from his native shores to the "holy experiment" of New England, Hooker became a leading light among the first generation of American Puritans. His training at Emmanuel had grounded him in the orthodoxy of Calvinism to which his life-long allegiance remained undiminished. Yet this physician to the soul also exhibited deep pastoral warmth and concern. Here was a model seventeenth-century pastor. Hooker was a man whose theology had a fierce and menacing side. From this he never shied away. Yet his constant ambition was to move the heart, not only to fear God, but to experience and "own" Christ's love and mercy. Thereunto, a soothing tenderness was often employed. Hooker likewise was obviously a man who personally knew his God.

> If mine hands were all of love, that I could work nothing but love, and if my eyes were able to see nothing but love, and my mind think nothing but love, and if I had a thousand bodies, it were all too little to love that God that hath immeasureably loved me, a poor sinful hellbound. (Hooker 1637c, 179-180)

As frequently as Hooker employed his morphology to urge others from their self-deceived confidence, did he use the same morphology to encourage the "poor doubter" that he could indeed expect unmerited grace from God. Whether in his study, pulpit, or parishioners' parlors, no other Puritan pastor so concerned himself with matters of doubt, hope, and despair. In the end, and whenever possible, a "charitable judgment" would be rendered by Hooker. Indeed, the rigors of the "relation" of the Bay Colony were not found at Hartford. Hooker remains a model of a tender-hearted minister, a man in whom great learning and wisdom were vivificated by zeal and holiness.

WORKS CITED

Adams, James Truslow. 1921. *The Founding of New England*. Boston: Atlantic Monthly Press.

Ahlstrom, Sydney. 1963. "Thomas Hooker and Democratic Citizenship," *Church History*. XXXII, 415-431. Press.

──────. 1972. *A Religious History of the American People*. New Haven and London: Yale University Press.

Albro, John. 1853. "The Life of Thomas Shepherd," *The Works of Thomas Shepherd*. New York. (AMS rpt. 1967).

Ames, William. 1643. *The Marrow of Sacred Divinity*. London.

──────. 1968. *The Marrow of Theology*. Translated and edited by John D. Eusden. Boston: Pilgrim Press.

Ball, John. 1644. *A Tryal of the New-Church Way in New England*. London.

Baker, J. Wayne. 1980. *Heinrich Bullinger and the Covenant: The Other Reformed Tradition*. Athens: Ohio University Press.

Battis, Emery. 1962. *Saints and Sectaries: Anne Hutchinson and the Antinomian Controversy in the Massachusetts Bay Colony*. Chapel Hill: University of North Carolina Press.

Bercovitch, Sacvan. 1979. *Puritan Origins of the American Self*. New Haven and London: Yale University Press.

Bouwsma, William J. 1986. *John Calvin: A Sixteenth-Century Portrait*. New York: Oxford University Press.

Bradford, William. 1952. *Of Plymouth Plantation*. ed. Samuel Eliot Morison. New York: Knopf.

Breitenbach, William. 1988. "Piety and Moralism: Edwards and the New Divinity," *Jonathan Edwards and the American Experience*. eds. Nathan Hatch and Harry Stout. New York: Oxford University

WORKS CITED

Burrage, Champlin. 1912. *The Early English Dissenters in the Light of Recent Research.* New York: Cambridge.

Bush, Sargent. 1972. "Thomas Hooker and the Westminster Assembly," *William and Mary Quarterly,* Third Series, XXIX (April), 291-300.

――――. 1973. "The Growth of Thomas Hooker's *The Doubting Christian,*" *Early American Literature,* VIII (Spring), 3-20.

――――. 1980. *The Writings of Thomas Hooker: Spiritual Adventure in Two Worlds.* Madison: University of Wisconsin Press.

Caldwell, Patricia. 1983. *The Puritan Conversion Narrative: The Beginnings of American Expression.* New York: Cambridge University Press.

Calvin, John. 1843. *Commentary on a Harmony of the Evangelists.* Translated by W. Pringle. Edinburgh: Calvin Translation Society.

――――. 1960. *Institutes of the Christian Religion.* LCC edition. Philadelphia: The Westminster Press.

Carter, Alice Clare. 1964. *The English Reformed Church in Amsterdam in the Seventeenth-Century.* Amsterdam: Scheltema and Holkema.

Cherry, Conrad. 1974. *The Theology of Jonathan Edwards.* Gloucester: Peter Smith.

Clarke, Samuel. 1683. *The Lives of Sundry Eminent Persons in This Later Age.* London.

Colonial Society of Massachusetts. 1932. "The Autobiography of Thomas Shepherd," *Transactions.* XXVII. Boston.

Connecticut Historical Society. 1850. *Public Records of the Colony of Connecticut.* Hartford: The Society.

Cotton, John. 1644. *Keyes of the Kingdom of Heaven.* London.

――――. 1659. *A Treatise of the Covenant of Grace.* London.

Davids, Thomas W. 1862. *Annals of Evangelical Nonconformity in the County of Essex.* London:

Jackson, Walford.
Denholm, Andrew Thomas. 1961. "Thomas Hooker: Puritan Teacher, 1586-1647." Unpublished doctoral dissertation, Hartford Seminary Foundation.
Dowey, Edward A. 1952. The Knowledge of God in Calvin's Theology. New York: Columbia University Press.
Edwards, Jonathan. 1957. Freedom of the Will. ed. by Paul Ramsey. New Haven and London: Yale University Press.
_____. 1979. The Works of Jonathan Edwards. Carlisle, The Banner of Truth Trust.
Emerson, Everett. 1955. "Thomas Hooker and the Reformed Theology: The Relationship of Hooker's Conversion Preaching to its Background." Unpublished doctoral dissertation, Louisiana State University.
_____. 1956a. "Calvin and Covenant Theology," Church History. XXV (June), 136-144.
_____. 1956b. "Notes on the Hooker Canon," American Literature. XXVII (January), 555.
_____. 1956c. "Introduction," Redemption: Three Sermons 1637-1656 by Thomas Hooker. Gainesville: Scholars' Facsimiles and Reprints.
_____. 1965. John Cotton. Boston: Twayne Publishers.
_____. 1967. "Thomas Hooker: The Puritan As Theologian," Anglican Theological Review. XLIV (April).
_____. 1977. Puritanism In America, 1620-1750. Boston: Twayne Publishers.
Fiering, Norman. 1972. "Will and Intellect in the New England Mind," William and Mary Quarterly. XXIX (October), 515-558.
_____. 1981a. Jonathan Edwards's Moral Thought and Its British Context. Chapel Hill: University of North Carolina Press.
_____. 1981b. Moral Philosophy at Seventeenth-Century Harvard. Chapel Hill: University of North Carolina Press.
Foster, Stephen. 1984. "English Puritanism and the Progress of New England Institutions, 1630-

WORKS CITED

1660," Saints and Revolutionaries: Essays on Early American History. eds. David D. Hall, et al. New York: Norton and Co.

Goodwin, Gordon. 1908. "Thomas Hooker," in Dictionary of National Biography, Vol. IX, edited by Leslie Stephen and Sidney Lee. New York: Macmillan Company.

Greene, M. Louis. 1905. The Development of Religious Liberty in Connecticut. Boston: Houghton Mifflin Company.

Habegger, Alfred. 1969. "Preparing the Soul for Christ: The Contrasting Sermon Forms of John Cotton and Thomas Hooker," American Literature, XLI (November), 342-354.

Hall, David D. 1968. The Antinomian Controversy 1636-1638: A Documentary History. Middletown: Wesleyan University Press.

_____. 1972. The Faithful Shepherd: A History of the New England Ministry in the Seventeenth-Century. Chapel Hill: University of North Carolina Press.

Haller, William. 1938, The Rise of Puritanism. New York: Columbia University Press.

Heartwell, Jaspar. 1647. Trodden Down Strength. London.

_____. 1654. The Firebrand Taken Out of the Fire, or the Wonderful History, Case, and Cure of Mrs. Joan Drake. London.

Helm, Paul. 1982. Calvin and the Calvinists. Edinburgh: The Banner of Truth Trust.

Heppe, Heinrich. 1978. Reformed Dogmatics: Set Out and Illustrated From the Sources. Grand Rapids: Baker.

Herget, Winfried. 1972. "Preaching and Publication: Chronology and the Style of Thomas Hooker's Sermons," Harvard Theological Review. 65, 231-239.

Hooker, Edward W. 1849. The Life of Thomas Hooker. Boston: Massachusetts Sabbath School Society.

Hooker, Thomas. 1627. "To The Reader," in John Rogers' The Doctrine of Faith. London.

_____. 1629. The Poore Doubting Christian Drawne

WORKS CITED

Unto Christ. London.
———. 1632. The Soules Preparation For Christ. London.
———. 1633. "Preface," to William Ames' A Fresh Suit Against Human Ceremonies in Gods Worship. London.
———. 1637a. The Soules Vocation or Effectual Calling To Christ. London.
———. 1637b. The Soules Humiliation. London.
———. 1637c. The Soules Implantation. London.
———. 1637d. The Soules Ingrafting Into Christ. London.
———. 1638a. Foure Learned and Godly Treatises. London.
———. 1638b. The Properties of an Honest Heart. London.
———. 1638c. The Sinners Salvation. London.
———. 1638d. The Soules Exaltation. London.
———. 1638e. The Soules Possession of Christ. London.
———. 1638f. The Stay of the Faithful. London
———. 1638g. The Unbeleevers Preparing For Christ. London.
———. 1638h. Three Godly Sermons. London.
———. 1638i. Spiritual Munition: A Funeral Sermon. London.
———. 1638j. Spiritual Thirst. London.
———. 1640a. The Christians Two Chief Lessons. London.
———. 1640b. The Patterne of Perfection. London.
———. 1640c. The Soules Implantation Into the Natural Olive. London.
———. 1641. The Danger of Desertion: A Farewell Sermon. London.
———. 1644. The Faithful Covenanter. London.
———. 1645a. A Briefe Exposition of the Lord's Prayer. London.
———. 1645b. Heavens Treasury Opened. London.
———. 1648. A Survey of the Summe of Church Discipline. London.
———. 1649. The Covenant of Grace Opened. London.

WORKS CITED

_____. 1651. *The Saints Dignitie and Dutie*. London.
_____. 1656a. *A Comment Upon Christ's Last Prayer*. London.
_____. 1656b. *The Application of Redemption* (Books I-VIII). London.
_____. 1656c. *The Application of Redemption* (Books IX-X). London.
Hoopes, James. 1988. "Calvinism and Consciousness from Edwards to Beecher," *Jonathan Edwards and the American Experience*. ed. by Nathan Hatch and Harry Stout. New York: Oxford University Press.
Hubbard, William. 1878. *A General History of New England From the Discovery to MDCLXXX*. Boston. (Reprinted New York: Arno Press, 1972)
Irving, John. 1989. *A Prayer For Owen Meany*. New York: William Morrow and Company.
Johnson, Edward. 1910. *Wonder-Working Providence of Sions Saviour in New England, 1628-1651*. New York: Barnes and Noble.
Kendall, R.T. 1979. *Calvin and English Calvinism to 1649*. New York: Oxford.
Levy, Babette. 1945. *Preaching in the First Half Century of New England History*. Hartford: The American Society of Church History.
Lillback, Peter Alan. "The Binding of God: Calvin's Role in the Development of Covenant Theology." Unpublished doctoral dissertation, Westminster Theological Seminary.
Lockyer, Roger. 1964. *Tudor and Stuart Britain*. New York: St. Martins Press.
Maclear, James Fulton. 1968. "The Heart of New England Rent," *The New England Puritans*. ed. Sydney V. James. New York: Harper and Row.
McGiffert, Michael. ed. 1972. *God's Plot: The Paradoxes of Puritan Piety, Being the Autobiography and Journal of Thomas Shepherd*. Amherst.
Massachusetts Historical Society. 1868. *Collections*. Fourth Series, VIII, 544-546. Boston: The Society.

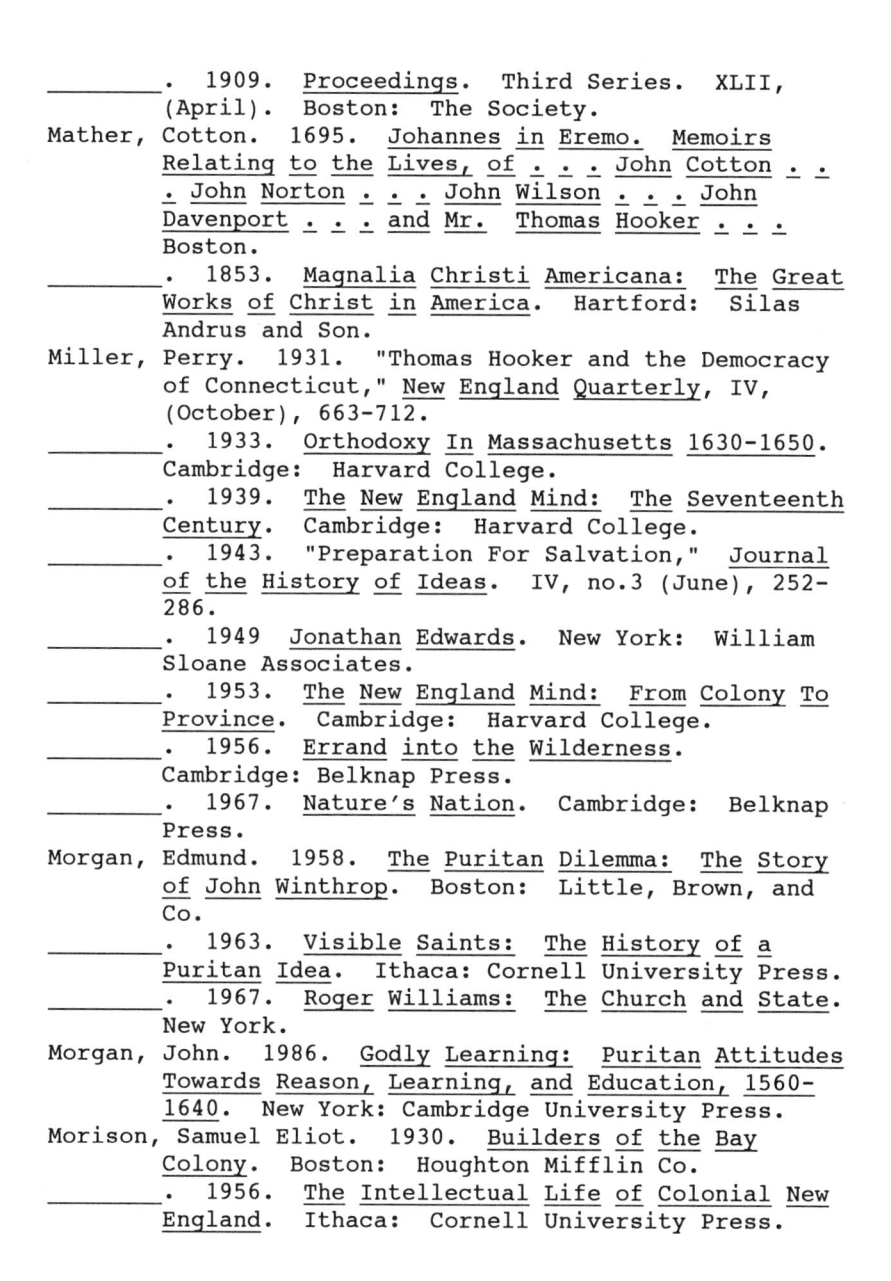

_____. 1909. Proceedings. Third Series. XLII, (April). Boston: The Society.
Mather, Cotton. 1695. Johannes in Eremo. Memoirs Relating to the Lives, of . . . John Cotton . . . John Norton . . . John Wilson . . . John Davenport . . . and Mr. Thomas Hooker . . . Boston.
_____. 1853. Magnalia Christi Americana: The Great Works of Christ in America. Hartford: Silas Andrus and Son.
Miller, Perry. 1931. "Thomas Hooker and the Democracy of Connecticut," New England Quarterly, IV, (October), 663-712.
_____. 1933. Orthodoxy In Massachusetts 1630-1650. Cambridge: Harvard College.
_____. 1939. The New England Mind: The Seventeenth Century. Cambridge: Harvard College.
_____. 1943. "Preparation For Salvation," Journal of the History of Ideas. IV, no.3 (June), 252-286.
_____. 1949 Jonathan Edwards. New York: William Sloane Associates.
_____. 1953. The New England Mind: From Colony To Province. Cambridge: Harvard College.
_____. 1956. Errand into the Wilderness. Cambridge: Belknap Press.
_____. 1967. Nature's Nation. Cambridge: Belknap Press.
Morgan, Edmund. 1958. The Puritan Dilemma: The Story of John Winthrop. Boston: Little, Brown, and Co.
_____. 1963. Visible Saints: The History of a Puritan Idea. Ithaca: Cornell University Press.
_____. 1967. Roger Williams: The Church and State. New York.
Morgan, John. 1986. Godly Learning: Puritan Attitudes Towards Reason, Learning, and Education, 1560-1640. New York: Cambridge University Press.
Morison, Samuel Eliot. 1930. Builders of the Bay Colony. Boston: Houghton Mifflin Co.
_____. 1956. The Intellectual Life of Colonial New England. Ithaca: Cornell University Press.

WORKS CITED

Murray, Iain H. 1978. "Antinomianism: New England's First Controversy," Banner of Truth. #179, #180, 1-75.
———. 1980. "Thomas Hooker and the Doctrine of Conversion," Banner of Truth. #206, 9-21.
Neal, Daniel. 1837. History of the Puritans. London.
Paige, Lucius R. 1877. History of Cambridge, Massachusetts. Boston: Houghton.
Parrington, Vernon Louis. 1927. Main Currents in American Thought: The Colonial Mind, 1620-1800. New York: Harcourt, Brace and Company.
Perkins, William. 1612, 1626. Works. London: Cambridge.
Pettit, Norman. 1966a. "Lydia's Conversion: An Issue in Hooker's Departure," Proceedings of the Cambridge Historical Society. XL (1964-1966), 59-83.
———. 1966b. The Heart Prepared: Grace and Conversion in Puritan Spiritual Life. New Haven and London: Yale University Press.
———. 1974. "Hooker's Doctrine of Assurance: A Critical Phase in New England Spiritual Thought," New England Quarterly. (March-December), 518-534.
Reid, James. 1811. Memoirs of the Westminster Divines. London: Stephen and Andrew Young.
Rogers, John. 1627. The Doctrine of Faith. London.
Rossiter, Clinton. 1952. "Thomas Hooker," New England Quarterly, XXV (March-December), 459-488.
———. 1953. Seedtime of the American Republic. New York: Harcourt, Brace.
Rutman, Darrett B. 1965. Winthrop's Boston, Portrait of a Puritan Town, 1630-1649. Chapel Hill: University of North Carolina Press.
Selement, George and Woolley, Bruce C. editors. 1981. Thomas Shepard's Confessions. Boston: Colonial Society of Massachusetts.
Shuffelton, Frank C. 1971. "Thomas Prince and his Edition of Thomas Hooker's Poor Doubting Christian," Early American Literature. V, 68-75.
———. 1972. "Light of the Western Churches: The

Career of Thomas Hooker, 1586-1647."
Unpublished doctoral dissertation, Stanford
University.
_____. 1977. Thomas Hooker 1586-1647. Princeton:
Princeton University Press.
Sibbes, Richard. 1864. The Works of Richard Sibbes.
ed. Alexander B. Grosart. Edinburgh.
Sprunger, Keith L. 1966. "Ames, Ramus, and the Method
of Puritan Theology," Harvard Theological
Review. LIX, (April), 133-151.
_____. 1972. The Learned Doctor William Ames:
Dutch Backgrounds of English and American
Puritanism. Chicago: University of Illinois
Press.
_____. 1973. "The Dutch Career of Thomas Hooker,"
New England Quarterly, XLVI (March), 17-44.
Stearns, Raymond. 1940. Congregationalism In The Dutch
Netherlands. Chicago: American Society of
Church History.
Stout, Harry. 1986. The New England Soul. New York:
Oxford University Press.
Trevor-Roper, Hugh. 1962. Archbishop Laud, 1573-1645.
New York: Macmillan.
Tyler, Moses Coit. 1878. A History of American
Literature. New York: G.P. Putnam's Sons.
Walker, George Leon. 1891. Thomas Hooker: Preacher,
Founder, Democrat. New York: Dodd, Mead, and
Co.
Wallace, Ronald S. 1959. Calvin's Doctrine of the
Christian Life. Edinburgh: Oliver and Boyd.
Williams, George H. 1967. "The Pilgrimage of Thomas
Hooker (1586-1647) in England, The Netherlands,
and New England," Bulletin of the Congregational
Library. Boston. XIX, No. 1, 5-15; No. 2, 9-
13.
_____. 1968. "Called by Thy Name, Leave Us Not: The
Case of Mrs. Joan Drake, A Formative Episode in
the Pastoral Career of Thomas Hooker in
England," Harvard Library Bulletin, XVI
(April), 111-128; (July), 278-300.
Williams, George H. et al. 1975. Thomas Hooker:
Writings In England and Holland, 1586-1633.

Cambridge: Harvard University Press.
Williams, Roger. 1963. "The Bloody Tenent Yet More Bloody," *The Complete Writings of Roger Williams*, IV. New York.
Winslow, Ola Elizabeth. 1940. *Jonathan Edwards 1703-1758*. New York: Macmillan.
――――――. 1957. *Master Roger Williams*. New York: Macmillan.
――――――. 1968. *John Eliot: Apostle To The Indians*. Boston: Houghton, Mifflin Co.
――――――. 1972. *Meetinghouse Hill*. New York: Norton.
Winthrop, John. 1908. *Winthrop's Journal*. ed. J.K. Hosmer. New York: Charles Scribner's Sons.
――――――. 1943. *Winthrop Papers*. ed. Samuel Eliot Morison, et al. Boston: Merrymount Press.
Young, Alexander. 1846. *Chronicles of the First Planters of the Colony of Massachusetts Bay, from 1623 to 1636*. Boston: Little and Brown.
Ziff, Larzer. 1962. *The Career of John Cotton: Puritanism and the American Experience*. Princeton: Princeton University Press.
――――――. 1973. *Puritanism In America*. New York: Viking.

INDEX

Adams, James Truslow, 1,6,49,50
Albro, John, 70
Ames, William, 24,30-33, 51,69,77,79ff,81,91,94,257
Antinomianism, 2,3,56-67,121,137,174,203,206,211,220
Arminianism, 82,204
Ashe, Simon, 9

Baker, J. Wayne, 76
Ball, John, 68
Battis, Emery, 45,200
Bercovitch, Sacvan, 53,250
Bradford, William 13
Breitenbach, William 258
Bush, Sargent, 2,68,86,99,202,242-243
Bullinger, Heinrich, 75

Calvin and Calvinism, 2,3,65,73ff,77,88-94,98,110ff,140,145,152,256
Cambridge Platform, 53
Chaderton, Laurence, 8
Charles I, 17,88
Cherry, Conrad, 93
Clarke, Samuel, 5
Collins, Samuel, 16,20,81
Conformity, 18ff
Cotton, John, 1,32-34,53,56-68,77-78,199,208
Covenant Theology, 74-81

Davenport, John, 32
Davids, Thomas, 20
Denholm, Andrew Thomas, 6-7,37,47,199,120
Dixie, Wolston, 7
Duck, Arthur, 16,20
Drake, Francis, 10,12,17
Drake, Joan, 1`0-13,30

Edwards, Jonathan, 3,73,90,93ff,257
Eliot, John, 20
Emerson, Everett, 2,65,66,76,84-86,120,247-248,250
Emmanuel College, 7-9,14,17,55
Endicott, John, 41-42

Faculty Psychology, 88-94
Fiering, Norman, 93
Forbes, John, 11,24
Fundamental Orders (1637), 49

Goodwin, Gordan, 16
Goodwin, Thomas, 95

Habegger, Alfred, 251
Hall, David D., 565ff,59-69,82,204,208,248
Haller, William, 178
Heartwell, Jaspar (pseudonymous), 10-11
Helm, Paul, 74
Herget, Winfried, 87
Hooker, Thomas: Answers To XX Questions, 25ff,98,128; The Application of Redemption, 44,82,84,85,87,91,131, 199,212-238; The Christians Two Chief Lessons, 36,90, 173ff,190; A Comment Upon Christ's Last Prayer, 85, 87,199,213,239ff; The Covenant of Grace Opened, 83,196,229; The Danger of Desertion, 14ff,184, 196,237; The Faithful Covenanter, 95,164ff; Four Learned and Godly Treatises, 44,141-142,181; The Patterne Of Perfection, 189ff; The Poore Doubting Christian Drawn Unto Christ, 99-103; The Properties Of An Honest Heart, 44; The Saints Dignite and Dutie, 82,86,173,199,204ff,209ff,250; The Sinners Salvation, 44,193ff,197; The Soules Exaltation, 44,86,161-173,182; The Soules Humiliation, 44,86-87,130,141, 181,214; The Soules Implantation, 44,86,143-149, 179,221-222,230,253; The Soules Ingrafting, 44,86, 142,221; The Soules Possession of Christ, 44,85,86, 173,183; The Soules Preparation For Christ, 31,44, 86-87,91,106,117-131,173,214,232,238,249; The Soules Vocation or Effectual Calling to Christ, 44,84,86, 88,90,149-161; Spiritual Thirst, 44,196, The Stay of The Faithful, 44,196; A Survey of the Summe Of Church

INDEX

Discipline, 1,23,26,32,38,52,67,69,167,196; Three Godly Sermons, 44,185ff,189,197; The Unbeleevers Preparing For Christ, 44,82,83,84,86, 87,98,106-117,120,132,218,226ff
Hubbard, William, 39,54
Hutchinson, Anne, 56-67,137,152,209

Irving, John, 62

Johnson, Edward, 247

Kendall, R.T., 74ff,98,109,120,153ff

Laud, William, 16,18,19,20,31
Lillback, Peter, 75ff
Lyford, John, 14

Mather, Cotton, 5,6,9,11,14,15-16,22,29,30,32-35,39,45, 47,54,63,67
Mather, Richard, 53
McGiffert, Michael, 201
Mildmay, Walter, 7
Miller, Perry, 1,6,50-56,69,79,81,91ff,125
Morgan, Edmund, 65,69,80
Morgan, John, 8,75,79
Morison, Samuel Eliot, 254
Murray, Iain H., 61-65,80

Neal, Daniel, 8
Norton, John, 33

Offwood, Stephen, 23,24,32

Paget, John 23-30
Paige, Lucius, 38
Parrington, Vernon, 1,6,50,53
Perkins, William, 2,79,81,251
Peter, Hugh, 23,133
Pettit, Norman, 65
Plain Style, 3,247-254
Pratt, John 47
Preston, John, 11,77-78

Ramus and Ramism, 11,79,81
Robinson, John, 69
Rogers, John, 11,14,19,28,95ff,128,231
Rossiter, Clinton, 1,7,54
Rutherford, Samuel, 68,70
Rutman, Darrett, 37

Shepard, Thomas, 1,13,33,48,65,69,70,75,82
Shuffelton, Frank, 2,6,9,15,20,21,22,37-38,42-43,
   61,94-96,99,120,199
Sibbes, Richard, 76-78,80,123,244-245
Sprunger, Keith, 6,22ff,29,30,79
Stearns, Raymond, 30
Stoddard, Solomon, 139
Stone, Samuel, 33-34,38,70
Stout, Harry, 250

Thirty-Years War, 18
Trevor-Roper, Hugh, 20
Tyler, Moses Coit, 247,248,253

Walker, George Leon, 1,6-7,9,15-16,24,31,36,70
Wheelwright, John, 57ff,207
Williams, George H. 6,10,11,16,19,21-22,25,26,28,30,32,
   34,35,86,96,99,150
Williams, Roger, 16,39-43,45,48,50
Winslow, Ola, 16,43,249
Winthrop, John, 1,5,35,38,39-43,45-50,56-68,69-70,
   200

Young, Alexander, 6,38,80

Ziff, Larzer, 65,97,199